PRELUDE TO POLITICAL ECONOMY

Prelude to Political Economy

A Study of the Social and Political
Foundations of Economics

KAUSHIK BASU

OXFORD
UNIVERSITY PRESS

OXFORD
UNIVERSITY PRESS

Great Clarendon Street, Oxford OX2 6DP
Oxford University Press is a department of the University of Oxford.
It furthers the University's objective of excellence in research, scholarship,
and education by publishing worldwide in

Oxford New York

Athens Auckland Bangkok Bogotá Buenos Aires Calcutta
Cape Town Chennai Dar es Salaam Delhi Florence Hong Kong Istanbul
Karachi Kuala Lumpur Madrid Melbourne Mexico City Mumbai
Nairobi Paris São Paulo Shanghai Singapore Taipei Tokyo Toronto Warsaw
and associated companies in Berlin Ibadan

Oxford is a registered trade mark of Oxford University Press
in the UK and certain other countries

Published in the United States
by Oxford University Press Inc., New York

British Library Cataloguing in Publication Data
Data available

Library of Congress Cataloging in Publication Data
Basu, Kaushik.
Prelude to political economy : a study of the social and political foundations of
economics / Kaushik Basu.
p. cm.
Includes bibliographical references and index.
1. Economics–Political aspects. 2. Economics–Social aspects. I. Title.
HB74.P65 B37 2000   330.1–dc21   00–044601

ISBN 0-19-829671-1

1 3 5 7 9 10 8 6 4 2

Typeset by Graphicraft Limited, Hong Kong
Printed in Great Britain
on acid-free paper by
T.J. International Ltd.,
Padstow, Cornwall

For
Karna and Diksha

Contents

Preface

This book is a critique of economics as social science. The need for such a critique stems not from the failure of economics but from its success, which has meant that the method of economics has spilled beyond its boundaries to many other social sciences. It is the anchor of the rapidly growing and varied concerns of the subject of law and economics; one sees its influence on the new institutionalism in sociology and anthropology; and, above all, it provides the foundations for the new positive political economy. This has led contemporary economists to ask questions that go well beyond traditional economics. These queries have resulted in plenty of answers; and, bolstered by this profusion, the literature has moved on rapidly.

The critique I am attempting in this book is unusual because it uses much of the same techniques that contemporary economics and positive political economy use. I rely on game theory, and more importantly, on game-theoretic reasoning. However, I do not share the confidence with which modern economists and political scientists have rushed to explain the rise and fall of nations, why one nation runs into a financial crisis and another not, why one economy remains stagnant and another takes off, why democracies appear when they do and do not when they do not. Seeing agreement among the practitioners, it is easy for the lay reader to believe that these answers must be right. But we must not forget that a group of people, all praising one another for their understanding of some phenomenon, can create a "cult effect," where knowledge is replaced by a shared illusion.

Contrary to the impression that the above paragraphs may create, this is an optimistic book. It is written in the belief that there is a large volume of knowledge that is within our grasp. And progress through this can enable us to craft better policy and, through that, a better society. What the book tries to do is to caution us that perhaps we are trying to move too fast, being too glib with our elegant tools of analysis. We have to be content with taking shorter steps as we advance to these larger questions concerning society and polity. And the hard part of this is not the mathematics, but the logic and reasoning over matters of conceptual intricacy. It must be recognized that markets and the economy are embedded in society, politics and the law; and an immense amount of research has to go into understanding the nature of this embedding before we can emerge with reliable answers. This is a large research agenda; and the present book is an attempt to develop some of the building blocks for the task. The demolition that is done is done entirely to make room for a more robust construction. My critique, therefore, is not meant to attack the belief of the new political scientist or the sociologist that economics has much to offer; it certainly does. Let me leave it at this. For me, as an economist, to labor the point that a critique of economics is not all loss will otherwise be reminiscent of Rimsky-Korsakov's widow, at her husband's funeral, consoling a weeping Stravinsky: "Pull yourself together, young man, we've still got Glazunov."[1]

I remarked above that the hard part of this research is not the mathematics. What is not often appreciated by economists is that good economics, and more generally social science, entails a kind of reasoning that is refreshingly independent and requires a skill that is different from one that a pure mathematician or a natural scientist needs. In a sense, it needs that and more. One factor behind this is that human beings – even those who can reason very well when they are talking of abstract entities, such as p and q – have a tendency to falter once the p's and q's are replaced by emotive words and propositions. A lot of contemporary social science requires very fine reasoning and, if one is innately prone to err where the terrain is one of direct human concern or emotional significance, which in the social sciences will frequently be the case, it is clear why we have to be extra careful in making our deductions and reaching conclusions.

The technical demands of this book are small; virtually anybody can read it. But it is not a book that can be read through quickly, at least not with comprehension. It is meant to be *worked* through. In places I have tried to say things that are difficult to articulate with full precision. My reason for persisting with such material is the belief that ideas are conveyed not just through the direct meanings of words, but in other ways as well. The human mind, unlike a computer, can and does receive messages beyond the literal. It is true not merely of poetry, but also of prose, that messages get transmitted not just through the lines but between them.

Economists are dismissive of ideas that cannot be fully formalized. This is a mistake; the body of human knowledge would be a fraction of what it is if formalism were the only way in which ideas were transmitted. I say this to caution the reader not to cast aside the less formal parts of this book as less important.

I hope that this monograph will be read by social scientists of all persuasions and that it will be used in courses on political economy, economics

---

[1] This is from a story told by Isaiah Berlin (Brendel A. (1997), "On Isaiah Berlin, 1909–1997," New York Review of Books, 44(20): 11).

and law – and even on economic theory. There are several ways of reading the book. The best is slowly, and all the way through. If it is being used for a graduate course, it can fit nicely into a single semester. For the reader in a hurry and with a modicum of familiarity with game theory, I would recommend Chapters 1, 4–6 and 8. For someone in a hurry and without that familiarity with game theory, one needs to simply add Chapter 2 to the above list. In the course of spelling out its central theses, the book presents and discusses several little paradoxes and puzzles, many of which remain unresolved. The reader who is not interested in the larger questions of the economy or in political philosophy will, I hope, nevertheless find the many smaller arguments and conundrums challenging enough to pause, think about, and perhaps even to join in and try to solve.

I began writing this book in the fall of 1993, when I gave a set of ten lectures to graduate students at the London School of Economics as part of a longer sequence in economic theory. I had called my lectures "Topics in Political Economy." I am grateful to Nick Stern for the invitation to visit LSE, and to Max Steuer and John Moore for the invitation to give the lectures and for tolerating this unconventional interpretation of what constitutes economic theory. The zest for such a large intellectual enterprise was also nurtured by my living quarters during my three months in London. By a stroke of good luck, it turned out to be an old high-ceilinged apartment, owned by London University, in the historic Bloomsbury area where, even on a short evening stroll, one was likely to come upon several plaques carrying the names of prominent thinkers from the 1920s and 1930s.

This book has been exceptionally long in incubation. The decision to write the book was taken well before the LSE lectures, in 1987 in Melbourne, after a series of long conversations on social norms and institutions with my friend and co-author, the economic historian Eric Jones. It was Eric who felt that I must write such a book and I immediately knew that he was right. A book could give me the space to articulate what I wanted to say, which journals, being more tradition-bound, would not allow. When I say "such a book" I do so with hesitation because there was no way of being sure, before actually producing the book, what Eric's intended "such" was. All I can say now is that, in case it was something else, he will have to live with the fact that he has made me lose more man hours on a single project than I ever have before.

As I worked on the monograph, I tested the emerging ideas and notes on a graduate class studying political economy at Cornell University. The students came, primarily, from economics and government departments and their different perspectives did a lot to enrich the material. The compulsion of weekly lectures forced me to read philosophy and other writings beyond economics – a task with which, left to myself, I would have been more tardy. Some of my ideas I got to test on an audience at the Institute for Advanced Study, Princeton, in May 1997, when I was invited to give a lecture at a conference to celebrate 25 years of social science at the Institute. I am grateful to Clifford Geertz, Albert Hirschman, Michael Walzer and Joan Scott for the invitation.

As the material for the monograph matured, a large number of economists and other social scientists read and commented on the notes, chapters, related papers and, in some cases, the entire manuscript. There are others with whom I have talked on these topics and from whom I have taken in wisdom handsomely. I cannot name them all, but I must thank especially Kenneth Arrow, Amiya Bagchi, Pranab Bardhan, Alaka Basu, Karna Basu, Larry Blume, Pinaki Bose, Sam Bowles, Dan Bromley, Partha Chatterjee, Mrinal Datta Chaudhuri, Avinash Dixit, David Easley, Patrick Emerson, Garance Genicot, Ashima Goyal, Joseph Halpern, Karla Hoff, Peter Katzenstein, Yvan Lengwiler, Luis-Felipe Lopez-Calva, Michael MacPherson, Sugata Marjit, Puran Mongia, Ted O'Donaghue, Claus Offe, Menno Pradhan, James Robinson, Emma Rothschild, Ariel Rubinstein, Andy Rutten, Amartya Sen, Neelam Sethi, Robert Solow, S. Subramanian (Subbu) and Eduardo Zambrano. Of these, two names that can bear repeating are Karla's and Subbu's, who read through and commented on the entire manuscript. If it were not for their help, the book would have been out sooner.

During the 1997/98 academic year, the sociologist David Strang and I directed a multidisciplinary research program on organizations and institutions at Cornell. This allowed us to bring in speakers and organize seminars and workshops. The interactions were invariably of value to me. From the point of view of this project, the visitors from whom I learned most were George Akerlof, Randy Calvert and Jean-Philippe Platteau.

Three readers for Oxford University Press made good use of the cover of anonymity and gave me some brutally frank criticisms and suggestions; at the same time they showed a confidence in the book that was heartening. I am also grateful to Andrew Schuller for not just accepting the book but for showing an appreciation of the project, much beyond what one has the right to expect from the publisher.

I had outstanding research assistance from Patrick Emerson, who also read and commented on several chapters. Secretarial support was provided with great skill by Paulette Carlisle. And, finally, I thank Alaka for being with me through the ups and downs.

The writing of this book has been for me an experience of unalloyed joy. I view the concerns expressed in the pages that follow not as a final word but as delineating a research agenda in an area of importance. I feel confident that I will work further on it in the future; and I hope that the book will lure at least a few others.

Kaushik Basu
December 1999

Part I. PRELIMINARIES

1. Introduction

1.1. Incident off Grand Trunk Road

The Grand Trunk Road is not quite as grand as it sounds, especially on the three odd hours' stretch between the towns of Bagodar and Dhanbad in eastern India. On a winter evening in the early 1990s I was traveling by taxi on this stretch, in order to catch a train to Calcutta, when we were forced to take a diversion. It was on this desolate road that we came across a ramshackle road-block. It was being manned by youngsters wielding *lathis*[1] and swords. In front of us, also stopped by the road-block, was a lorry, and the young men were talking to its occupants. From the sight of some distant lanterns I figured we were close to a village. While we waited for our turn, my taxi-driver turned towards me and in a whisper said that these youngsters were hoodlums collecting *rangdari* tax by threatening to beat up passengers and drivers. He asked me not to talk; to leave it all to him.

I had read and heard about the illegal *rangdari* tax – extortion that occurs in some parts of rural India – but I had not met anybody who had direct experience of it. Such is the human urge to be first, that, despite the tense circumstance, I was quite excited at the prospect of encountering it ahead of my friends.

Eventually, one of the youngsters strode up to our car and asked me to lower my window. He had a wad of paper in one hand and a *lathi* in the other. He explained that they were collecting a small sum of money, as *rangdari* tax, from every vehicle. After we paid it, which, he politely explained, we would have to, he would give us a receipt and we would be free to go.

The end of the story is unimportant for my present purpose, but here it is for completeness. Not wanting a showdown, I reached for my pocket but my driver, made of sterner stuff, would have none of it. To my dismay he got into an altercation and was asked to get out of the car and talk to the boss, who stood nearby. After some animated discussion with the boss, the driver returned. The road-blocks were removed and as we sped away in the direction of Dhanbad my driver proudly told me how we had escaped

---

[1] Rods, usually iron or wood.

extortion. He said he had told the young men and their boss that I was a visitor from Delhi and forcing me to pay the "tax" would sully my impression of the region. This struck a chord of local chauvinism in his listeners and, like some visiting dignitary, I was allowed to proceed tax-free.

Innocuous though this incident was, it has a lot to say to a trained economist – provided, of course, that she is not trained beyond repair. Note that at one level these youngsters were doing something quite normal in an economy; they were selling a product. The product itself, however, was unusual. It consisted of uninjured scalps, untwisted arms and other bodily harms not done. This is because what the youngster with the *lathi* in one hand and receipts in the other was, effectively, telling us was that if we gave him a small amount of money, he would let us go unharmed. Indeed, viewed in this way, it was a bargain, as the lorry driver, ahead of us, well realized.

In economics books, why do we almost never encounter such trades? The reason is that, for each person, certain things are assumed to be his endowment, which only he can sell. This includes not only his house and his watch but his head and arms as well. While for many economic contexts this assumption is a harmless one, it turns out to be untenably strong when one considers primitive economies, modern international economic relations, and societal relations in general. In these contexts, individuals often encroach on one another's endowments, selling to a person what in most societies would be considered as belonging to that person. In subtle and not-so-subtle ways, big countries bully small countries, big business extorts from powerless consumers, and husbands coerce wives, using as pawns and bringing into exchange (often unobtrusively) goods that in standard economics are assumed to be beyond the reach of the market. With the rise in interdisciplinary research, which straddles economics, politics and sociology and, for good or for bad, increasingly uses the method of economics, it is essential to confront this assumption frontally.

Another matter to which the incident off Grand Trunk Road draws our attention is the meaning of government, law and social norms. Indian newspapers and magazines have written about the *rangdari* tax as illegal extortion, conducted by hoodlums. At one level that is true, but it was impossible for me not to see that it was not quite like stray banditry either.

The existence of the village near the road-block suggested that the tax collectors had some legitimacy in the eyes of the villagers. It is very likely that they spend part of their booty on the local villages and part for their own merriment, which is rather like what real governments do. I could not determine the purpose of the receipts, but one conjecture is that other members of the same group had set up road-blocks elsewhere and, if one was unfortunate enough to run into more than one road-block on the same day, one could show the receipt and save oneself from being double-taxed.

All this reveals that the collectors of *rangdari* tax are almost like a government in a microcosm. They have local legitimacy, and they collect taxes by threatening punishment, and they have organization. The reason why we think of such an activity as illegal is because we treat the larger government to be the real one. But there is nothing immutable about this. There are times when competing claims to legitimacy are widely recognized. In 1971 when the East Pakistan leaders declared the government in West Pakistan as illegal and collected money to run their own efforts, it was no longer obvious who was the real government and who were the collectors of *rangdari* tax. Once the nation of Bangladesh was born, gradually it seemed to the citizens that that was the only legitimate state they had ever had.

In economics, we have typically been glib about the meaning and constitution of government. Government has been treated as a crucible of exogenous variables; a posse of bureaucrats, policemen and planners carrying out the functions of the state. It is the agency towards which economists direct their advice. It provides policy economists with their *raison d'être*. In reality, however, the individuals who comprise government are also "players" in the economy game, with their own motivations, strategies and game plans. Once one recognizes this, advising government appears to be as futile as advising consumers or entrepreneurs of firms. One is then forced to consider the question that dates back at least to Hume: Who will police the policeman?

For successful social science we need a better understanding of the state, the law, social norms and the role of policy advice. This is precisely what the present book strives to achieve.

1.2. Positive Political Economy

The dissatisfaction with mainstream economics that provokes this enquiry has been felt by others and has given rise to the nascent, but rapidly growing, field that is frequently called "positive political economy."

Mainstream economics was founded on many strong assumptions. Being concerned with the functioning of markets, it ignored questions concerning the nature of government. For the most part institutions and politics were treated as immaterial; government was construed as an exogenous "black box;" social norms were equated with decorations. As an initial gambit and for certain restricted purposes this was fine. But living with such assumptions of convenience has the risk of these beginning to *appear* real after some time. As the horizons of our enquiry have broadened and the different social sciences have trespassed across their boundaries, these assumptions have become a hindrance rather than an aid. In particular, if we want to understand why some economies have succeeded and some failed, or why some governments are so effective and others not, the first step is to recognize the importance of institutions.

It is this recognition that has given rise to the literature on positive political economy. And to the extent that the present book is also founded on this recognition, it may be thought of as belonging to this new discipline. But I would be wary of such a label. Starting from the right motivations, positive political economy has moved on far too quickly, far too confidently. Barring a few important exceptions, these new writings have the deficiency of having too much to say. Given the demand for this kind of inquiry, this is not an unnatural development. But at the same time it has the risk of developing into a new orthodoxy, with its concomitant retinue of consultants offering results and solutions.

When Voltaire was dying, the Jesuit priest by his bedside urged him to denounce the devil; but Voltaire's response was characteristically burlesque: "This is no time for making new enemies" (Holmes, 1995: 55). In venturing out into this new field of enquiry by denouncing potential friends, I am aware that I am flouting Voltaire's wise advice. But there is no other option. This monograph is founded in much deeper skepticism than the new political economy. It is more oriented to shifting our methods of enquiry than to offering new results. The new results presented are few and tentative. Furthermore, this book has a broader brush than positive political economy, being interested in social situations that lie beyond economics *and* politics. In this sense, my interest is closer to the *old* "political economy" – for instance, that of John Stuart Mill.

The present book, however, uses techniques that were not available to writers in the nineteenth century. I refer here especially to the techniques of strategic analysis, which became available with the rise of game theory. Hence, the present book may be viewed as an attempt to provide the groundwork for reconstructing the old political economy using modern methods of analysis.

The emergence of game theory has undermined one of the central tenets of conservative economics: that individuals left to strive for their own selfish ends automatically bring about social optimality. The first Fundamental Theorem of Welfare Economics, from which this folk wisdom is allegedly derived, never really said or implied this, as has been emphasized by some of the economists who actually worked to refine and formalize the theorem (see Hahn, 1984, esp. Ch. 5). Nevertheless, this became part of conservative orthodoxy. This orthodoxy withstood repeated attacks by Marxist economists and acquired the reputation of resilience and, through that, more followers. But it is clear now that it withstood these attacks not because it was the truth but because the attacks were inadequate and theoretically ill-founded. The traditional wisdom has now finally begun to crumble, ironically because of further developments in economic theory and, in particular, the advent of game theory and strategic analysis.

These developments are changing the very nature of the debate. The term "intervention," so often associated with government, betrays an implicit view of government as an agency exogenous to the economy. Once we take an inclusive view of government, as this book suggests we should, the subject of government intervention acquires a certain parallel with the subject of consumer intervention or entrepreneur intervention. The goodness or badness of all these interventions ought to be discussed on similar footings. The fact that, in conventional discourse, the former is debated with so much ardor and the latter is treated as beyond the pale of discussion is a direct outcome of our flawed conception of government.

1.3. An Overview

I used to have a jogging book, written by a jogging expert, which insisted that, if one did not want to injure oneself, one must first warm up by doing stretches for a few minutes before jogging. The trouble was that the book said nothing about how to do stretches properly. Then, on June 27, 1997, I was pleased to find our local daily, *The Ithaca Journal*, carrying a full-length article on stretching. As I read the article, however, my pleasure turned to disappointment. The article was written by a stretch expert. He warned that stretches were not to be taken lightly and, if one were not to injure oneself, one must first warm up by doing ten minutes of jogging. Alas, there seemed to be no way that I could get a little exercise without injuring myself.

In organizing the various topics in this book I face some of the same dilemma. Like the jogging and stretching experts, social scientists of different specializations tend to argue for the primacy of place for their own kind of social science. But once one takes an inclusive view of the state, the markets, and the social norms espoused in this book, there is no natural starting point. I have responded to this dilemma by drawing a somewhat artificial line between received wisdom and what is more novel, and by placing most of the traditional ideas in the initial chapters as warmups. The central message of this book, where I have new things to say, therefore comes a little later, so that the core of the book consists of Chapters 4 to 8. It is easy to interpret this as taking a somewhat dismissive attitude towards individual rationality and strategic decision-theory, but that will be a mistake. I have placed these topics in the preliminary chapters simply to give the reader the option of going over what is generally known in the economics literature before going to the central theses of this book, and not as a signal of their being secondary in understanding markets and the economy.

The formal game theory that is used in this book is minimal, though game-theoretic reasoning permeates the pages. So that no reader is handicapped because of a lack of knowledge of game theory, Chapter 2 provides a straightforward primer on game theory. As with all major intellectual ventures, it is only a tiny portion of the enormous literature on game theory that is relevant for the real world. So the researcher who is interested primarily in real-world economics and politics needs to understand only a small selection of that vast subject. Chapter 2 is my (admittedly idiosyncratic) choice for such a reader. Chapter 3 begins by presenting and discussing standard notions of individual rationality, and the power of the economist's rationality axiom.

Part II of the book, consisting of Chapter 4 alone, situates the individual in a social setting. It consists of an extended argument that an economy or a market is invariably embedded in a social setting, with all its attendant norms, institutions and beliefs. This is not just empirically so; but is also true in our theoretical models, which *seem* to function in an institutional vacuum but which are invariably founded on institutional assumptions. If we do not choose these assumptions consciously, it simply means that they get selected unwittingly.

Part III (Chapters 5–8) grapples with the idea of "the state" and laws. It argues that the standard view is fundamentally flawed; that social norms and the law are much closer than appears at first sight; and that the state is nothing but a set of beliefs. This last idea echoes some of Hume's views, but it is buttressed with techniques of analysis that were not available in Hume's day. And, as a consequence, it is possible to subject this idea to more rigorous scrutiny and to give the argument a more formal structure.

Despite the greater rigor, these chapters cannot claim any more than to take very small positive steps. I believe they are important because they are steps in the right direction, and I hope that that will compensate for the absence of anything that can be described as definitive. One can only hope that, as Robert Nozick (1974: xii) put it so eloquently, "there is room for words on subjects other than last words."

The two chapters (9 and 10) that comprise Part IV discuss a few special topics in welfare economics. They examine the problem of interpersonal comparison and construct an unconventional argument against consequentialism and, in particular, utilitarianism. These chapters also discuss the role of individual rights and propose an approach to modeling these, which is a direct outcome of the view of law and economics put forward in Part III.

While the central message of this book – the need to take a more inclusive view of social norms and the state in studying economics, and that such an enterprise may be harder than it appears at first sight – occurs in Chapters 4–8, the book has an important corollary proposition to report. This concerns the domain over which individuals maximize utility (or whatever it is that they maximize) and the domain over which utilitarianism and other consequentialist ethics are applied. This second message emerges gradually, in bits and pieces comprising spinoffs from the effort to develop and defend the central message. Hence, there is a need to pick up the threads of this corollary and state it as clearly as possible. This is done in Part V, Chapter 11. It is argued in that chapter that human beings do not use their rationality calculus over all available actions but only over a subset of them. This is not just an empirical matter but also may be an inherent feature of the world – an implication of the fact that the collectivity of all available actions is often unmanageably large and may not even constitute a set at all. This corollary proposition is a somewhat inarticulate criticism of normal economics. It needs to be polished, sharpened and made rigorous. But to the extent that it is fallout from my arguments, it is impossible to ignore, especially because it may have important implications for the economist's view of the free-rider problem and the design of incentive-compatible mechanisms and policy in general. I have resolved the dilemma of handling a proposition that can only be inarticulately spelled out at this stage, but that is nonetheless important in practice, by relegating it to the concluding chapter, amidst leads and pointers to future research.

Even though this book is a critique of conventional economics and positive political economy, it is not meant to detract from the many achievements of modern economics. The discipline's rigor and comprehensiveness have undoubtedly enriched our understanding of the marketplace. In matters of everyday economics, such as the control of inflation or the tracking of the inefficiencies of the market, we have learned much from our texts. But this very success has had a regrettable consequence: the confidence it inspires has spilled over to domains where we have little reason to be confident. Today's economists and political scientists are often called upon to advise on major policy changes for transition economies, to analyze why some developing countries make a mockery of the epithet "developing" by refusing to do any such thing, and to design large reform packages. Thanks largely to mechanisms of herd behavior, a vast majority of economists and many international organizations seem to speak in one voice, giving outsiders the impression of a deeply-held common understanding. The East Asian crisis of 1997, the state of the Russian economy in the year 2000 and the obstinacy of poverty in sub-Saharan Africa are all testimony to the inadequacy of conventional wisdom.

If we want to address these larger questions, we have to take seriously the fact that the market and the economy are embedded in society and politics. We have to recognize that the market system does not – and, more importantly, cannot – function solely on the basis of the individual pursuit of self-interest (Arrow, 1972, 1982; Stiglitz, 1999). It is increasingly being realized that institutions matter. But to give this simple-sounding idea proper shape requires us to reexamine the social and political foundations of economics. This is precisely what this book attempts. Hence, although the book is, at one level, a fairly abstract exercise, it is also motivated by mundane concerns of policy and social progress.

2. Games and Misdemeanors: Game Theory for the Uninitiated

2.1. Motivation

Consider these three scenarios. John F. Kennedy and Nikita Khrushchev pondering their next moves over Cuba; Garry Kasparov and Vishwanathan Anand confronting each other across a chess board; the manufacturers of Absolut Vodka and Stolichnaya working out their marketing strategies. There is much that is disparate in these three scenarios: One involves war, one sport and one business; one concerns nations, one individuals and one firms. Yet there is also something that is common to all three descriptions. "Game theory" is a subject that deals with the common element. From the point of view of game theory, in each of these scenarios, agents are trying to optimize something, while taking into account the fact that others are also doing the same; this is the essence and the other things are details.

For economics, the rise of game theory over the last few decades has been as momentous as the appearance of marginalist analysis towards the end of the nineteenth century. For good or for bad, game theory has permeated virtually all branches of economics. It has also, for the first time, given economics a method of analysis that is not borrowed from the natural sciences. On the contrary, nurtured and developed within economics, this method has spread to other disciplines, such as political science, sociology, psychology, ethics and even biology.

The origins of game theory go back to at least 1913, when the mathematician Ernst Zermelo published a remarkable paper on chess.[1] There were some contributions after that, notably by Emile Borel in 1921, but the big break came in 1944 with the publication of von Neumann and Morgenstern's book on the subject. For the next thirty years or so, game theory was considered a major *intellectual* breakthrough but it nevertheless remained a curio. It was only from the mid-1970s that it really began

[1] The work that took place in the nineteenth century and even earlier was mainly that of probabilists, often analyzing card games. An important contribution was a minimax solution to a card game by James Waldegrave in the early eighteenth century, which got to be known by word of mouth and letters between mathematicians of that time. Waldegrave, who subsequently went to Vienna and Versailles as the British ambassador, abandoned mathematics and did not pursue this line of thought any further.

establishing itself as an essential methodological tool for economists, soon thereafter spreading to other related social sciences.

This book uses some game theory and a lot of game-*theoretic* reasoning; and the present chapter prepares the reader for this. It covers a little more than is strictly needed for this book, but it should provide one with the tools needed to read beyond this book and, more importantly, to develop one's own ideas and research agenda.

2.2. Hex

Legend has it that the game of Hex developed as a pastime among mathematicians at Princeton University, who played it on the hexagonal tiles covering the bathroom floor at Fine Hall.[2] The mathematicians included John Nash to whom is attributed a brilliant theorem about this game.

The rules of the game are simple. Consider the 14-by-14 hexagonal board shown in Fig. 2.1. There is nothing magical about the number 14; it can actually be any *n*-by-*n* board. Two players play this game. Player 1 (or White) has white counters and player 2 (or Black) has black counters.

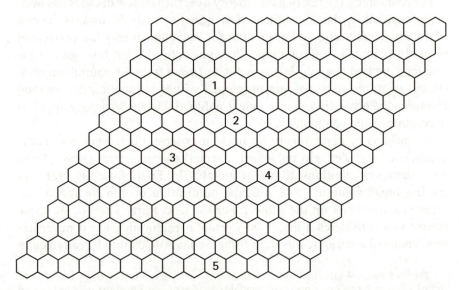

Figure 2.1 A sample Hex board, with a game started

[2] The game was probably invented by the Danish poet and polymath, Piet Hein.

White has the first move. This involves placing a white counter inside any of the 196 hexagonal boxes. Then Black places a black counter in any of the remaining 195 boxes. Then White places a white counter; and then Black; and so on. They play till all boxes are full (with 98 white counters and 98 black counters).

If there is an unbroken chain of hexagonal boxes with white counters from the top edge to the bottom edge then White is declared the winner. If there is an unbroken black chain from the left edge to the right edge then Black is the winner. It is easy to see that both White and Black cannot be winners. Less easy to see but also true is the fact that this game can never end in a draw. That is, once the board is entirely covered with black and white counters, there will be either an unbroken chain of white counters from the top edge to the bottom edge or an unbroken chain of black counters from the left edge to the right edge.[3]

Despite its easy rules, Hex is a fascinating game to play and the reader is encouraged to photocopy Fig. 2.1, whiten out the numbers, and play the game by writing in W and B in lieu of placing white and black counters.

The theorem that is attributed to John Nash is that, in the game of Hex, *White can always win.* What is fascinating about this theorem is that it can be proved even without knowing *how* White can win. Consider the game of Noughts and Crosses also known as tic-tac-toe. Anybody familiar with this game knows that in this game both players can always ensure a draw. This is proved by actually showing *how* each player can ensure a draw. In Hex, on the contrary, I may not (indeed I do not) know how to win if I were playing White but I nevertheless know that White can ensure a win.

Before I prove the theorem, let me introduce some terminology, which is anyway useful for later purposes. In a game, a **strategy** is a statement of a player's full plan of action for all contingencies that may arise. Thus White's strategy could be this. Place the first white counter in the (hexagonal) box marked 1 in Fig. 2.1. If Black then places a counter in box 2, place a white counter in 3; if Black places a counter in 4 instead, place a white counter in 5; and so on. Black's strategy can be something like this. If White places the first counter in the top left box, place a black counter in 1. If White places the first counter in the second box from the upper left hand corner, place a black counter in 1; and so on. So – and this is important to understand – if White writes down a strategy in a book and goes away, then someone else (by using the book) can play for White the entire game, no matter how Black plays. Likewise for Black's strategy.

---

[3] For a proof, see Beck, Bleicher and Crowe (1969: 329–338).

The theorem that was mentioned above may be stated formally as follows:

In the game of Hex, White has a winning strategy.

In other words, White can write down a strategy that ensures victory, no matter how Black plays. In yet other words, if both players are perfect, White is bound to win.

Here is an outline of the proof by contradiction. Suppose that Black has a winning strategy. What this means is that Black can write a book that describes a strategy that ensures a win for Black. Suppose now that Black has written such a book and White has photocopied this. White's plan is to follow this book. For the first move, White will of course not find any instruction in this book, since this is a book giving Black's strategy (and so it will have instructions on how to make the second move, fourth move and so on). So let White place the first white counter anywhere, say in the box marked 1 in Fig. 2.1; and let him in his mind refer to this as a "grey" counter. The second move is, of course, Black's. Black places a black counter wherever she wishes. Suppose she places it in the box marked 2. Now White pretends that Black's move was the first one (that is, he ignores the grey counter) and looks up (the photocopy of) Black's book to see how he should play. This book will have instruction on how to play move 2 since it is Black's book. Let White place a white counter as this book instructs (of course, with symmetric reversal of the board since his aim is to link the top edge to the bottom edge). Next Black moves. White again ignores the grey counter, treats Black's move as if it were the third move in the game and consults Black's book on how to play the fourth move.

In following the instruction in Black's book in this manner, White can run into one hitch. If at some point the book says "Place a counter in box 1," then, recalling that White had placed a counter in box 1 in the first move and was playing as if that move were never made, he is in trouble. That box is not empty. But this is no real problem. All White has to do is place a counter in any open box, think of this new counter as grey, and start thinking of the first counter (the one in box 1) as white. Hence, White can follow Black's book to a T. But since Black's book can ensure a win, this means that White can always win. Hence, if Black has a winning strategy, then White has a winning strategy. This is a contradiction. So our initial assumption that Black has a winning strategy cannot be true. And since in Hex, as noted earlier, there can never be a draw, it follows that White has a winning strategy. This completes the proof.

Some people may find the penultimate sentence of the previous paragraph confusing. Rightly so, because it is based on a presumption, namely that in a game such as Hex, if both players are perfect, then either White always wins, or Black always wins or there is always a draw. Fortunately, this is true and, in the case of Hex, fairly transparently so (although we know that the third option is purely academic in Hex). This also happens to be a consequence of Zermelo's (1913) theorem on chess, which says that in chess either White has a winning strategy, or Black has a winning strategy, or both players can ensure a draw; in brief, the outcome of chess is said to be **determined**.

At first sight this sounds like a dull tautology. In actuality it *is* a tautology, but not dull; it says something very interesting. If it said that in every game of chess either White will win or Black will win or there will be a draw, that would be a dull tautology. But Zermelo's theorem says that either White *has a winning strategy* or Black *has a winning strategy* or both players *have a strategy to ensure at least a draw*. In other words, what Zermelo's theorem says is that chess is actually as humdrum a game as Noughts and Crosses. If perfect players play the game, the outcome will always be the same. Indeed, there would be no point in playing the game once it is known who is playing with white. What makes this theorem interesting is that it tells us that the outcome is *determined* without being able to tell us as to which way it is determined. The reason why chess continues to fascinate us is because the perfect player has not yet been born. Neither Deep Blue nor Kasparov is anywhere near that ideal.

Zermelo's theorem extends to a large class of games, which includes Hex. In fact, Zermelo's theorem is very easy to prove for Hex. This can be done by backward-induction as follows. Define first a game called "t-Hex," where t is a non-negative integer less than 196, as follows. In a game of t-Hex, one starts with a board on which the first t moves are glued on the usual Hex board by the manufacturer. Depending on where the t counters are glued one can have different t-Hex boards (and, therefore, games). The two-players play a game of t-Hex by taking the first t moves as given and playing from there on.

Thus it should be clear that there can be 196 1-Hex games, depending on where the one white counter is glued in. At the other extreme, note that for every 195-Hex game the outcome is determined. To see this, consider a 195-Hex game. There is one empty box where Black has to place his counter. Hence, for every play of this 195-Hex, one of the following three must be true: (a) White can always win. (b) Black can always win. (c) The players can always ensure a draw.[4] So, in brief, every 195-Hex game is determined.

---

[4] Of course, as we have already noted, (c) in fact never happens.

Now consider a 194-Hex game. This begins with White's move. After White moves, the board gets converted into a 195-Hex game. Since all 195-Hex games are determined, it follows that, in the 194-Hex game, for every possible move by White the outcome is known. If all these outcomes result in Black winning, in the 194-Hex we can say that Black always wins. If at least one outcome results in White winning, we can say that in the 194-Hex White can always win (he simply has to make *that* move); and if at least one outcome results in a draw and no outcome results in White winning, we can assert that in the 194-Hex White can ensure a draw. Hence, 194-Hex games are also determined.

Continuing to induct backwards in the same way, we establish that the 0-Hex game is determined. But 0-Hex is nothing but Hex. So this establishes Zermelo's theorem for Hex.

We shall have occasion to return several times later to backward-induction arguments of this kind. But it is time now to move away from parlor games, like chess and Hex, to the kind of games that underlie social analysis.

2.3. Normal-Form Games

Before we can analyze real-life conflicts, such as the Cuban missile crisis of 1962, as a game, it is essential to cast these real conflicts into the formal mold of a "game." One standard kind of game is called a normal-form (or, equivalently, strategic-form or single-shot) game. Such a game is best thought of as one that is played simultaneously by all players and at one point of time. Before describing a normal-form game formally, consider some examples.

The best-known such game is the Prisoner's Dilemma (PD): Two individuals arrested for some joint crime or misdemeanor are locked up in separate rooms and read out an eccentric sentence by the magistrate. Each of them has to say either that he (D) did commit the crime or that he (C) is clean. If both choose to say D, they will get ten years each in jail. If both choose C the magistrate will presume they did not commit the crime, as they attest, but nevertheless consider them guilty of some minor misdemeanor and so put them in jail for two years each. If one person chooses C and the other D, then the former (the magistrate presumes) has not only committed the crime but tells lies, and so will get 20 years in jail, while the latter is so good in comparison – he has committed the crime but look at his honesty – that he will go scot-free.[5]

The information contained in the magistrate's sentence can be summarized in a "payoff matrix" as shown in Fig. 2.2. In this payoff matrix, prisoner (or player) 1 chooses rows and 2 chooses columns. The two numbers in each box denote the players' payoffs: the left figure is player 1's payoff and the right is 2's payoff. So if 1 chooses D and 2 chooses C we have a box showing (0, 20). Hence prisoner 1 gets 0 years and prisoner 2 gets 20 years in jail.

Prisoner 2

		C	D
Prisoner 1	C	2, 2	20, 0
	D	0, 20	10, 10

Figure 2.2 Payoff matrix (jail terms)

Though I have called the table in Fig. 2.2 a payoff matrix, strictly speaking it is not so. This is because in a payoff matrix the numbers denote utility or money earned – essentially something that a person wants to *maximize*. In the above table, the numbers are jail years – something that people try to *minimize*. We can, however, alter the story so that the magistrate announces fines instead of jail years and we could then think of the payoffs as money that will be left with each player after paying the fine. If both players have ten units of money to start with, we can think of a set of punishments that in relative terms is identical to the jail terms described above and that results in each player ending up with the money shown in the payoff matrix in Fig. 2.3. If both players choose C they get eight units of money; if player 1 chooses C and player 2 chooses D, they get 0 and 10

[5] The Prisoner's Dilemma was conceived in 1950 when A. W. Tucker was visiting the mathematics department of Stanford (on leave from Princeton) and because of some space problems was given an office in the psychology department. His neighbors, curious about his research, asked him to give a talk to their department. Tucker, who wanted to demonstrate to the psychologists how a dominant-strategy equilibrium could be suboptimal, invented the Prisoner's Dilemma. It is now known that the *mathematics* of the Prisoner's Dilemma (that there can be dominant strategies for each individual which result in a Pareto suboptimal outcome) was known to scientists at the Rand corporation even before Tucker's talk. But given that what is exciting about the PD is not its arithmetic but its social interpretation, Tucker may rightly be treated as its founder.

	C	D
C	8, 8	0, 10
D	10, 0	1, 1

Figure 2.3 Payoff matrix (Prisoner's Dilemma)

units of money respectively. Strictly speaking, the payoffs are not meant to be in money units but whatever it is that individuals seek to maximize. This is often described by the once-neutral term "utils." The risk of tautology associated with this approach is discussed in Chapter 3.

From now on we shall take the payoff matrix indicated in Fig. 2.3 to be that for the Prisoner's Dilemma (PD), and label it game G_1. Each player wants to maximize his or her payoff. This is what we mean by saying that a player is "rational."[6] Now, how will rational players play the PD game? Put yourself in the shoes of player 1 (i.e. the player choosing rows in Fig. 2.3). Now suppose in the other room the other prisoner has chosen C. Clearly, as player 1 you can either get 8 dollars (by choosing C) or 10 dollars (by choosing D), and so it is better to choose D. If, on the other hand, the other prisoner chooses D, you can get 0 dollars (by choosing C) or 1 dollar (by choosing D). So it is better to choose D. But this means that, no matter what the other prisoner chooses, you are better off choosing D. The Prisoner's Dilemma is no real dilemma at all.

Since this game is symmetric between the two players, the other player will also choose D. So rationality in the PD leads to the outcome (D, D), where each player gets 1 dollar each. The "good" outcome, where they get 8 dollars each, eludes them. So, unlike in traditional neoclassical economics, where individual rationality leads to social efficiency, the PD encapsulates a situation where the opposite happens. This is the reason why the Prisoner's Dilemma is such an important game. It shows up clearly the qualitatively different results we get once we adopt a game-theoretic approach to the economy (with strategic behavior on the part of agents and where externalities are the norm rather than the exception) as opposed to the traditional, neoclassical approach.

Another example of a normal-form game is the Battle of the Sexes. A woman and a man have to decide whether to go to the Ballet (B) or a Sumo wrestling match (S). They would both rather go to the same place but the

---

[6] "Rationality" is a complicated idea and a detailed discussion of it is deferred to Chapter 3.

	B	S
B	4, 2	0, 0
S	0, 0	2, 4

Figure 2.4 Payoff matrix (Battle of the Sexes)

man (player 2) prefers S and the woman (player 1) prefers B. Their benefits are summarized in the payoff matrix in Fig. 2.4. As is the convention, player 1 chooses rows and player 2 chooses columns. If both choose B, the woman gets 4 utils and the man 2 utils. What will be the outcome of this game? In reality a lot depends on who the man is and who the woman is. If they are a married couple of whom the woman is known for her stubbornness, one may expect the outcome to be (B, B). If the man is known to be unbending, perhaps it will be (S, S).

A large part of game theory is concerned with predicting outcomes of games. And the central idea used for prediction is the "Nash equilibrium," due to John Nash. To define a Nash equilibrium without risk of misunderstanding it is important to describe a normal-form game a bit more formally.

A **normal-form game**[7] is fully defined in terms of three components. First, there must be a set of **players**, $N = \{1, \ldots, n\}$. Next, for each player i there has to be a well-defined set S_i of **actions** or **strategies**. At times, S_i will be a finite set that can be denoted by numbers or letters. Thus if player i has three strategies, we can write $S_i = \{1, 2, 3\}$ or $S_i = \{A, B, C\}$. There will be occasions when S_i is infinite. In this book we shall always confine S_i to the set of real numbers. Thus S_i may be an interval $[a, b]$. Finally, in a game every player i must have a **payoff function** P_i. Once every player has chosen a strategy, then P_i specifies a real number denoting the dollars or utils or payoff that player i gets. Thus if $s_j \in S_j$ is chosen by player j $(j = 1, \ldots, n)$, then $P_i(s_1, \ldots, s_n)$ denotes the payoff for player i.

Now, it is easy to see that the Battle of the Sexes (or the PD) is indeed a game in this formal sense. The set of players is $N = \{1, 2\}$; $S_1 = \{S, B\}$ and $S_2 = \{S, B\}$ and the payoff functions are summarized in Fig. 2.4. Thus, for instance, $P_1(S, S) = 2$ and $P_2(B, S) = 0$.

---

[7] Throughout this book, attention is confined to *noncooperative* games; so it is harmless to drop the adjective "noncooperative."

Let us now turn to the "Hawk–Dove" game. If the Prisoner's Dilemma is popularly perceived as the game that helps us understand the arms race, the Hawk–Dove game is viewed as a model of actual conflict. It is the game most commonly cited in strategic evaluations of the Cuban missile crisis of 1962. The Hawk–Dove game is described fully by the payoff matrix shown in Fig. 2.5.

	D	H
D	2, 2	0, 4
H	4, 0	−1, −1

Figure 2.5 Payoff matrix (Hawk–Dove game)

In this game an individual can either be aggressive (choosing strategy "Hawk", or H) or be timid (choosing strategy "Dove", or D).[8] Think of there being a resource worth 4 units. If both participants choose D, they share the resource; that is, they get a payoff of 2 each. If one chooses H and the other D, the payoff is (4, 0), since the aggressor gets it all. If both choose H, there is war and both are worse off in the end, with −1 each: they destroy the resource *and* hurt themselves.

In the abstract world of game theory, there is no difference between the Hawk–Dove game and the "Chicken" game, which apparently used to be played by pairs of degenerate teenagers. They have to drive on a narrow road towards each other at full speed. The one to swerve off loses. If neither swerves, they have a massive accident – which is the worst outcome. If both swerve off, it is a draw. By calling the strategy "swerve" (D) and the one "not to swerve" (H), we can think of the Chicken game exactly as that of the payoff matrix in Fig. 2.5. If you believe the other player will swerve, it is in your interest to be aggressive and to drive through. You get 4 utils. If on the other hand you expect the other player to play H, it is in your interest to play D. A wrong expectation on the part of any player can cause a disastrous outcome.

The analogy with the Cuban missile crisis is based on the latter interpretation. To take an aggressive line with nuclear weapons is to risk war where no side will emerge as victor. But of course if the other side backs down, as Russia fortunately did in 1962, you emerge as victor.

---

[8] This game has shot into prominence because of its use in evolutionary game theory by biologists (*see* Maynard-Smith, 1982).

The crisis began when American U-2 reconnaissance aircraft flying high above Cuba photographed Soviet medium-range ballistic missiles (MRBMs). This information was delivered to President John F. Kennedy on October 16, 1962. The discovery of MRBMs was a shock to Kennedy, who had been assured by Nikita Khrushchev, President of the USSR at the time, that the Soviets would not place offensive weapons in Cuba. These ballistic missiles could deliver nuclear bombs as far as Washington, and so this arming of Cuba was considered unacceptable by Kennedy. This discovery was kept a secret from the larger public as Kennedy and a small coterie of top advisers discussed what the US options were. On October 22, Kennedy went public on this subject and in a televised speech outlined his plans, the central elements of which were to blockade the seas around Cuba in order to prevent any ship carrying arms from reaching Cuban shores and to demand that the Soviet Union begin to dismantle the missiles in Cuba. He also sent a letter to Khrushchev saying much the same.

This aggressive gambit lurched the world closer to a nuclear war than ever before or after. Troops and aircrafts the world over were put on alert, and nuclear submarines left port so as to survive a first assault. The big question was whether the Soviets would try to break the blockade or refuse to dismantle the missiles. If they did either, the United States would, in all likelihood, attack Cuba or even the USSR, perhaps by bombing some small Russian city as a demonstration of resolve; and this could escalate within hours into fully-fledged nuclear war.

The first reaction of Khrushchev was one of indignation. Thus his cable to Kennedy on October 23, 1962 said that the United States was violating "the Charter of United Nations" and "international norms of freedom of navigation on high seas" (May and Zelikow, 1997: 321). Khrushchev insisted that the arms sent by the USSR to Cuba were to enable Cuba to respond to external aggression. And, indeed, the United States had been involved in a variety of overt and covert action against Cuba, the most aggressive covert action being the one codenamed "Mongoose" by the CIA.[9] The Soviets treated Kennedy's announcement as an "ultimatum" and at first gave the impression that they would not give in. They argued that there were US missiles in Turkey, which could hit the USSR within minutes, and if that be so they had the right to interact with Cuba in the way they wished.

The world waited with mounting tension. Then, on October 29, the USSR announced that it would concede to the US demands. Their ships would

---

[9] Robert Kennedy, who zealously promoted Mongoose, had argued that, in the effort to overthrow Castro, "No time, money, effort – or manpower – was to be spared." (May and Zelikow, 1997: 34).

turn around, as some had already done, and the USSR would dismantle the missiles in Cuba; in return, the United States assured the Soviets that they would not invade Cuba. The crisis had blown over.

To reduce this complex conflict to a simple two-player game is, of course, simplistic. Though Khrushchev, from all accounts, took most of his decisions alone, Kennedy used a team of advisers. Moreover, Kennedy also had one eye on the Republicans – he did not want them to make him out to be weak. So, at the minimum, this was not a *two*-player game. In addition, the payoffs were not known to all parties. Were the Russians emotionally committed to protecting Castro? Or were they interested in geographical expansion? There was no way for the United States to know the answers to these questions. And, as Jervis (1976) pointed out, the course of history may have been very different depending on what the Americans thought were the Russian interests. But despite all this, collapsing the game into a simple 2-by-2 game highlights useful aspects of the conflict. For one, it clarifies the role of resolve, or appearing to be resolved. Kennedy understood this, thanks to the enormous amount of advice that he took during those crucial days (one of the inputs in fact coming from the game theorist Thomas Schelling). And Kennedy's making clear that he would play the Hawk strategy, come what may, ensured that the outcome of the game would be (H, D) – H for the United States and D for the USSR.[10]

Given the formal description of a game as given above (before the digression on the Cuban crisis), we can now define a Nash equilibrium. When every player has chosen a strategy, let us call that an "outcome" of the game. Thus an **outcome** is $(s_1, \ldots, s_n)$ where $s_j \in S_j$ for all j. An outcome is also referred to as a "strategy n-tuple," or a "strategy pair" when $n = 2$.

Given a normal-form game, an outcome $(s_1^*, \ldots, s_n^*)$ is a **Nash equilibrium** if, for every player i,

$$P_i(s_1^*, \ldots, s_{i-1}^*, s_i^*, s_{i+1}^*, \ldots, s_n^*) \geq P_i(s_1^*, \ldots, s_{i-1}^*, s_i, s_{i+1}^*, \ldots, s_n^*) \text{ for all } s_i \in S_i.$$

In words, a strategy n-tuple or an outcome is a Nash equilibrium if no player can benefit through a *unilateral* deviation to some other strategy.

In the payoff matrix in Fig. 2.3, clearly (D, D) is a Nash equilibrium, for if any player deviates he gets 0 instead of 1. In Fig. 2.4, there are two Nash equilibria: (B, B) and (S, S). Which are the Nash equilibria in the Hawk–Dove matrix? And do all games have to have at least one Nash equilibrium?

---

[10] It should be evident from this that the *sequence* of moves plays an important role in these conflicts. This is indeed true, as we will see in Section 2.4.

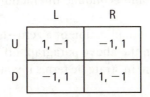

	L	R
U	1, −1	−1, 1
D	−1, 1	1, −1

Figure 2.6 Payoff matrix (zero-sum game)

The answer to this last question is "no" and this is easily illustrated with the example of a "zero-sum" game, as shown in Fig. 2.6 and to be labelled "G_4."

In game G_4, player 1 can choose U (Up) or D (Down) and player 2 can choose L (Left) or R (Right). The payoff matrix shows the payoffs. If the outcome were (U, L), player 2 would benefit by deviating to R. From (U, R), player 1 would want to deviate; from (D, R), player 2; and from (D, L), player 1. So the game has no Nash equilibrium.

There is one way around this non-existence problem. This entails allowing players to use a "mixed strategy." A **mixed strategy** is one in which a player randomizes his strategies. In G_4, a mixed strategy for player 1 can be to play U with probability $\frac{1}{4}$ and D with probability $\frac{3}{4}$. This may be written in brief as $(\frac{1}{4}, \frac{3}{4})$. Basically, a mixed strategy for player 1 is (p_1, p_2) where $0 \le p_i \le 1$ $(i = 1, 2)$ and $p_1 + p_2 = 1$.

If in G_4 player 1 uses the mixed strategy $(\frac{1}{2}, \frac{1}{2})$ and player 2 uses the mixed strategy $(\frac{1}{2}, \frac{1}{2})$, that is, she plays L with probability $\frac{1}{2}$ and R with probability $\frac{1}{2}$, then clearly player 1's expected payoff is 0 and player 2's expected payoff is 0. Note further that no player can do better through a unilateral deviation to another mixed strategy. Hence, if we allow players to use mixed strategies, then $(\frac{1}{2}, \frac{1}{2})$ for player 1 and $(\frac{1}{2}, \frac{1}{2})$ for player 2 constitute a Nash equilibrium.

Finally, a word on nomenclature. The reason why G_4 is called a **zero-sum game** is that no matter what the outcome is, the payoffs of all the players always sum to zero. *This implies that, when we move from one outcome* (e.g. (U, L)) *to another* (e.g. (U, R)), *one player's gain is always exactly offset by another's loss.* Thus, in a zero-sum game everybody can never gain or lose by moving from one outcome to another. The PD described in Fig. 2.3 is clearly a non-zero-sum game and, more significantly, a variable-sum game since shifting from, for instance, outcome (D, D) to (C, C) makes total payoff rise from 2 to 16. If all economic interactions between nations were zero-sum games, then if country A's trading partner (say country B) celebrated after completing some trade, country A would have reason to moan. Fortunately, trade and economic interactions are seldom zero-sum games.

Note that the significant implication of a zero-sum game is the sentence that is written in italics in the above paragraph. If that be so, then even if a game were not zero-sum, in strategic terms it would be no different from a zero-sum game.

Consider the game shown in the payoff matrix of Fig. 2.7, denoted "G_5." The payoffs in G_5 always sum to 6. So one person's gain is always another's loss. So when we want to refer to a game in which all players can gain or lose, it is, strictly speaking, not enough to describe the game as a non-zero-sum game. What we are really talking about then is a **variable-sum game**. Indeed, since in game-theoretic terms there is so little to distinguish between G_4 and a game like G_5, at times we refer to G_5 (representing any constant-sum game) as a zero-sum game.

	L	R
U	4, 2	2, 4
D	2, 4	4, 2

Figure 2.7 Payoff matrix (constant-sum game)

2.4. Extensive–Form Games

One important distinction between the games discussed in Section 2.3 and chess, Hex, and the Cuban missile crisis as happened in reality is that the latter games are all played "in time." That is, they involve moves in a sequence, or at least at different points of time. The games in Section 2.3 are, on the other hand, played at one point of time, all at once. Games that are played over time are called **extensive-form games**. I will not formally define an extensive-form game but introduce it through a series of examples.

The diagram in Fig. 2.8 illustrates an extensive-form game (labeled Γ_1) with two players. The game has five nodes, of which three are **terminal nodes** and x and w are **nonterminal nodes**. Also, w is called the **initial node**. As indicated, at node w, player 1 has to choose between two actions, L and R. If she chooses L, the game ends (that is, they reach a terminal node) and both players get one dollar (or one util) each. If player 1 chooses action R, the game reaches node x, where player 2 has to choose between actions

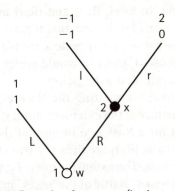

Figure 2.8 Extensive-form game (basic, two players)

l and r. After that, the game ends with payoffs as shown. In an extensive-form game, a player's (pure) strategy is a specification of the player's choice of action at every node where the player is supposed to move. So, in Γ_1, player 1 has to specify a choice between L and R and player 2 has to specify a choice between l and r. It is important to realize that to know player 2's strategy we must know what player 2 would do at node x, even if we know that player 1 has chosen L and so player 2's choice is really academic. This idea of a "strategy" is very important to understand. It is the same idea that was introduced in the context of Hex. Essentially it is a plan of action for all contingencies that may arise.

A game like Γ_1 can also be reduced to a normal form in which player 1 has to choose a strategy from {L, R} and player 2 has to choose from {l, r}. The normal-form counterpart of Γ_1 is given by G'_1, as illustrated in Fig. 2.9.

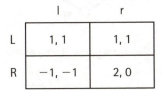

Figure 2.9 Payoff matrix for the normal-form counterpart of game Γ_1

To find the Nash equilibrium of an extensive-form game, we use the same principle as the one used in the previous section. We look for a strategy-pair such that no player can gain from a unilateral deviation. Thus in Γ_1, player 1 playing L and player 2 playing l is a Nash equilibrium; also player 1 playing R and player 2 playing r is a Nash equilibrium. These are, in fact, the only Nash equilibria. In brief, (L, l) and (R, r) are the only two Nash equilibria. To verify the case of (L, l), note that if player 1 chooses L, player 2 has no incentive to play r instead l at node x for player 2 will get 1 either way. And if player 2 chooses l, player 1 would prefer not to deviate from L, for she will get -1 through such a deviation.

There is another method for spotting the Nash equilibria of extensive-form games. This is by reducing the extensive-form game to a normal-form game and then looking for a Nash equilibrium of the normal-form game. Thus, in G_1', clearly (L, l) and (R, r) are the only two Nash equilibria.

Consider another example. The extensive game Γ_2, illustrated in Fig. 2.10, is a variant of the well-known "Battle of the Sexes" in which player 1 moves first and player 2 moves second. Note that, in Γ_2, player 2's strategy requires him to specify what he will do at x and also at y. Hence, player 2 has four possible strategies: BB', BS', SB' and SS'. Hence the normal-form description of Γ_2, G_2', is as shown in Fig. 2.11. G_2' looks different from the equivalent in Fig. 2.4 because it captures the idea that the players move in a sequence, instead of simultaneously as in the Battle of the Sexes. I leave it to the reader to find the Nash equilibria of Γ_2.

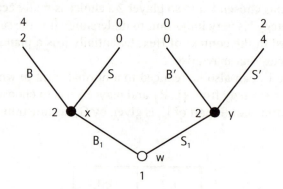

Figure 2.10 Extensive-form game (Battle of the Sexes (variant))

| | | Player 2 | | | |
		BB'	BS'	SB'	SS'
Player 1	B_1	4, 2	4, 2	0, 0	0, 0
	S_1	0, 0	2, 4	0, 0	2, 4

Figure 2.11 Payoff matrix for the normal-form counterpart of game Γ_2

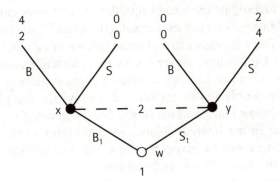

Figure 2.12 Extensive-form game (Battle of the Sexes (standard))

What happens if we want to represent the Battle of the Sexes proper (that is, Fig. 2.4) as an extensive-form? Can this be done? The answer is "yes" and Γ_3 in Fig. 2.12 is one such representation. When two or more nodes are connected by a broken line, the collection of such nodes is called an "information set." Hence $\{x, y\}$ is an information set in Γ_3. An **informa-tion set** is a collection of nodes such that the player who has to make a move does not know which particular node he is at. Thus, in Γ_3, when player 2 chooses between actions B and S, he does not know whether he is at x or at y. In other words, he chooses between B and S without knowing whether player 1 has chosen B_1 or S_1. To most game theorists, this is the same as players 1 and 2 moving simultaneously. I think one may legitim-ately want to distinguish between (a) a simultaneous-move game and (b) a game where player i moves first and player j moves second but player j does not know what player i has chosen when player j makes his move. We shall, however, follow the standard game-theory convention.

It is worth pointing out that when we have a nonterminal node that is not connected to another node by a broken line, the convention is to refer to the set containing that single node also as an information set. Thus, in Γ_2, the information sets are $\{x\}$, $\{y\}$ and $\{w\}$. In Γ_3, the information sets are $\{x, y\}$ and $\{w\}$. Note also that in Γ_3 the set of actions available at node x is the same as the set of actions available at y, namely $\{B, S\}$. This is always the case for nodes belonging to the same information set. Basically, player 2 is asked to choose an action from the set $\{B, S\}$ when the informa-tion set $\{x, y\}$ is reached. Throughout, the branches in a game tree will be called **actions**. Thus, in extensive-form games we distinguish between actions and strategies.

Let us now investigate the idea of equilibrium a bit more carefully in the context of extensive-form games. Consider the game Γ_1 and the Nash equilibrium (L, l). There is reason to feel some unease in calling this an equilibrium. In this equilibrium, player 2 says that she will choose action l at node x. She does not lose through this choice *because player 1 chooses L at node w*. In other words, in this equilibrium she says she will play l at node x *because she knows that x will not be reached*; however, if x *were* reached, playing l is not in her interest. Hence, we could think of the equilibrium (L, l) as being sustained by player 2's threat that she will play l at node x and note that this threat is not really credible.

The important concept of "subgame-perfect equilibrium" (due to Selten, 1975) is basically that of a Nash equilibrium that does not rely on incredible threats of the above kind. In Γ_1, (R, r) is subgame-perfect but (L, l) is not. Let us proceed to formalize the idea of subgame perfection a little more.

Given a game tree, such as Γ_1, Γ_2 or Γ_3, consider clipping off a "subtree" by cutting just below any node and picking up the bough, the way that we at times cut out a branch from a tree to decorate a room. Persisting with the sylvan analogy, think of an information set as a set of nodes linked by a cobweb. If we can pluck out a bough without breaking a cobweb, then the bough (with all the properties of the original game tree, including the cobwebs within the bough) is called a **subgame** of the original game. Incidentally – and this is purely a matter of convention – if we pluck the tree from its root, what we have is also called a subgame of the game even though it is the whole game tree.

Now consider Γ_1 again. This has two subgames. One is the game itself and the other is shown (as Γ_4) in Fig. 2.13. In Γ_4, player 2 begins and has to choose l or r. Either choice ends the game. If she chooses r, then player 1 gets 2 utils and player 2 gets nothing; if she chooses l, both get −1 util. This is a silly game but nevertheless a game. This makes it clear that a subgame is a game in its own right.

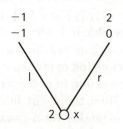

$$\begin{matrix} -1 & & 2 \\ -1 & & 0 \end{matrix}$$

l   r

2 ◯ x

Figure 2.13 Subgame of game Γ_1

Note that Γ_2 has three subgames: Γ_2 itself, the subgame with root at x, and the subgame rooted at y. What about the game Γ_3? As per our definition, Γ_3 is itself one subgame. Consider also the subtree emanating from x, as shown in Fig. 2.14. To pluck this from the tree entails breaking a cobweb or, less lyrically, cutting up an information set. Hence the game in Fig. 2.14 is *not* a subgame of Γ_3. As should be amply clear now, Γ_3 has only one subgame – itself.

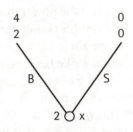

Figure 2.14 A subtree from game Γ_3

Consider a two-person extensive-form game. A strategy-pair specified for this game is a **subgame perfect equilibrium (SPE)** if it constitutes a Nash equilibrium for every subgame of the game. Since a game is a subgame of itself, an SPE is always a Nash equilibrium. But not every Nash equilibrium is an SPE. For this reason, subgame perfection is described as a "refinement" of Nash, and the Nash equilibrium as a "coarsening" of subgame perfection.

To see the definition of SPE in action, return again to Γ_1 (*see* Fig. 2.8). Consider first the strategy-pair (R, r). We already know this is a Nash equilibrium of Γ_1. Now consider the subgame with root x, that is, the game Γ_4. Note that (R, r), applied to game Γ_4, will take the game to the terminal node marked (2, 0). Player 1's choice of R is inconsequential in this game; player 2's choice takes the game to (2, 0). This is a Nash equilibrium of Γ_4. No one can do better through a deviation. Hence (R, r) is an SPE of Γ_1.

Next consider (L, l). This is a Nash equilibrium of Γ_1 but not a Nash equilibrium for the game Γ_4. Player 2 can do better by deviating. Hence, (L, l) is not an SPE of Γ_1.

In Γ_3 whatever is a Nash equilibrium is also an SPE because Γ_3 has no *proper* subgame.

Let us digress once more back to the Cuban missile crisis. Though in its simplest model it is described as the Hawk–Dove game, what the United States and the Soviets really played was a complex extensive-form game.

There were moves and countermoves. Indeed, to understand one of the crucial doctrines of nuclear conflict, that of "second strike," one has to use an extensive-form structure. According to the **second-strike doctrine**, for a nation to have a nuclear arsenal does not guarantee deterrence from outside attack unless it has the demonstrable ability to survive a first nuclear attack and strike back. Indeed, to have a nuclear arsenal and *not* have the power of second strike may encourage other nations to attack it and destroy its nuclear capability. It is for this reason that both the United States and the USSR worked rapidly to acquire the power of second strike. It is for this same reason that, in the 1960s, 180 US planes carrying nuclear bombs had standing orders to take off and remain in the air, when an attack was imminent, so that they would be able to strike back rapidly.

The Cuban crisis was a series of moves and countermoves. Not only did the US planes leave the bases and prepare for a second strike when the tensions peaked after the US "ultimatum," but there are analysts who have argued that the game had begun much before October 1962, with events of the past, like the Bay of Pigs incident, and the construction of the Berlin Wall, which had influenced the players' beliefs and colored their thinking. But even ignoring what happened before October 22, a first cut at an extensive-form characterization of the Cuban crisis would require us to recognize that the United States had the advantage of the first move, since the Soviet authorities did not know that the United States knew about the MRBMs in Cuba. Hence, we should think of the Cuban crisis more as the Hawk–Dove game played in a sequence, with the United States having the first move to play H or D. The Soviets then had the choice of responding with the Hawk action or the Dove action. Hence, we can describe the Cuban Missile Crisis game as Γ_5 (*see* Fig. 2.15), in which player 1 is the United States and player 2 is the USSR, and H stands for the aggressive (Hawk) action and D for the timid (Dove) action, with the single and double primes being used to distinguish actions at different nodes. The payoffs are understood easily by referring to the matrix in Fig. 2.5.

Faced with this game, what action would game theory predict? To answer this, we have to use the idea of subgame perfection just introduced. A little bit of thought will reveal that the only subgame perfect equilibrium is one in which player 2 chooses H′ at node x and D″ at node y, and player 1 chooses H at the initial node. The outcome of the game would then be the one in which player 1 plays the aggressive move and player 2 the timid move, as exactly what happened in 1962.

Returning to formal game theory, note that one useful way of finding the subgame-perfect equilibrium is to use "backward induction." This entails

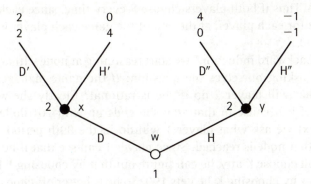

Figure 2.15 Extensive-form game (Cuban Missile Crisis)

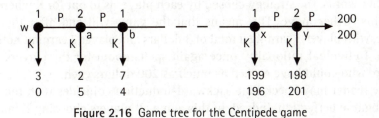

Figure 2.16 Game tree for the Centipede game

working backwards from terminal nodes and locating rational actions. One game on which this method of analysis works well is the so-called "Centipede" game (Rosenthal, 1981). There are two players, labeled 1 and 2; and suppose that player 1 has a parcel in his hand. The first move is player 1's. He can pass the parcel (choosing action P) or keep it (choosing action K). If he keeps it, he gets 3 dollars, player 2 gets nothing, and the game ends. If he passes the parcel, each player gets 2 dollars and it is then player 2's move. Player 2 can pass (choosing P) or keep (choosing K). If she keeps it, she gets 3 dollars and the game ends. If she passes it, they again get 2 dollars each; and now it is again player 1's move. The game continues exactly like this till the hundredth move, after which the game always ends.

What would you expect the outcome of this to be? Put yourself in the shoes of one of these players and think. Most of us would reach the conclusion that we will choose P lots of times and earn $200 or nearly $200. Let us see what formal game theory predicts. For this, it is useful to describe the Centipede as a game tree. This is done in Γ_6, illustrated in Fig. 2.16. Note that the payoffs at the terminal nodes show the *accumulated* earnings of the players. Thus if both players choose P every time, since each choice of P yields $2 for each player, at the end of the game each player would have earned $200.

To use "backward induction" we start reasoning at node y (that is, the last period) by asking ourselves the question: *If* the game manages to reach node y, what will player 2 do if she is rational? Clearly she will choose K instead of P because in that way she ends up with 201 dollars instead of 200. Next we ask what player 1 will do in the 99th period, that is, at node x, *if* that node is reached. Since player 1 can see that if he chooses P player 2 will choose K at y, he can figure out that by choosing P he will get 198 whereas by choosing K he gets 199. So he is better off choosing K. It is easy to see now that, by a similar argument, player 2 will choose K in the 98th move, player 1 will choose K in the 97th move, and so on all the way. In other words, the strategy chosen by each player is to opt for K whenever it is his or her move. This means that the game will end after the first move, with player 1 earning a total of 3 dollars and player 2 earning nothing at all. Individual rationality once again spells doom for the players as a group, who could have earned as much as 200 dollars each.

The reader may check that backward-induction coincides with the idea of subgame perfection. Indeed, in this game all players choosing K (and so bringing the game to a close after the first move) is the only Nash equilibrium and the only SPE.

It is a useful exercise to apply the backward induction argument to Γ_5 (*see* Fig. 2.15). This entails first determining how player 2 will choose at nodes x and y and then using this information to determine how player 1 will choose at the initial node.

It is interesting to see how the backward induction can be used in the finitely-repeated PD. A "repeated PD game" involves two players repeatedly playing game G_1 set out in Fig. 2.3. Let us first consider the *infinitely* repeated PD, where players 1 and 2 play G_1 once, earn payoffs, and then play G_1 again, earning more payoffs, and then play G_1 again and so on *ad infinitum*. What is interesting is that players in the "infinitely-repeated Prisoner's Dilemma" may play cooperatively (that is, (C, C) in each game G_1) in equilibrium. This is because, though in any particular game a player can always do better by playing D, doing so may make the other player retaliate in such a way in the future as to make it not worthwhile deviating in any particular game. The talk of the "future" should make it clear that this argument holds only for the *repeated* PD. Thus repeated play makes it possible for the two players to cooperate without any need for third-party intervention.

To see this formally, assume that each player has a time-discount factor of δ, which is less than unity.[11] An alternate interpretation of δ is that it denotes, in each period, the probability that the game will continue for one more period. Hence the probability of the game continuing for two more periods is δ^2, three more periods δ^3, and so on. Whether we treat δ as the discount factor or the continuation probability, the algebra is unaffected. Some economists prefer the probability interpretation because that makes the probability of the game never stopping equal to zero. Suppose each player decides to play what is called a "trigger" strategy. Such a strategy involves starting in period 1 by playing C and then continuing to do so as long as neither player plays D. If, however, anybody plays D in any period, then from then onwards the player plays D in all future periods. In other words, a player cooperates as long as the other player cooperates. And once cooperation breaks down, it breaks down for ever. It is like a trigger being pulled. To summarize and to state this more precisely, a **trigger strategy** is one in which, in any period t, the player looks at the history of play in all previous periods and if he sees that D has been played somewhere (by either player) then in period t he plays D; otherwise, he plays C.

Let us now check whether both players using the trigger strategy constitutes a Nash equilibrium. Suppose, without loss of generality, that player 2 is using a trigger strategy. Then, if player 1 also uses a trigger strategy, clearly the outcome in every period will be (C, C). Hence the present value of payoffs earned by player 1 in our G_1 example (*see* Fig. 2.3) will be

$$\frac{8}{1 - \delta} = 8 + 8\delta + 8\delta^2 + \ldots.$$

If player 1 deviates from this strategy and plays D in one period, he will earn 10 utils in that period; but since from then on cooperation will break down, he will in all future periods earn only 1 util. So the present value of payoffs earned by player 1 will be

$$10 + \frac{\delta}{1 - \delta} = 10 + \delta + \delta^2 + \delta^3 + \ldots.$$

Hence a unilateral deviation is not worthwhile as long as

$$10 + \frac{\delta}{1 - \delta} \leq \frac{8}{1 - \delta},$$

[11] If the discount *rate* is r, then $\delta = 1/(1 + r)$. If a person expects to earn D dollars in the next period and has a discount factor of δ, the present value of those D dollars is δD.

or, equivalently, as long as $\delta \geq \frac{2}{9}$. Therefore, if $\delta \geq \frac{2}{9}$, the trigger strategy on the part of both players is a Nash equilibrium. In fact, it is also a sub-game perfect equilibrium. Hence, if $\delta \geq \frac{2}{9}$, the players may cooperate in the PD of their own accord. This technical argument from game theory has been widely used in the debate on anarchy versus the state.

Suppose now the PD is being played a finite number of times – say 100 times – and this is common knowledge. Interestingly, in this case cooperation can be shown to break down in equilibrium. To see this, we once again use the backward-induction argument. Consider the 100th period. That being the last, each player has reason to maximize his or her earnings in it. So they will play as if it were a single-shot Prisoner's Dilemma. So the outcome will be (D, D). Now consider the 99th game. Since the outcome in the 100th game is a foregone conclusion, each player may as well play D in this one too. The argument unfolds inexorably backwards and the outcome is (D, D) in every game. While this prediction shows the power of game-theoretic reasoning, it also leaves many (lay persons as well as experts) with an uncomfortable feeling. Will rational players *really* play as game theory predicts, or is game theory missing out on something?

This brings us to the brink of some deep philosophical debates. It is an area of considerable research involving economics, philosophy and the science of artificial intelligence. It will be too much of a digression to go into it here.[12] Let me instead simply draw the reader's attention to some of the underlying epistemics of the problem.

Note first that rationality, in itself, is not enough to drive the backward-induction argument, be it in the repeated Prisoner's Dilemma or the Centi-pede game. Translating to the Centipede game an argument of mine (Basu, 1977) made in the context of the PD, note that player 1 chooses K at node x because player 1 is rational and player 1 *knows that player 2 is rational* (and so will choose K at node y). And at the node just before x (not shown in Fig. 2.16), our argument was based on the implicit assumption that player 2 *knows* that player 1 *knows* that player 2 is rational. The assumptions of mutual knowledge of rationality keep growing in this manner (in fact, to a hundredfold) for us to show that player 1 will choose K in the first move. Indeed, game theorists, explicitly or unwittingly, have assumed that players are rational, that they know that they are rational, that they know that they know that they are rational, and so on *ad infinitum*. When this assumption is true, we say that rationality is **common knowledge** among

---

[12] The interested reader may wish to consult Reny (1986), Binmore (1987), Bicchieri (1989) and Basu (1990).

the players. Backward induction is usually predicated on rationality being common knowledge (Aumann, 1995; Asheim, 1999). Yet, in a somewhat inarticulate way, I feel uncomfortable with the assumption of rationality being common knowledge. Is this a consistent assumption? I comment on this briefly in Chapter 3 when discussing individual knowledge and rationality.

The algebra of common knowledge is now well developed (*see, for instance,* Fagin *et al.,* 1995) but its philosophical status is still open to important questions. I will, on occasions, have to refer to the common knowledge of rationality, but for the most part I shall try to steer clear of its philosophical conundrums. We have many other things to keep us busy in the chapters that follow.[13]

---

[13] For the reader who wishes to pursue game theory a step further in the quasi-formal manner in which the subject has been pursued in this chapter, a useful reference is Gibbons (1997).

3. Individual Rationality

3.1 The Concept of Rationality

As we have just seen, much of game theory is based on the **assumption of rational behavior** on the part of individuals. This is quite natural since game theory is largely an offshoot of economics and individual rationality is one of the central axioms of economics. Yet, the kind of rationality assumptions that have been used in economics go well beyond the concept that we encountered in Chapter 2. In economics, this innocuous-looking assumption has turned out to be extremely powerful. It is amazing how many of the laws of the market can be deduced from the assumption. Not surprisingly, given its rich dividends, social scientists working in neighboring disciplines – particularly, politics and sociology – have been lured into using this assumption. The so-called "rational actor model" is now quite pervasive in political science, and rational choice is often treated as the mainspring of positive political economy.[1]

Nevertheless, in recent years the logic and empirical validity of the assumption have been increasingly called into question. Some of this is a natural reaction to the overzealousness with which many mainstream economists have championed the assumption. But, while for large areas of standard economics the axiom of rationality is useful, once we move out to terrains beyond everyday economics, the axiom can be restrictive and misleading. It can still give lots of answers but it is not clear how much faith we should place in those answers. To grapple with questions like why one nation is democratic and another not, or why one tribe succeeds and another fails, it is essential to recognize that human behavior is influenced not solely by the attempt to maximize an unchanging utility function but also by social norms, culture, psychology and personal histories. One must be careful in interpreting a remark like the one just made. The fact that a human being is endowed with psychology and social norms does not, in itself, invalidate standard – even textbookish – utility theory, because a person's utility function can *embody* many of these features. However, as Kahneman (1994), Schlicht (1998) and many others have reminded us,

---

[1] This new approach has been both celebrated and lamented: see Shepsle and Bonchuk (1997) and Green and Shapiro (1994).

there are also many instances in life where our psychology thwarts our rationality calculus. Most of us have had the experience of stepping onto a stationary escalator and stumbling a little to adjust to the fact of its stationarity, even though we could see this in advance and so had all the information needed not to make the mistake of stepping on it as if it were the usual moving escalator. Likewise, social norms are not *always* compatible with conventional rationality. We shall see illustrations of this in Chapter 4. The present chapter evaluates the logic and internal consistency of the textbook view of the "rational man."

Unfortunately, what is often criticized as the "economist's view" of rationality is no one's view. So let me briefly describe the standard economist's conception of rationality so that, when we criticize it, it is not a straw man that we take our aim at.

In economics a person is taken to be rational if that person, given his information, chooses the action that maximizes his objective, *whatever that objective happens to be*. So, to describe a person as "rational" is not to condone or criticize him but simply to say that the person is good at choosing the actions that lead to whatever it is that he or she wishes to maximize. That whatever-it-is-that-he-or-she-wishes-to-maximize is usually given the name of **utility** (with the units being referred to as **utils**). In game theory, as we have already seen, it is called "payoff." In some specific contexts, we treat profit or income as the relevant maximand. The term "utility", though, has the advantage of being open to alternative interpretations. At times this flexibility has been overused and economists have gone further than game theorists by arbitrarily redefining a person's utility so as to accommodate all possible behavior under its rubric. In her critique of neoclassical economics, Joan Robinson (1962: 47) wrote (her italics), "*Utility* is a metaphysical concept of impregnable circularity; *utility* is the quality in commodities that makes individuals want to buy them, and the fact that individuals want to buy commodities shows that they have *utility*."

While it is true that many neoclassical economists fall into this tautological trap, the founders of utility theory did not offer it as an unfalsifiable truth. If it were an unfalsifiable claim, then no testable proposition would emerge from it. To avoid this predicament, utility must be given content by saying, for instance, that the utility level achieved by a person depends on the amount of goods and services consumed by the person. In game theory, utility (or, equivalently, payoff) is described more arbitrarily; but, nevertheless, it depends on the actions or strategies chosen by individuals; and, in addition, the utility earned from different strategies is specified in advance. So we can conceive of actions that falsify the assumption of rational behavior.

Modern economics has, however, increasingly moved away from the utility-maximization-based idea of rationality to consistency-based definitions. To understand this, suppose that a person has to choose between alternatives x and y, and the person chooses x. Given the axiom of individual rationality, we can then say that x gives the person more utility than y. Next, suppose the person is given a choice between x, y and z; we can predict (keeping in mind the previous choice) that the person will not choose y but may choose x or z.[2] Thus, if individuals are maximizers of utility, we can expect them to conform to certain **consistencies** in their choice. It is this realization that led Samuelson (1938) to construct a theory of consumer behavior that treats consistency of choice as its first axiom. Thus while the choice of axioms is *motivated* by the presumption of utility maximization, Samuelson's "revealed preference approach" was, in fact, an attempt to found the theory of consumer behavior purely on axioms of "internal consistency."[3]

To get a foretaste of this, consider one consistency assumption that Samuelson used, called the Weak Axiom of Revealed Preference (WARP). According to WARP, if a person chooses x and rejects y, then he will not on another occasion, in which x is available to him, choose y.[4]

The first set of critiques of rationality that we shall encounter in this chapter is directed at the above conception of rationality. It is, of course, to be expected that the assumption of selfish utility maximization will run into heavy weather as soon as we allow for social norms and cultural constraints. It may, however, seem that the consistency axioms are immune to the introduction of norms since, whether one is maximizing one's own utility or utility tainted by social norms, this should not affect the consistency of choice. However, as Sen (1993) and Akerlof (1991) have argued persuasively, this is not so. Internal consistency can run into difficulty when we try to allow for norms and the limitations of human psychology. The next two sections present formally the idea of consistency-based definitions of rationality and then discuss their shortcomings.

Different kinds of complications arise when we move to strategic contexts where several individuals have to take account of one another's actions in order to determine what is the rational course. We have already

---

[2] Strictly speaking, if a person chooses x and rejects y, we cannot say that x gives more utility than y but that it gives at least as much utility as y. I am, however, following Samuelson (1938) in using the assumption of strict preference. The consequence of weakening this was examined by Hicks (1956).

[3] To what extent Samuelson succeeded in this has been questioned: see Sen (1973).

[4] For formal analysis of the implications of WARP, see Arrow (1959) and Suzumura (1983).

encountered this problem in Chapter 2 on game theory, and we shall also grapple with some puzzling implications later in this chapter.

3.2. Internal Consistency

Ever since the work of Samuelson (1938) and Hicks (1956), the practice of equating rationality with consistent choice behavior has found increasing favor among economists. Before evaluating this approach, it is useful to spell out some definitions and notations. It is usually assumed that the alternatives $x, y, z, \ldots$, from among which an individual makes her choice, are full descriptions of possible states of the world. But if we insist on this strict characterization, the model would be quite unusable in practice. Thus usually we think of alternatives as "partial descriptions" of the world, implicitly assuming other things to be constant. Thus in consumer theory the alternatives can be different baskets of goods, for instance, x and y. So when we describe a consumer as choosing between x and y, we mean she chooses between x and y with other things remaining the same (to the extent that this is possible).

The choices that an individual actually makes are codified in the "choice function." A person's **choice function**, C, is a function such that for every set S of alternatives $C(S)$ is an element of S.[5] The interpretation is that $C(S)$ is the element that the person chooses from S.

Essentially, rationality is a property of the choice function. That is, to say whether an individual is rational or not, we need to have information not on the color of his hair or whether he finds sunsets beautiful but his choice function. As we have already seen, according to one line of thinking the rationality of C depends on how well it matches up to something external to C. For instance, we may want C to be such that it chooses the alternative that maximizes utility from among the set of available alternatives – and in this case C has to be consistent with something *external* to C (namely an exogenously specified utility function). According to the line of thought emerging from Samuelson (1938), **rationality** is defined as a trait of how C behaves on different parts of its domain – and in this case what we are seeking is a kind of *internal* consistency of C.[6] Sen (1993) calls these two approaches those of external and internal consistencies, respectively.

---

[5] In the choice-theory literature, unlike in consumer theory, $C(S)$ can consist of more than one element. However, it is convenient for us in this context to wear the consumer-theory hat.

[6] For an interesting related discussion on the "internalist interpretation" of rationality, and its weakness, see Satz and Ferejohn (1994).

One example of internal consistency that we have already encountered is WARP.

Suppose an individual has a choice function that over the sets $\{x, y\}$ and $\{x, y, z\}$ chooses as follows:

$$C(\{x, y\}) = x; \tag{3.1}$$

$$C(\{x, y, z\}) = y. \tag{3.2}$$

Clearly, this person violates WARP. By his choice of x from x and y he reveals a preference for x over y and he violates this when he chooses y from among x, y and z. So if WARP were our requirement of rationality, the person who chooses as above must be deemed irrational.

Sen (1993) argues that while this approach of internal consistency *may* be fine in certain limited spheres of consumer choice, it is inadequate if we are analyzing "political actions" or "collective bargaining" or choices involving "social concerns." In other words, in taking the method of economics to political economy, it is important not to found our analysis on the assumption of *internal* consistency. Sen's argument, in essence, is that, at times, the *feasibility set* can give one information that changes one's choice. A devout Muslim, for instance, may decide not to eat anything in a restaurant after learning that the restaurant also serves pork.

One does not have to go to the larger issues of political economy to understand Sen's argument. In Sen's own example, a person you barely know asks you whether you would like to go to his home and have some tea (x) or go away (y); and you choose x. Now suppose, instead, that the same person had asked you whether you would like to go to his home and have some tea (x), go away (y), or snort some cocaine with him (z). It would not be unreasonable for you to now choose y, even though x is available and earlier you had revealed a preference for x over y. Hence, your choice is exactly as in (3.1) and (3.2). But your choice is easy to understand and there is nothing irrational about such a choice. This is the basis of Sen's claim that internal consistency, which requires that a person will not choose as in (3.1) *and* (3.2), is not a reasonable criterion of rationality.

Before I give my response to Sen's claim, let us look at a standard response that one finds from economic theorists. Several theorists, with whom I have discussed Sen's example, express disagreement with Sen on the ground that, in the above tea–cocaine example, choosing x from the set $\{x, y\}$ is not the same thing as choosing x from $\{x, y, z\}$. In the second case you have some additional information: that you may be having tea in the home of a drug addict. Hence, the x is not the same in both choice situations. Thus, if $\{x, y\}$ is written as S and $\{x, y, z\}$ as T, then we may think of x chosen from S and T as two separate options, which may be written as x/S and x/T, respectively. Hence, when x is chosen from S, the person reveals a preference for x/S over y/S. This does not place any restriction on how he should choose from among x/T, y/T and z/T.

I find this objection to Sen's example not persuasive because it amounts to a defense of WARP by reducing WARP to a tautology.[7] Whenever something like (3.1) and (3.2) happens, this approach would say that x in (3.2) is not the same as x in (3.1). But once WARP is reduced to a tautology, it can no longer have any explanatory power. This is the same "tautological trap" – mentioned in Section 3.1 – that traditional neoclassical economists often fell into while discussing utility maximization. So this objection can be dismissed.

In my opinion, the two more-reasonable responses to Sen's argument are the following. First, note that for any axiom to have explanatory power it must be "falsifiable." That is, we should be able to conceive of situations where the axiom is invalid. We could now concede Sen's example as a reasonable one where WARP turns out to be invalid. But as long as we are ready to maintain that this is a marginal possibility, then all that the tea–cocaine example shows is that WARP is falsifiable. Then this is no longer a reason to reject WARP. The power of this argument turns on the empirical question of how marginal the cases of violation of internal consistency are likely to be. The answer clearly depends on the domain of analysis. My own guess is that in the domain of political economy they will not be marginal at all.

The second response is to accept Sen's claim. But in that case what has to be noted is that if we take his argument a natural step further, it turns out to be even more destructive than Sen had supposed, because it calls into question the very existence of a choice function. In fact, it is arguable that the existence of a choice function is a kind of internal consistency requirement and in that case it is natural that an argument against internal consistency will also tend to dislodge the existential claim.

---

[7] This is not to deny that one can conceive of other descriptions of z, where one would agree with Sen's critics that y/S is not the same as y/T and so the example is not a falsification of WARP. This would be the case if, for instance, z represented "Go to the restaurant and have tea because that way the tea would not be laced with arsenic." This offer of z reveals something too drastic about x. The distinction between this and Sen's example is not one of hard definition but a matter of judgment. The tautological trap that one must guard against is that of taking this escape route (of claiming that an alternative is distinct depending on the menu in which it appears) *whenever* there is a seeming violation of WARP.

To see this, suppose first you are given a choice between x (tea) and y (go away) exactly as in Sen's example; and you choose x. Next assume that a person again offers you a choice between x and y but, this time, while making this offer to you, he rummages through his sling bag and takes out his cocaine pack. You may, very reasonably, now choose y. Hence your choices were:

$$C(\{x, y\}) = x;$$

$$C(\{x, y\}) = y.$$

This simply means that the individual does not have a choice *function*. That is, given a set S, he does not have a well-defined choice.

What I am arguing is that the additional information, which in Sen's example comes from expanding the menu by adding z to it, can also come in other ways, which leave the menu unchanged. Hence Sen's argument as to how a rational person may reject WARP can be extended to the claim that a rational person may not have a choice function at all.

Of course, the critique of Sen's model, discussed above, can be leveled against my claim as well. That is, it can be argued that if we describe *fully* the alternatives, then the x and y from which the individual has to choose in the two situations turn out to be different x's and y's; and so there is no conflict of choice. But, as I pointed out above, this amounts to a defense of traditional theory by reducing it to a tautology. Indeed, if we define states of the world sufficiently fully, so as to include mental states as well, then the existence of the choice function becomes a direct consequence of the philosophy of determinism (discussed in the Appendix to this book). It would then have very little to do with our view of decision making and choice; it would stand or fall depending on our attitude to determinism.

A special case where a reasonable person may violate internal consistency and may not even have a choice function is in choosing over a period of time. This can explain several real-life phenomena such as procrastination and drug addiction, and that is the subject matter of the next section. Hence, the models in the next section illustrate how, when we move to domains of decision making beyond economics, it may be essential to abandon the view of rationality that equates it with internal consistency.

3.3. Procrastination and Addiction

A tiny irrationality can, at times, result in behavior that is grossly irrational. This is especially worrying because the tiny irrationality may be quite a natural part of the human psyche. Drawing on a body of literature in psychology, Akerlof (1991) argued that certain bits of information (and therefore costs and benefits) can acquire "salience" in the human mind, thereby causing a small "miscalculation".[8] Akerlof illustrated this with his own experience.

I recount this experience, with some minor rewriting of history in order to bring out its central message more clearly. When Akerlof was in India, Stiglitz, who was also then in India but about to leave for the United States, gave A (for Akerlof) a parcel to mail to S (for Stiglitz). A found that each morning the cost of having to take the parcel to the post office, waiting in a queue and so on seemed prohibitive. On each day, the transactions cost of mailing the parcel on that day acquired "salience" – that is, the cost appeared larger than it really was. So each day he would postpone the mailing of the parcel by "one more day." Finally, he took the parcel with him when he was leaving for the States. In retrospect, A regretted that he did not mail the parcel earlier; but this *massive* procrastination was the outcome of the *tiny* irrationality of postponing the mailing one day at a time.

This model of dynamic inconsistency is important because, by breaking away from the standard axioms of rationality such as WARP, it can explain several real-life phenomena – for example, how a person becomes a drug addict by taking a series of small decisions, or how a person grows into a major criminal by committing larger and larger crimes over time. But before discussing some of these implications, it is useful to formalize the model of procrastination.

Suppose there are N days left for Akerlof's departure from India when Stiglitz hands him a parcel to be mailed. It is useful to label the days, starting from when the parcel is given to A up to when A leaves for the States, by numbering them backwards. Thus the days are labeled as follows:

$$N \quad N-1 \quad N-2 \quad \ldots \quad 2 \quad 1 \quad 0$$

In short, we are using a calendar exactly of the kind that we actually use for the period "Before Christ," though in this case the event that occurs at date zero is rather less momentous.

Assume that A empathizes totally with S and so gets the same benefit as S gets from the use of the parcel. Let us denote the benefit (or mental satisfaction) that S gets from having the parcel for each additional day, up to day 0, by x and the total utility he gets from having the parcel with him

---

[8] An earlier work that posed the same question in an intergenerational setting and reached the same conclusion is that due to Phelps and Pollak (1968).

after day 0 by X. Let c be the cost (mainly transactions cost) of sending the parcel. On each day this cost acquires "salience" and so *seems* larger. Let p (> 0) be the salience premium. What this means is the following: If on day n Akerlof decides to send the parcel on *that* day, the cost to him appears to be $c(1 + p)$. If, however, he decides to send it on some other day t ($< n$) – don't forget we are in a period equivalent to BC – then the cost to him (on day n) seems to be c. This encapsulates the idea of us wanting to postpone tasks that are unpleasant.

I will now assume

$$pc > x \tag{3.3}$$

and

$$xN > pc. \tag{3.4}$$

These are arbitrary assumptions, but the interesting case arises when these hold true. So, I am not asserting that (3.3) and (3.4) *are* true, but simply confining attention to this case.

Consider, on any arbitrary day n, A's decision problem. If he sends the parcel on that day, the net benefit is $X + xn - (1 + p)c$. It is assumed, for simplicity, that the parcel reaches S instantaneously. If A sends it the following day, the net benefit is $X + x(n-1) - c$. Hence he will postpone the task by a day if $x < pc$. In other words, given (3.3), he *does* postpone it by a day. But this happens every day. Each morning he calculates whether he should send it that day or the next, and he chooses the latter. And the parcel does not get sent till day 0. On day 0 it is worth sending the parcel if $X - (1 + p)c > 0$.

If, on day N, A had to decide whether to send it on that day (with a net benefit of $X + xN - (1 + p)c$) or on day 0 (with a net benefit of $X - c$), he would clearly prefer to send it on day N because of (3.4). Hence this illustrates how, given salience, he takes a sequence of decisions such that the totality of what happens turns out to be suboptimal by his own evaluation.

It is interesting to see that this dynamic inconsistency is also a case of internal inconsistency, since it violates WARP, discussed in Section 3.2. Assume $N = 2$ and consider A's choice problem on day 2 (i.e. day N). He has to decide whether to send it on day 2, 1 or 0. Evidently he will choose day 1. Next consider his choice on day 1. He has to choose between day 1 and 0, and we know he will choose 0. Hence, in the language of the previous section,

$$C(\{2, 1, 0\}) = 1$$

$$C(\{1, 0\}) = 0.$$

These choices are exactly like in (3.2) and (3.1) above and so constitute a violation of WARP. Nevertheless, Akerlof's (1991) individual gives us some deep insights into human behavior and folly.

Is this kind of dynamic inconsistency rare or unusual? The answer is: "probably not." Most of us have had the following kind of experience at some time or the other. Suppose on March 1 you have to decide whether you will undertake an onerous task on April 7 or April 14, given that the reward from doing it on April 7 is expected to be slightly higher. Most of us would choose to do it on April 7. However, if the same decision were presented on April 6, many of us would choose to do the task on April 14. This explains why so many people in the United States file their tax returns on April 14, though doing this at the eleventh hour always means some risk that one will need some information that it will then be too late to get.

There is actually some evidence that such inconsistency may be hard-wired into our psyche, since it has been observed in animals and birds (see O'Donoghue and Rabin, 2000, for references). An interesting study by Ainslie and Herrnstein (1982) confirmed this in the case of pigeons. In essence, each of several pigeons was given the option to peck on a green key or a white key. If it chose the former, after t seconds it would get some food; and if it chose the latter, after $t + 4$ seconds it would get a larger amount of food. They were made to play this game at various levels of t. First t was set at 0.01 seconds. In other words, pecking the green key would almost immediately bring it a small amount of food. It was found that, after some initial rounds of unstable, random pecking, the pigeons tended to stabilize on the green key. That is, they were willing to sacrifice quantity in order to get the food soon. Then the value of t was raised to 2, 4, 5, 8 and 12 seconds, at each level the "subjects" were given many rounds of trial, so that they got to understand the implications of pecking green and white. It was found that as t increased, the preferences reversed. That is, the pigeons began preferring the white key. In brief, if pigeons had to file tax returns, the task for the IRS would be no simpler; the pigeons would tend to leave it till the last minute.

Apart from the general phenomenon of procrastination, there is one commonly observed behavior that this model explains very well. Most of us have had the experience of letters remaining unanswered for unwarranted lengths of time. Then just before we go away for a seven-day holiday we answer all these waiting letters. What is interesting is that if we did not go away for the holiday then the letters may have remained unanswered for the seven days and more. Why does the holiday change our decision? The reason is that, in the absence of a seven-day holiday, we do not answer the letters because we can procrastinate one day at a time. On the other hand, the day before a holiday begins we are forced to choose between replying "now" and replying after at least seven days. This inability to procrastinate a little bit at a time is what makes us clear our desk tops.

Most people do not flinch from pilfering small objects from hotel rooms – soaps, matchboxes, pens and sewing kits. Defying standard economics, some people find innate pleasure in such theft. I know people who, every time they go to a hotel, use soaps and shampoo acquired during their previous hotel sojourn. The prominent Indian journalist and writer Khushwant Singh claimed that the prospect of these pickings was the sole reason he attended conferences. Few people, however, steal larger objects such as towels, bedsheets, blankets and curtains. My guess, prompted by the above model, is that if hotel rooms had a range of moveable objects, starting from tiny, less-valuable things such as soaps, to progressively larger and more-valuable objects, going all the way to table lamps, curtains and alarm clocks, there would be more people stealing table lamps, curtains and alarm clocks. In other words, there are at least some people whose failure to graduate from pilferage to pillage must be because of the lack of stepping stones *en route*.

When climbing the last stretch of Mount Everest in the fateful summer of 1996, the Spanish mountaineer Araceli Segarra was so overcome by exhaustion that she was on the verge of abandoning the climb. But she kept telling herself that she would do "ten more steps" and that would be it. She did that all the way up to the peak. Evidently, she was using an Akerlof-type reasoning, though in reverse. She knew that, if at the start of that last exhausting climb she contemplated whether to take the thousands of steps needed to reach the top or to give up, she would choose the latter. So she jettisoned that line of reasoning and opted to think of ten steps at a time.

This model can also explain why some politicians who first enter politics with an unblemished record have, after a certain lapse of time, been found guilty of large acts of corruption. The "lapse of time" in this explanation is crucial; that is what makes it possible to slide gradually, one step at a time, into big acts of corruption.

Akerlof has discussed other examples of small erroneous decisions blowing up into large regrettable actions. Drug or cigarette addiction is a good example. Since a smoker can postpone quitting cigarettes one day at a time, it is easy not to quit cigarettes at all. If, however, there was a mechanism that ensured that if you do not quit smoking now you cannot quit for a year, then there would be many more who would kick the habit.

I believe this problem is even more widely applicable than Phelps and Pollak (1968), Akerlof (1991) and O'Donoghue and Rabin (1999) suggest, because it can occur even without salience. That is, a person can take a series of completely rational decisions that in its totality she regrets. In other words, what I am claiming is that dynamic inconsistency can arise even without salience. In what follows I prove this paradoxical claim with an example.[9]

Suppose a person faces the following decision problem: starting on day 1, whether to have a cigarette or not on each day. Since he does not know when he will die, we shall treat this as an infinite-horizon problem. Of course, we may interpret the infinite horizon, as is usually done in game theory, by supposing that for every date t there is a probability $\delta < 1$ of his being alive for one more day. Then the δ simply appears like a discount factor in the computation of present value.

More formally, if N is the set of positive integers, then for each day $t \in N$ the person has to choose between action 1 (having a smoke) and action 0 (desisting from smoking). If we denote his choice of action on day t by x_t (that is, $x_t \in \{0, 1\}$) then his choice of an action sequence is an infinite vector of zeros and ones. Hence an **action sequence** is a vector: $(x_1, x_2, \dots)$. We shall use Δ to denote the set of all possible action sequences. Thus each element of Δ is a plan of action for one's entire life.[10]

The decision problem that the person faces is to choose an element from Δ. Let u be a utility function or a payoff function, which, for every element x of Δ, specifies the utility $u(x)$ that the person gets. The person's problem is to choose x so as to maximize utility.

The question that is being raised is whether there exists a utility function, u, such that a person can be maximizing it and yet exhibit time inconsistency in the sense of Akerlof. More formally, consider the following properties of a utility function.

Property A: If $x, y \in \Delta$ are such that there exists t so that $x_t = 1$, $y_t = 0$ and, for all $k \neq t$, $x_k = y_k$, then $u(x) > u(y)$;

Property B: If $x, y \in \Delta$ are such that, for all t, $x_t = 1$ and $y_t = 0$, then $u(x) < u(y)$.

Property A asserts that, the actions chosen for all other days remaining the same, if the person decides to smoke on *one* day on which he had previously decided not to smoke, he is better off. This captures the idea that

---

[9] Despite being based on rational behavior, my argument is quite distinct from that of Becker and Murphy (1988).

[10] The fact that there are infinite decision points does not mean that the game has to be played out over an infinite amount of time. Let the interval [0, 1] represent a year. Let D be the countably infinite set in [0, 1], such that $D = \{1 - (1/t) | t$ is a positive integer$\}$. If a person has to take a decision at each point in D, then there will be an infinite number of decisions to be taken in one year.

one day's procrastination in kicking the addiction or, equivalently, one additional day's indulgence in smoking or taking a drug, enhances utility. This is not an unrealistic assumption. As Shedler and Block (1990: 626) note, for impulsive and alienated individuals "the temporary effects of various drugs 'numb out' feelings of isolation and inadequacy; they offer transient gratification to individuals who lack deeper and more meaningful gratifications. . . ."

Property B asserts that smoking every day leaves the person worse off than not smoking at all. Outside a small tobacco lobby, this is well accepted.

The question we are asking is whether A and B are compatible; that is, whether there exists a utility function such that each additional day's smoke enhances utility but smoking every day gives less utility than not ever smoking. The answer is "yes" and this is now demonstrated constructively. The construction has a seemingly paradoxical quality, explored in Basu (1994b) and analogous to Escher's painting of the waterfall, reproduced in Fig. 3.1. We shall return to such a construction in a different context in Chapter 10.

Let u be defined as follows:

$$u(x) = \begin{cases} f(x_1) + \delta f(x_2) + \delta^2 f(x_3) + \dots & \text{if } \Sigma x_t < \infty \\ g(x_1) + \delta g(x_2) + \delta^2 g(x_3) + \dots & \text{if } \Sigma x_t = \infty, \end{cases}$$

where $\delta \in (0, 1)$ and f and g are real-valued functions such that $f(1) > f(0) > g(1) > g(0)$. It is simple to verify that this u satisfies properties A and B. Since a single switch from 0 to 1 cannot shift us from the case where $\Sigma x_t < \infty$ to $\Sigma x_t = \infty$ or vice versa, property A is immediate. Next note that $u(1, 1, \dots) = g(1)/(1 - \delta)$ and $u(0, 0, \dots) = f(0)/(1 - \delta)$. Hence, property B is satisfied.

One way of interpreting this utility function (though that is not needed for the proof above) is this. If a person chooses to smoke on a finite number of days, call him an "experimenter." Otherwise call him a "frequent user."[11] The pleasure a person gets from smoking on a particular day depends on whether he is headed towards being an experimenter or a frequent smoker. Since this is a model without uncertainty, this is not an unreasonable assumption (though it is unusual in economics). After all, if a person knows that she will have painful surgery next year, she would typically be a little sadder this year itself. And this is true not only in the sense of diminished present value but diminished joy from *this* year's activities and consumption.

---

[11] The terminology is a mild misuse of categories defined by Shedler and Block (1990) to distinguish between occasional and regular users of drugs.

Figure 3.1 *Waterfall* by M. C. Escher

What the above model demonstrates is that if a person takes a rational decision each day, he will have reason to regret. A rational decision taken on a day-by-day basis, or "atomistically," would result in his choosing to smoke (action 1) every day. But he clearly would be better off if he chose not to smoke on any day. Thus the rule "Do not ever smoke," while it may not be optimum, dominates the outcome that would emerge from atomistic rationality.

This is paradoxical in somewhat the same way as Escher's waterfall. If one studies the water's flow at any point in the famous picture, the water is plainly flowing down in a counterclockwise direction. Yet the downward flowing stream ends up at the highest point – the top rung of the tower. "It is hard to get children not to wade too deep into the water; it is easier to tell them to stay out of the water" wrote Thomas Schelling (1985: 368), thereby illustrating how at times it may be worthwhile for us to bind ourselves to some simple, rule-based behavior, even though we know that marginal infringements of the rule may be rewarding.

For a whole range of "vices" we try to stop ourselves at a point that is typically suboptimal in the sense that, if we could indulge ourselves a little more *and stop*, we would be better off. We do so because we do not trust our own ability to stop. The fact that addicts often express regret for their addiction and procrastinators for their procrastination shows that we have reason to be wary of our ability to exercise self-control. This also fits well with the widely observed phenomenon of individuals making vows or giving others the authority to impose restrictions on them.[12]

How does one explain these sorts of battles within the self? One way is to allow for absentmindedness or changes in human preference (Schelling, 1984, 1985). Akerlof (1991), as we just saw, explained this by allowing for the fact of "salience" in our perception of the goodness (or badness) of actions. What is ingenious about Akerlof's argument is that he shows how the small irrationality can explain grossly time-inconsistent behavior.

The purpose of the model I constructed above was to investigate whether the kind of inconsistency that Akerlof and Schelling write about can be generated without salience or preference change. The model answers this in the affirmative by showing that perfectly rational human beings, taking small decisions at a time – e.g., whether to have one more cigarette, whether to go one more step into the rapids, or whether to postpone mailing a box by a little more time – can take a series of decisions that, in terms of their

---

[12] For a recent formal model of self-control, see Gul and Pesendorfer (1999). See also Dasgupta (1988).

own preferences, is suboptimal where an individual could have done better by adherence to simple rules.

It is worth stressing here that though I constructed my example for a decision problem involving an infinite length of time, this is not necessary. What the construction crucially needs is an infinite number of decision points. To the extent that there is an infinite number of points of time in a year at which you can mail a parcel, or there is an infinite number of lengths between zero feet and 8 feet of water that a child can wade into, these decision problems can be modeled the same way that I modeled the smoker's problem (see also footnote 10).

I establish my claim within a certain context, which is by no means all-embracing. My aim is not to dismiss the role of salience or preference change in understanding human behavior but to demonstrate that there are contexts where the same behavior can be accommodated within the economist's standard model of *Homo economicus*. My explanation also helps us distinguish between what may be called "act optimization" and "rule optimization," which are analogs in the domain of utility maximization of the well-known concepts of act utilitarianism and rule utilitarianism (Gibbard, 1965; Smart and Williams, 1973; Sen, 1987: 88).

My model calls for a distinction between act optimization and rule optimization. **Act-optimizing behavior** is one where a person takes an optimizing action at each decision node (in my example, each day). On the other hand, **rule optimization** is the choice of a rule from among a set of simple rules in order to maximize utility. Examples of simple rules are: Never smoke; always smoke; smoke only on Sundays; and so on.[13]

In conventional contexts, act optimization will always (weakly) dominate rule optimization. What the above model demonstrates is that there can be contexts where a person would do strictly better by rejecting optimizing act by act and resorting to the use of simple rules to guide action.

3.4. The Traveler's Dilemma

Still pursuing the theme of how standard definitions of rationality are inadequate for explaining human behavior, let us now move beyond the individualistic context to interactive or strategic environments, by drawing on some of the techniques of analysis introduced in the previous chapter.

---

[13] While *simple* rules are difficult to design rigorously, they play a major role in our perception of the world and our choices (Schlicht, 1998).

In such situations, not only do the standard definitions of rationality run into difficulties of the kind encountered in the above sections but they actually give rise to some deep paradoxes, precursors of which we have already encountered in Chapter 2. One of the things that we will find is that formal rationalistic reasoning leads us to expect less cooperation among individuals than we would expect on the basis of introspection or experience. Let me illustrate this with a game that I developed in Basu (1994a) and christened "The Traveler's Dilemma."

Two travelers returning home from a remote island, where they bought identical antiques (or, rather, what the local tribal chief, while choking on suppressed laughter, described as "antiques"), discover that the airline has managed to smash these, as airlines sometimes do. The airline manager, who is described by his juniors as a "corporate whiz" (by which they mean a man of low cunning), assures the passengers of adequate compensation. But since he does not know the cost of the antique, he offers the following scheme.

Each of the two travelers has to write down on a piece of paper the cost of their antique. This can be any integer value between 2 units of money and 100 units. Denote the number chosen by traveler i by n_i. If both write the same number, that is, $n_1 = n_2$, then it is reasonable to assume that they are telling the truth (so argues the manager) and in that case each of these travelers will be paid n_1 (= n_2) units of money.

If traveler i writes a larger number than the other (i.e., $n_i > n_j$), then it is reasonable to assume (so it seems to the manager) that j is being honest and i is lying. In that case the manager will treat the lower number, n_j, as the real cost and will pay traveler i the sum of $n_j - 2$ and pay j the sum of $n_j + 2$. Traveler i is paid 2 units less than the adjudged cost as a penalty for lying, and j is paid 2 units more as reward for being honest in comparison with the other traveler. Given that each traveler or player wants to maximize his payoff (or compensation), what outcome should one expect to see in the above game? In other words, which pair of strategies, (n_1, n_2), will be chosen by the players?[14]

In order to answer this question, it is useful first to express this game as a payoff matrix. A part of this matrix is displayed in Fig. 3.2. At first sight, both players feel pleased that they can get 100 units each. To get this, each player simply has to write "100." But each player soon realizes that if the other player adheres to this plan then he can get 101 units of money by writing "99." But, of course, both players will do this, which means that

[14] It is interesting to note that the Traveler's Dilemma is, in a sense, a generalization of the Prisoner's Dilemma. If the players were asked to confine their choice to the numbers 2 or 3 (instead of any integer from 2 to 100), we would have exactly the Prisoner's Dilemma.

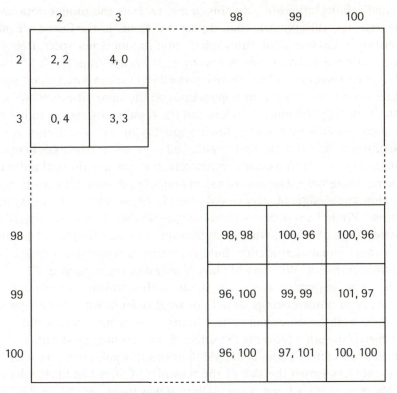

Figure 3.2 The Traveler's Dilemma

each player will in fact get 99 units. But if both were planning to write "99," then each player will reason that he can do better by writing "98;" and so on. The logic is inexorable, and there is no stopping until they get to the strategy pair (2, 2), that is, each player writes "2." Hence, they will end up getting two units of money each. This illustrates how backward-induction, at the level of introspection, works even in a one-shot game.

It is easy to check that all standard solutions predict outcome (2, 2). This is the unique strict equilibrium of the game and the only Nash equilibrium. Yet it seems very unlikely that any two individuals, no matter how rational they are and how certain they are about each other's rationality, each other's knowledge of each other's rationality, and so on, will play (2, 2). It is likely that each will choose a large number in the belief that so will the other, and thereby they will both get large payoffs.

In the finitely repeated Prisoner's Dilemma, it has been shown that cooperation in the early games is possible if one uses the (single-shot) rationalizability criterion.[15] In this game, (2, 2) is the unique rationalizable outcome. Observe also that, unlike this game, in the Centipede game described in Chapter 2 the "unwanted" equilibrium is not strict. Hence, in terms of formal analysis there seems to be no escape from (2, 2).

But even knowing all this, there is something very rational about rejecting (2, 2) and expecting your opponent to do the same. This is the essence of the Traveler's Dilemma.[16] This is also the reason why escape routes that are made possible by allowing for irrationality or the expectation of irrationality (see, for example, Kreps *et al.*, 1982) are not of relevance here even though they may be important empirically. It is not an empirical point that is being made here. The aim is to explain why, despite rationality being common knowledge, players would reject (2, 2), as intuitively seems to be the case. While I am unable to resolve the paradox, I want to suggest two possible lines of attack, which call into question our traditional assumptions about human knowledge. But before that, it is worth dwelling on the empirical question: Why would players in reality reject playing 2?

The most important answer is to do with altruism. For a mere two dollars, most human beings would not want to let down the other person, certainly so if the other person is a friend or an acquaintance, but this is true even if the other player is a stranger. Some recent experiments with the Traveler's Dilemma (Capra *et al.*, 1999) brings this point out very well. The experimenters varied the size of the reward and punishment, R, which in the above account is fixed at two dollars. It was found that when R is large, players tend to play as predicted by game theory; but when R is small, they play much more cooperatively. That is, they choose large numbers.

It is interesting to note that such cooperative behavior is probably the outcome of a combination of altruism and conformity.[17] In addition to having, arguably, an inherent amount of altruism, if a person believes that others are altruistic, the person's altruism is reinforced. Interesting evidence for this comes from the experiments that show that economists tend to play games more selfishly than other social scientists (Frank, Gilovich and Regan, 1993). In all likelihood this is a reflection of different beliefs among different classes of academics. Repeatedly encountering in microeconomics textbooks the assumption of how human beings are relentlessly selfish,

[15] The idea of rationalizability was not discussed in Chapter 2 on game theory. The interested reader may consult Bernheim (1984) or Pearce (1984).

[16] For interesting extensions of this game and the development of some related games, see Zambrano (1998) and Colombo (1999).

[17] Both altruism and conformity have enormous literatures. See, for instance, Axelrod (1984) and Schlicht (1998). It is also worth noting that the altruism here is taken as occurring between the players and not something that extends to the airline company or the organizer of the game.

economists often come to believe that that is the norm. And their own behavior is then, in part, an attempt to conform to the norm.

I shall have much more to say on the formation and persistence of social norms in the next chapter, but, for now, let us pursue a question of greater *logical* intrigue. So *assume* (what is admittedly not true in reality) that the players are ruthlessly selfish. It seems, on the basis of intuitive thinking, that, even then, the players will not play (2, 2). This is much harder to explain. It is not a question of reality but of logic. How do we reconcile selfishness being total and rationality being common knowledge with the possibility of the players choosing to play large numbers?

Note that though the Traveler's Dilemma is a normal-form game, it nevertheless can be thought of as having the "unreached-node problem" encountered in extensive-form games. To see this, begin by (a) defining rational play in the usual way and then (b) assume that rationality is common knowledge. Since (2, 2) is the only rationalizable outcome, it follows that that is what one should expect since rationalizability is the consequence of (a) and (b). Now suppose player 1 wants to decide how he would do if he rejected playing 2 and went instead for a larger number. It is not clear that this question is at all answerable. If it is true that (a) and (b) imply that player 1 will choose strategy 2, then a world where (a) and (b) are true and the player chooses some other strategy may not be conceivable, and so such introspective experiments may not be possible.

One possible line of attack that this suggests is to argue that the implicit assumptions, (a) and (b), which underlie so much of game theory, may by themselves be inconsistent. In Basu (1990) I showed that, in the context of games like the Centipede, the problem stemmed from assuming that rationality is common knowledge and that every game must have a solution. The method was to write down some properties of a solution, given that rationality is common knowledge, and to demonstrate that these properties cannot be together satisfied. However, there I made critical use of the extensive-form structure of the game. The Traveler's Dilemma challenges one to construct similar theorems without recourse to the sequence of play.

To end on an optimistic note, I shall now consider a more novel line of attack. Observe that in the Traveler's Dilemma there cannot exist a well-defined set of strategies, T_i, except in the special case $T_i = \{2\}$, such that: (i) a rational player may play any strategy in T_i and will never play anything outside it; and (ii) such a T_i can be *deduced* from an examination of the game. To see this, suppose that T_1 and T_2 are such sets. Since player 2 is perfectly rational, he can deduce what the game theorist can deduce. Hence, by (ii), he can deduce T_1. Let t be the largest number in T_1. Since player 1 will never play any number above t, it never pays for player 2 to play t. Hence T_1 and T_2 are not identical. But since this game is symmetrical and T_1 and T_2 are deduced purely from examing the game, T_1 must be the same as T_2. This contradiction establishes that no such (T_1, T_2) exists.

Note that this whole exercise was for well-defined (i.e., the usual kind of) sets. Hence, there *may* exist ill-defined sets that *would* work. There seems to be some *a priori* ground for believing that there may be an escape route here. Harking back to an idea that was touched on earlier, suppose that player 1 believes that player 2 will play a large number. Then, if player 1 were simply deciding whether he himself should play a large number or not, it would be in his interest to play a large number. Thus (large, large) seems to be a kind of Nash equilibrium *in ill-defined categories*. The ill-definedness is important here because, if the set of large numbers were a well-defined set, one knows from the previous paragraph that this argument would break down.

I am here interpreting "large" in the sense of everyday language, which is different from the fuzzy-set-theoretic interpretation. The latter implies that the set of integers that are certainly *not* large is a well-defined or "crisp" set. The everyday use of the word "large" clearly does not conform to this. Once this is taken seriously, many objections concerning the idea of Nash equilibrium in ill-defined categories, which immediately come to mind, cease to be valid.

Consider a question like this: "If the other player is playing a large number, should I ever play a number that is one less than a large number?" Once one starts answering questions like this, the argument as to why (large, large) is a kind of Nash equilibrium will quickly break down. What I am arguing, however, is that the question like the one above is not permitted in this framework. Given the everyday use of the word "large," "a large number minus 1" is a meaningless term. All I am claiming here is that if a player is told that the other player will choose a large number and is then asked whether he will choose a large number or not, he will say "yes."

The use of imprecise categories does not mean forgoing rationality. What was argued in this section was that one way of holding on to the rationality assumption in the face of paradoxical games such as the Traveler's Dilemma may be to allow players to use ill-defined categories in doing their reasoning about how to choose in game-theoretic situations.

The analysis of the Traveler's Dilemma, as well as the Centipede and the repeated Prisoner's Dilemma discussed in Chapter 2, makes implicit use of some intricate assumptions concerning knowledge. It is, for instance, implicitly assumed that player 1 knows that player 2 is rational, that player 1 knows that player 2 knows that player 1 is rational, and so on. I had tried to draw attention to these assumptions in Basu (1977) – see also Schick (1977). But a good way to see the relation between knowledge assumptions and the behavior of players in a game is to study Rubinstein's (1989) "Electronic Mail Game." After studying this game, I shall try to demonstrate how our standard knowledge assumptions can be tenuous and so may be a factor behind some of the conundrums of rationality.

3.5. The E-mail Game – Almost

What I present here is a simplified version of Rubinstein's (1989) celebrated paradox. See also Osborne and Rubinstein (1994: Ch. 5).

Two friends, 1 and 2, have planned to go either to a bistro (B) or to an amphitheatre (A) that is near 1's home. If the weather near 1's home is sunny (s) they prefer to meet at A. If it is rainy (r), they prefer B as the meeting place. The payoffs that the individuals get are shown in Fig. 3.3.

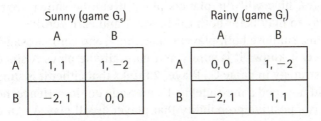

Figure 3.3 Payoff matrix (simplified E-mail game)

As per the usual convention of game theory (spelled out in Chapter 2), player 1 chooses rows and player 2 chooses columns. Thus, for example, if the weather is rainy (game G_r), and 1 chooses A and 2 chooses B, then player 1 gets a payoff of 1 and player 2 a payoff of -2. Note that game G_s has one Nash equilibrium, (A, A), and G_r has two Nash equilibria, (A, A) and (B, B). Of these two equilibria, (B, B) yields greater payoffs to both players, namely (1, 1) instead of (0, 0), in the game G_r. If it were common knowledge that it is rainy, it is not unreasonable to expect both players to play B and earn a payoff of 1 unit each.

As in a standard game, each player chooses his strategy (in this case "A or B") independently. However in the E-mail Game, before choosing their strategies, player 1 gets to know what the weather condition is and tries to communicate this information to player 2. The communication occurs through the following technology. Each player possesses a computer. If it is rainy, player 1 sends a message (saying that it is rainy) from 1's computer to 2's computer. No message is sent if it is sunny. Both computers are programmed so that whenever a computer receives a message it sends out a message (of acknowledgement). However, the transmission lines between the two computers are not flawless: Every time a message goes out from a computer there is a small probability, ε, that the message is lost in transmission, so that it does not reach the other person's computer.

To sum up, if the weather is sunny, no messages are sent. If it is rainy, player 1 sends a message for sure. Then player 2 sends a message with probability $1 - \varepsilon$ (that is, if she receives the message from 1); and player 1 sends another message with probability $(1 - \varepsilon)^2$, and so on. After the machines stop sending messages, each player sees how many messages were sent from his or her machine; and then chooses between the strategies A and B.

Suppose both machines send ten messages. Then clearly it is rainy; both players know that it is rainy; both players know that both players know that it is rainy, and so on up to ten times. The question is: After receiving those ten messages, how will the players play? It can be shown that the only rational way to play is for both to choose A and earn zero![18]

To see this, suppose both player's machines send zero messages. Then it means player 1 knows it is sunny and naturally he plays A since A is the dominant strategy in game G_s. Player 2 thinks that either it is sunny (hence player 1 did not send a message) or 1's message got lost. Hence, he believes that there is a positive probability that player 1 will play A. An examination of game G_r (see Fig. 3.3) makes it obvious that, given such a belief, A is the only rational move for player 2.

Next consider the case in which player 1's machine sends exactly one message. This means that either the message from 1 fails to reach 2 or 2's message (i.e. 2's acknowledgement of 1's message) fails to reach 1, because if neither of these had happened then 1's machine would have sent more than one message. It follows that player 1 will know that either 2's machine sent zero messages or one message (both events having positive probability). If the former happens, we know from the preceding paragraph that 2 will play A. Since player 1 knows this, 1 will also play A.

Now consider the case in which 2's machine sends exactly one message. Then player 2 will know that either 1's machine sent one message or two messages. And we can continue in this fashion. By such induction, it is evident that no matter how many messages go from each player's machine, each player plays nothing but A.

If state r (rainy) having occurred were common knowledge, it is a Nash equilibrium for both players to choose B and earn 1 unit each. But anything short of common knowledge, as we just saw, destroys this outcome. Both may know r, know that they know r, and so on a hundred times; but the only rational play will be (A, A).[19]

After discussing the E-mail Game and other paradoxes of backward induction, Osborne and Rubinstein (1994: 84) go on to argue that the "discrepancy between our intuition and the [game-theoretic] analysis lies in the fact that mathematical induction is not part of the reasoning process of human beings." While that may well be so, I believe that, more significantly, the paradoxes show that human beings have the ability to reject inductive thinking when it is advantageous to them. If this were not so, we would have to maintain that those trained in inductive thinking (e.g., mathematicians) would play the game differently. But that does not seem likely. This point of view is difficult to formalize because we do not as yet have a model of what it means for an agent to reject induction or, more generally, to consciously reject the use of "rational" computation. But this is a direction in which these paradoxes nudge us.

Paradoxical results of this kind have also drawn our attention to the close relation between knowledge and rationality. This is now an area of active enquiry involving game theory, economics and the science of artificial intelligence (see Fagin et al., 1995). How a person chooses or acts clearly depends on what a person knows or believes. Economists and game theorists have traditionally been very cavalier in making assumptions about knowledge and erred in the direction of assuming too much.

One frequently used assumption is that, among the players of a game, rationality is common knowledge. Innocuous though this assumption sounds, as the simplified E-mail Game above illustrates, it is an enormously powerful assumption.[20] In addition, I believe that this assumption may, in some situations, have problems of internal logical consistency. Indeed, its cavalier use may be the source of some of the paradoxes of rationality that we have encountered above, such as the Traveler's Dilemma. With me this remains no more than a hunch; it is not something that I can prove. What I do in the next section is illustrate some of the deep paradoxes of knowledge in order to emphasize that we cannot simply pick our knowledge assumptions out of thin air.

---

[19] This outcome can be true even if, everything else remaining the same in G_s and G_r above, the payoffs from (A, A) in G_s and (B, B) in G_r were (1.5, 1.5).

[20] I discussed this in the context of the Prisoner's Dilemma in Basu (1977).

3.6. The Paradox of Cognition

It is a banal observation that human perception is less than perfect. Thus a person typically cannot tell the difference between a cup of coffee with n grains of sugar and a cup of coffee with $n + 1$ grains of sugar. Yet if we keep adding one grain at a time for quite a while, the person will know the difference ultimately. After all, most people can tell the difference between a cup of coffee with no sugar and a cup with two spoons of sugar. This observation is closely related to the well-known Sorites paradox, or Heap paradox, which is associated with the name of the Greek philosopher Eubulides, who lived in the fourth century BC. It is also related to the problem of intransitivity of indifference, which has been widely discussed in economics. But I want to draw the reader's attention to a related but new problem. I call it the "paradox of cognition."

For brevity, I shall from here on refer to "a cup of coffee with n grains of sugar" as simply "n." Thus, what we noted in the above paragraph is that, for any non-negative integer n: (a) people cannot distinguish between n and $n + 1$; and (b) they can distinguish between n and $n + m$ if m is a sufficiently large integer. Without loss of generality, let us suppose that statement (b) is true as long as $m \geq 10$; that is, a person cannot tell the difference between n and $n + m$ if and only if $m < 10$.

Now suppose a person is given a cup of coffee with 20 grains of sugar. Given the assumption in the above paragraph, the person will not know if the cup has 11, 12, . . . , 28 or 29 grains of sugar. If it had any more or any less he would know since he can perceive differences of 10 grains or more. *But when he finds himself wondering whether what he has got is 11, 12, . . . , 28 or 29, he should be able to deduce that he has 20 because only at 20 will he know that he has something in the set $\{11, . . . , 29\}$ and yet not know which particular amount he has.* Thus he should know he has 20. In brief, since he does not know whether he has 11, 12, . . . or 29, he should know that he has exactly 20. This is the paradox.

There are different ways of trying to resolve this paradox, which I have discussed in Basu (1995b). Here, I shall elaborate on one particular resolution that is most closely related to the discussion at the end of the previous section (3.4). This involves rejecting what is often called the "axiom of transparency." This axiom says that if a person knows something, then the person knows that he knows it. This axiom is an integral part of the standard algebra of knowledge and "S5 logic" that game theorists use.[21]

---

[21] While this axiom remains largely unchallenged, a few writers – notably Sorensen (1988) and Williamson (1994) – take a line very similar to the one I take here.

Observe that, in the paragraph previous to the one above, the italicized sentence is not as self-evident as it may appear at first sight. It implicitly uses the axiom of transparency. For a person wondering whether he has 11, 12, ..., or 29 grains to know that he has 20, he must know what he knows. This is because he must know that it is only at 20 that he will know he has got 11, 12, ..., or 29. So if we reject the axiom of transparency, the italicized line ceases to be valid and the paradox does not arise anymore.[22]

There is another independent reason for rejecting the axiom of transparency. Consider what I will call a person's "imperception relation" T, which may be interpreted (roughly speaking) as follows. For two states of the world x and y, if $x \, T \, y$ is true, then it means the person cannot tell the difference between states x and y. Thus, if state x is a world where a person gets a cup of coffee with n grains of sugar, and y is a world where the person gets a cup of coffee with $n + 1$ grains of sugar, with everything else between the two worlds being the same, then for any typical person's imperception relation T, $x \, T \, y$ is true. The concept of imperception relation is closely related to the idea of "accessibility" in modal logic.

From the discussion earlier in this section, it is clear that it is unrealistic to think of T as transitive. But we know from modal logic that the transitivity of T is virtually[23] equivalent to the axiom of transparency. Hence, if T is intransitive we have to reject the axiom of transparency.

This is the main lesson I would like to derive from the paradox of cognition. There are other possible ways out, but they seem to me to be either too destructive or too prone to circularity. Let me illustrate my point with two other ways of resolving the paradox.

---

[22] There is another problem about the italicized sentence that may strike some readers. It suggests that when a person sips a cup of coffee with 20 grains of sugar, he cannot tell whether it has 20 or 19 grains, but he can tell that it does not have 10 grains of sugar. This seems unrealistic, because it is one thing to be able to distinguish between the sugar content of two cups of coffee and quite another thing to be able to tell the numbers of grains of sugar in the cups. This is akin to the music expert who can tell the difference between any two notes but cannot on hearing a note tell you which one it is. While this is a valid point, this "matching problem" can easily be solved while leaving my paradox untouched. For that solution, we could assume that on a table we have cups of coffee with, respectively, zero grains of sugar, 1 grain of sugar, 2 grains, 3, 4 and so on; and these cups are labelled 0, 1, 2, 3, 4 and so on, respectively. These cups are like the *tanpura* in the background during an Indian classical music concert. When now we perform the experiment of giving the person an unlabelled cup containing 20 grains and ask how much sugar it has, let us allow him to sip from the labelled cups freely for reference. Now the matching problem is solved but the paradox remains. I am grateful to Jean Dreze and Bob Frank for drawing my attention to this matching problem.

[23] The "virtually" warns the reader that the formal result requires a mild condition to be satisfied (Basu, 1995b).

First, we could challenge the very existence of an **imperception relation**, defined as a binary relation that captures a person's inability to perceive differences between states of the world. This in turn would suggest that, given a state x, there is no well-defined set $\bar{T}(x)$ of states such that the person in question cannot tell the difference between state x and elements of $\bar{T}(x)$. Recall that, in my construction above, $\bar{T}(20) = \{11, 12, \ldots, 29\}$. If the existence of such sets is called into question, then the paradox of cognition cannot be constructed. If one introspects on this matter, the existence of sets like $\bar{T}(x)$ does indeed seem doubtful in reality. But I am tempted to avoid this line of resolution because it destroys the very basis of the algebra of knowledge. The rejection of the axiom of transparency, on the other hand, resolves the paradox while practicing damage minimization.

To appreciate the other line of attack, let us define Ω to be the set of all possible states of the world. In our coffee example, $\Omega = \{0, 1, 2, \ldots\}$, since a state of the world was defined simply in terms of the number of grains of sugar in a cup of coffee. Now we can consider a resolution of the paradox by expanding the state space Ω to allow for variations in perception and knowledge. Thus we could, for instance, think of each element of Ω being an ordered pair of integers, (r, s), where r is the number of grains of sugar in the coffee and s is the number of grains that a person feels there is in the coffee. Thus, in the example described above, we shall have information sets such as $\{(20, 11), (20, 12), \ldots, (20, 29)\}$ and $\{(21, 12), (21, 13), \ldots, (21, 30)\}$. Hence, there will be no overlaps or intersections between information sets and, as a consequence, the paradox of cognition disappears.

If one takes the line that Aumann (1976) takes, which is to treat each element of Ω to be a complete description of a state of the world, including details of people's knowledge and perception, one would have to take the approach of expanding Ω as just explained.

However, this is a problematic route to take. It is an attempt to cling on to the partitions approach at all cost. It is reminiscent of the effort of early economists (and, regrettably, even some contemporaries) to fit all human choice and behavior into the rubric of utility maximization. They kept adjusting the specification of the utility function every time their attention was drawn to some non-utility-maximizing behavior, thereby trivializing the utility function. Likewise, Ω becomes a vacuous concept if we keep expanding it to retain the information partitions approach. Moreover, we cannot then treat Ω as a primitive – that is, we cannot write down Ω and then go on to consider alternative knowledge structures or imperception relations – because variations in the latter would require us to return to Ω and make changes in its specification. Also, the requirement of complete description implies that we cannot consider simple structures of Ω of the kind discussed above, where each element of Ω is an integer that tells us simply the number of grains of sugar in a cup of coffee. Likewise, Fagin *et al.* (1995: 16) argue that Ω can have a "concrete interpretation" in situations such as "a poker game [where possible states of the world] are simply all the possible ways the cards could have been distributed among the players." Hence, even apart from the philosophical difficulties of *complete* descriptions (see Binmore and Brandenburger, 1990), this line of resolving the cognition paradox seems to be unsatisfactory. It is interesting to note here that Shin (1993) *begins* with states that are complete descriptions of *objective features* and then *iteratively* fills in the knowledge of individuals.

In the light of this, I prefer the argument for jettisoning the axiom of transparency. The rejection of this axiom has lots of implications for the analysis of knowledge and behavior in strategic environments. What is of special interest here is that many events that were earlier taken to be obviously common knowledge cease to be so. To see this, consider a one-person society. In such a society, suppose the person knows that some event E has occurred. In the traditional approach, which takes the axiom of transparency to be valid, this will immediately mean E is common knowledge. This is because for a person to know E implies (by the axiom of transparency) for her to know that she knows E, and so on by repeated application of the axiom. In other words, in a one-person society, knowledge is common knowledge. However, this is no longer true once this axiom is discarded. In fact we cannot from the fact that a person knows E deduce that he knows that he knows E. To see this, return to the example above and set $E = \{11, 12, \ldots, 29\}$. Clearly, the event that the person knows E is given by $\{20\}$. But he can never know this event.

Hence, once we, realistically, discard the axiom of transparency, even in a one-person society, common knowledge becomes extremely hard to come by. Moreover, very often a person simply does not know what he himself knows, let alone higher orders of such knowledge.[24] Hence, we have to be even more suspect of *inter*personal knowledge, because it includes all the problems mentioned above, plus the problem of "other minds." Thus the widespread use of the assumption that rationality is common knowledge among players in a game is open to serious question.

There is an interesting connection between this analysis of self-knowledge and the problem of self-control discussed later in Section 4.3. In a series of

---

[24] A different and novel approach to modeling the lack of self-knowledge and its implication occurs in Benabou and Tirole (1999).

papers (see, for instance, their 1999 paper), O'Donoghue and Rabin have distinguished between two kinds of people among those who lack self-control (that is, basically all of us). There are those who know that they lack self-control and those who do not. They call the former "sophisticated" and the latter "naive." In general, it is better to know oneself (there is a nice resonance to the prescription "Know thyself"), and so the sophisticated persons do better. Basically, they know how to deal with themselves.

O'Donoghue and Rabin derive many interesting results, including how in some situations being sophisticated can exacerbate the problem of self-control. I wish, however, to draw the reader's attention to something else here. In their paper, what they do not distinguish between are: (1) a person who knows that he lacks self-control and knows that he knows that he lacks self-control, and so on all the way to common knowledge; and (2) a person who knows that he lacks self-control but he does not know that he knows that he lacks self-control. In the traditional setting, this is an unnecessary distinction because no one can be of type 2. The axiom of transparency guarantees this. In a one-person decision problem, as soon as you know your preference, there is common knowledge of it.

Once, however, we reject the axiom of transparency, we can subdivide the people who know that they have a self-control problem into many different kinds and, in particular, between types 1 and 2, as described above. It can then be shown that in many situations, including some of the kind discussed by O'Donoghue and Rabin, persons of type 2 behave differently not only from those who are naive but those who are sophisticated in the sense of (1) above.

The rejection of the axiom of transparency cannot only help us resolve the paradox of cognition but can give us new insights into human behavior.

Part II. SOCIETY

4. Social Norms, Culture and Beliefs

4.1. Of Mice and Men

Economists usually write as if social norms do not matter. In reality, social norms and institutions play an important role in influencing not just polity and society but economics and outcomes in the marketplace. The prosperity and progress of an economy are not just a matter of guns and butter – or, for that matter, tariff levels, fiscal deficit and macroeconomic stability – but also our attitude towards work, level of mutual trust, standard of ethics, and social norms. What is more surprising is that a norms-free economics may not simply be empirically flawed but analytically so. Some may even argue that a norms-free economics is not possible. Hence, when we write up models with no reference to norms and institutions, it is likely that we are nevertheless using norms and institutions but doing so unwittingly.

This is reason enough for taking social norms seriously. Another reason is that a hand-waving use of norms runs the risk of going to the other extreme and explaining everything in terms of social norms. As Solow (1995: 318) warns us, it is easy to fall into the trap of explaining "any kind of behavior (and its opposite) by postulating a social norm that says 'Do this' (or its opposite)." In other words, a norms-based explanation can run into the same risk of tautology as an individual-rationality-based explanation, as was discussed in the previous chapter. This is no reason to deny the use of norms, as economists often do, but to study norms as they are and limit ourselves to using social norms that stand the test of scrutiny and realism. In giving that explanation, Solow was urging the use of norms in economics rather than any abstention.

The importance of social norms as foundation for economic activity is best illustrated by the act of exchange. According to the first principles of economics, two agents will exchange or trade goods if the following assumptions are true: (a) each individual prefers having more goods to less; (b) each person satisfies the law of diminishing marginal utility;[1] and (c) the initial endowment of goods is lopsided – for example, one person has all

---

[1] Strictly speaking, what we need is the convexity of preference. But since this turns out to be equivalent to the law of diminishing marginal utility if the utility function happens to be additively separable, I shall here use the more familiar condition of diminishing marginal utility.

the butter and the other all the bread. To many economists, (a), (b) and (c) are indeed sufficient conditions for trade to occur. What they do not realize is that these are sufficient *only* when the agents are already embedded in a certain institutional environment and characterized by adequate social norms. For instance, exchange is greatly facilitated by the ability to communicate or, even better, to speak and understand a common language. And given that language is very likely an evolved social convention,[2] trade and exchange are predicated on social conventions.

The importance of these implicit requirements for trade can be inferred from some experiments in economics, which were conducted originally for a different purpose. Experiments have shown that rats prefer more to less – a fact that I suspected well before I read experimental economics. Furthermore, experiments have established that rats also satisfy the law of diminishing marginal utility or, more precisely, have convex preference. This was established by some innovative experiments conducted by Kagel *et al.* (1975) on white albino rats, belonging to the – this for the connoisseur – Wistar and Sprague–Dawley stock. So, rats satisfy assumptions (a) and (b). All that remained to be done to check the exchange hypothesis was to give different kinds of food to different rats, which would fulfil assumption (c), and see what the rats did. It seems some relentless researchers did just that (reported in Warneryd, 1995). They presumably placed two rats at some distance apart, with each possessing a different food item. The researchers discovered that, though these rats satisfied assumptions (a), (b) and (c), they did not, alas, indulge in trade and exchange. I feel I could have predicted this from my occasional encounter with rats, but it is anyway good to have these things experimentally confirmed.

Facetious though it may sound, the above account does amount to a very substantial critique of traditional economics. It shows that even in models that seem transparently free of any requirements of norms and institutions, that is not the case. The example, by showing that "rattiness" is bad for trade, alerts us to the possibility that "the Protestant ethic" or "Rastafarianism" may be good for trade (or, for that matter, bad). Market-related activity, trade and other economic functionings have to be embedded in institutions and social norms. If we refuse to embed our models consciously, we will still be doing so, only unwittingly. And given that the latter is not such a wise approach, it is important that we recognize the role that social norms play and try to build these in consciously and in keeping with reality.

---

[2] This view of language, which I adhere to, is not undisputed; but it has the respectability of age, dating at least as far back as to the writings of David Hume. Warneryd (1990) has formalized this in terms of evolutionary game theory.

The recognition that markets and economic activity are embedded in social institutions and norms can make an enormous difference to the way in which formal theorems of economics are interpreted. Let me illustrate this with an example. Consider the **First Fundamental Theorem** of welfare economics, which may be stated, taking the liberty of colloquialism, as follows:

> If individuals maximize their own selfish utility, then (given that certain technical conditions are satisfied), the competitive equilibrium that arises is always Pareto-optimal.

In itself, this is a mathematical theorem that tells us nothing about the world we live in. Its application to the real world depends on how we interpret it *beyond* what it actually tells us. One popular interpretation of this theorem is that it shows that if individuals are left free to choose whatever they want, then society attains optimality. And, conversely, taxes and other government interventions that limit the feasible sets of individuals tend to result in suboptimality. In defense of this interpretation, one would typically point out that in the standard competitive model in which the theorem is established, it is assumed that individual consumers are free to choose any point (or basket of goods) from within their budget sets (or what their incomes permit).

Let us now think for a moment what are the kinds of choices a person can in reality make. It is true that a person can choose from a variety of alternative baskets of goods that lie within his budget; but a person can also choose to rob, steal and plunder; he can try to take away the endowment of another individual, invoking the age-old principle of more being better than less; he can commit blackmail, larceny, and arson; he can spread rumors, slander, and, disregarding Auden's proscription, "sit with statisticians" or "commit a social science."[3] Hence, when we allow an individual to choose any point within his budget set, there are two ways of viewing this. We could view this as giving him great freedom: he can choose *any* point. Or we could view it as very restrictive: he is not allowed to choose anything (from the large menu of options he has in life) apart from choosing a point from his budget set. If we follow the latter course, then here is an interpretation of the fundamental theorem that is a "dual" to the popular interpretation described above: The fundamental theorem shows that society

---

[3] From W. H. Auden's poem, "Under which Lyre: A Reactionary Tract for the Times" (reprinted in his *Selected Poems*, Vintage International, New York, 1989).

Bowles and Gintis (1993: 96) are referring to the same problem when they note that the Walrasian model "arbitrarily precludes malfeasance."

attains optimality if individual choice is severely restricted and in particular confined to choosing points from within the budget set.

One may argue that the restriction of not allowing theft, larceny and blackmail is not a restriction at all because it may be in the self-interest of the individual not to indulge in these things. If that is so, then we need to formally show this by starting with a model where all these "extra-economic" activities are allowed but are, somehow, rejected voluntarily by the individuals. My belief is that, once we start from such a large domain to get to the case where the pure general equilibrium model works, we need either social norms that effectively restrict the set from which one chooses, or the institution of government, with coercive powers, or some other related institution, in order to prevent individuals from finding some of these extra-economic activities worthwhile.

Since this exercise of embedding the market model has not been performed thus far,[4] we do not really know whether the model of the market, abstracted from its social and political moorings, can ever be realized. This would be an easy agenda item if government were conceived of as an exogenous body that makes it costly for individuals to steal and rob. But, as argued in the next few chapters, that would not be a reasonable method of analysis. We have to allow for the fact that government is run by individuals who respond to incentives, and explain the survival of government and government's power from a model of individual decision-making. The endogenization of government is the subject matter of the next four chapters. The present chapter is concerned with social norms.

As an important digression I want to stress that this problem of the vastness of actions and strategies available in reality to agents is underplayed in our models, and probably handicaps our ability to understand reality. The assumption, in general equilibrium and game-theory models, that agents face well-defined strategy sets or feasibility sets and are cognizant of this, is not realistic in many cases. As I have just argued, individuals in reality choose not just from budget sets but from a bewildering range of possibilities. Consider the Cuban Missile Crisis. As discussed in Chapter 2, this has often been analyzed as a game, in particular as the Hawk–Dove game. But to describe the missile crisis as a game is to make several simplifying assumptions, many of which were pointed out in Chapter 2. A deeper criticism is that the agents in the "game" that was being played in reality did not have well-defined sets of possible actions. Let us take the US side of the

---

[4] Even though its importance has been stressed time and again: see, for instance, Polanyi (1944), Granovetter (1985), Platteau (1994), Emigh (1999) and Nee and Strang's discussion of "context-bound conceptions of rationality" (1998).

game, about which we now know a lot. The interminable deliberations that Kennedy and his advisers went through were not just sessions to weigh the costs and benefits of the various strategies available to them, but, in large measure, to *discover* the set of strategies available to them. And this set kept expanding rapidly as they discussed. They could invade Cuba and destroy the missile sites; they could invade Cuba and bomb the entire island in order to ensure that there would not be any retaliation from some unknown military base; they could do these things suddenly without notice or by warning the USSR and Cuba; they could offer to the USSR to remove the missiles in Turkey in exchange for the Soviet missiles being removed from Cuba. Indeed, interestingly enough, the action that was finally taken, namely to blockade the sea around Cuba and give the USSR a limited time to remove the missiles from Cuba, was not even mentioned in the first few hours of trying to enlist the set of available strategies. In fact, what we can really say is that the United States used the action it thought best *from among the ones it had discovered.* And no doubt the same was true for the USSR. In fact, if anything, the USSR probably considered a more limited set of options, since it does not appear that Khrushchev had the kind of brainstorming sessions that Kennedy had to explore alternative courses of action.

With this caveat about the use of game-theory models in explaining complicated real-life conflicts, let us now turn to the dazzling array of norms that one encounters in life. There are norms of honesty, hard work and diligence. There are norms of ownership and property. Sugden (1989) has written about the norm that prevailed in a Yorkshire fishing village, whereby the first person to arrive on the shore after a high tide could collect the driftwood and, by placing two stones on the pile, leave it for later collection with general societal recognition that the driftwood was the property of the person who placed the stones. There are norms of politeness, like enquiring how a person is, despite no interest in the answer. In most industrial nations, it is a norm not to ask strangers personal questions; it is considered impolite to behave otherwise. In many developing nations, on the other hand, when you meet a new person, it is considered impolite *not* to ask personal questions; that would show a lack of interest in the person. In the years when I traveled regularly between Delhi and Calcutta by train, I was more than once impressed by how my co-passengers managed to extricate information about my salary before we passed Ghaziabad station (approximately 30 minutes from Delhi).

Social norms are closely related to customs. Schlicht (1998) has written about numerous customs – for instance, the norms of driving on the highway, which go well beyond what is required by the law but which we all live by unwittingly. And it is only through some detachment and introspection that one becomes aware of them.

Just the fact that norms are abundant in reality is no reason why economists should be concerned about them. However, there are several norms that influence market outcomes and economic functioning more profoundly than has been appreciated by economists; and this is the reason why we need to understand them. In order to analyze and understand the role of norms in an economy, a useful first step is to classify the myriad norms that remain even after we omit the ones that are unimportant from the point of view of *economic* analysis.

I find it useful to distinguish between three kinds of social norms: Rationality-limiting norms, preference-changing norms and equilibrium-selection norms.[5]

A **rationality-limiting norm** is a norm that stops us from doing certain things or choosing certain options, irrespective of how much utility that thing or option gives us. Thus, most individuals would not consider picking another person's wallet in a crowded bus. This (lack of) action they would take not by speculating about the amount the wallet is likely to contain, the chances of getting caught, the severity of the law and so on, but because they consider stealing wallets as something that is *simply not done.*

In traditional economics, the **feasible set** of alternatives facing an individual (from which the person makes his or her choice) is defined in terms of technological or budgetary feasibility. Thus a consumer's feasible set is the collection of all the combinations of goods and services that the consumer can purchase given his or her income. From the above discussion it should be evident that a rationality-limiting norm further limits the feasible set, because now certain alternatives may be effectively infeasible to an individual not just because they are technologically infeasible (like walking on water) or budgetarily infeasible (like buying a Jaguar car) but because they are ruled out by the person's norms. Indeed, a person endowed with norms may forgo options that could have enhanced his utility and thus such a person would be considered irrational in terms of mainstream economics. Basically, such norms limit the domain over which the rationality calculus is applied.

Some may argue that instead of thinking that such norms limit individual rationality, we can simply redefine our utility function, so that what I described above as normatively infeasible is described instead as an option

---

[5] For a related classification, see Posner (1997).

that gives a very low utility – perhaps negative infinity. But if one does this *invariably*, one runs the risk of reducing utility theory to a tautology. Moreover, in reality there are certain things we would love to do but our norms get in the way. Nevertheless, this does not mean that norms never change our preferences or utility functions. Certain norms do get internalized. There are many individuals whose religion requires them to be vegetarian, and they tell you that they find non-vegetarian food revolting anyway. More often than not, this is no coincidence; a religious norm adhered to over a stretch of time often gets internalized, so that one begins actually to prefer what the norm requires one to do. This can explain why one finds systematic variations in taste across regions and nations. What starts out as a norm or a custom can over time become part of one's preference. Such a norm may be referred to as a **preference-changing norm**. The main reason for recognizing this kind of a norm as a separate conceptual entity is that it can give us an understanding of how some of our preferences are formed. This can enormously enrich the traditional model of economics, which treats preferences as primitives.

Finally, consider the norm, in many countries, of driving on the right on the roads. It is true that this norm is additionally fortified by the law; but it is arguable that even if this were just a norm or a convention and not the law, people would still drive on the right. This explains why the police have to be vigilant in enforcing the Stop-sign rule or the speeding rule but not the drive-on-the-right rule. The first two are laws that are not always in people's self interest to obey (they may of course be in their *group* interest). But the third is a norm that, once it is in place, happens to be entirely compatible with self-interested behavior. In the absence of such a norm, there are at least two possible equilibria: everyone drives on the left, and everyone drives on the right. This norm is very different from the two discussed above because it simply helps people *select* an equilibrium when more than one equilibrium is available. It is for this reason that this is called an **equilibrium-selection norm**. This is the norm the study of which is currently in vogue in economics and has generated a lot of literature, to the extent that economists tend to forget about the other kinds of norms – conveniently so, since the equilibrium-selection norm is the one that is most compatible with conventional economics.

We return to all three kinds of norms in the sections that follow, rationality-limiting norms and preference-changing norms being discussed in Section 4.2 and equilibrium-selection norms being the subject matter of Section 4.4. The remaining sections discuss some of the implications of these ideas and their foundations.

4.2. The Bridge on Forest Home Drive

On Forest Home Drive in Ithaca there is a bridge on which two cars cannot cross each other. When we were in school in Calcutta we were told how in the Andes there are pathways along steep mountains that are so narrow that two people cannot pass each other; and so when two persons happened to come face to face on one of these paths, the one with the quicker draw survived by shooting the other person.

In Ithaca a different norm is used. Cars pass in small convoys, three or four at a time, and the convoys alternate from the two directions. That is, after the third or fourth car ahead goes, one just stops and waits for three or four oncoming cars, and then starts again. This stopping and waiting is against one's self-interest. So this is an example of a rationality-limiting norm. One possible reason why we find norms of this kind prevailing in Ithaca and not the norm of a shootout is that this is evolutionarily more stable. This is also the reason why the Andean custom probably exists nowhere at all and was simply a tale meant for children.

The evolutionary basis of these norms is discussed in Sections 4.5 and 4.6. Whatever the basis of rationality-limiting norms, that such norms play an important role in shaping human behavior is undeniable. I have discussed elsewhere how it is difficult to explain why we pay taxi drivers after a taxi ride, especially when we know that we are likely never again to meet the driver, if we do not want to concede the fact that human beings do at times adhere to norms, even when these are not in their self-interest (see also Basu, 1983b; Schlicht, 1998). It is hopeless to say that we pay because otherwise the taxi driver will beat us up and that the cost of the beating exceeds the meter reading. If the fear of a thrashing is the only reason we pay, it becomes unclear why, after passengers pay up, taxi drivers do not threaten to beat up passengers the same way that they would if the passengers had not paid, unless they pay a second time. Somewhere, we have to make room for norms.

The power of one agent to punish another is often essential for certain kinds of transactions to be possible. In the context of international lending, where there is no effective world government to enforce contracts, it has been pointed out that lending occurs only when the lender has the power to punish the borrower. Otherwise, borrowers would renege on their repayments; and knowing this, the lender would not lend in the first place. Once again, as an argument based on pure rationality this is problematic. If the lender has such power, why does he not collect "repayment" without lending any money in the first place but by threatening to punish borrowers in the same way that he would if the borrower had borrowed money and not repaid. There may be convoluted pure-rationality arguments to explain international lending, but I am skeptical that that would be the right argument. Even in the ruthless world of international politics, there are norms and it would enrich our understanding of trade and exchange if we tried to take account of the norms explicitly (Basu, 1991).

As discussed in the previous section, closely related to the idea of rationality-limiting norms is the concept of preference-changing norms. These latter have been modeled, yielding considerable insight into certain kinds of economic activity.[6] According to this approach, a person's actual preference is the outcome of his selfish preference *and* social norm. While selfish preferences are assumed to be primitives, the norms respond to the prevailing fashions and mores in the society. We are here talking of norms that have been internalized and so are not enforced through social sanctions and shame. Usually this happens when a norm has been around for some time. In many societies a smoker refrains from smoking in public areas – for instance, in hospital waiting rooms – because of what others would think or say; but when this norm persists for a long time, smokers may themselves *prefer* not to smoke in public areas and so a smoker would follow this norm even when he happens to be alone.

We may at first think that preference-changing norms or internalized norms are not interesting because, in the end, they are just like preferences and so no different from what economists learn in their first courses. This would, however, be wrong, because a recognition that a part of our actual preference is shaped by norms allows us to understand how preferences are formed and how individual preferences may change in response to changes in society.

Consider the example of a norm that gives rise to diminished utility to a person who is unemployed and has to draw unemployment benefit. This can happen because of stigma, or loss of face, or a sense of shame. But let us suppose that this is internalized as a part of the person's preference. It is quite reasonable to suppose that this stigma cost becomes smaller the larger the number of people who draw on unemployment benefit. If all your neighbors are on welfare, it may not feel quite as bad to be on welfare. Let us make this assumption. It is now easy to see that macroeconomic or society-level changes (for instance, the amount of unemployment in the

---

[6] See, among others, Granovetter and Soong, 1983; Basu, 1987; Elster, 1989; Sugden, 1989; Besley and Coate, 1992; Durlauf, 1996; Lindbeck, Nyberg and Weibull, 1999; Lopez-Calva (1999); and Cooper and Garcia-Penalosa, 1999. See Mansbridge (1990) for a discussion of different mechanisms for bringing altruism in line with self-interested behavior.

economy) can cause changes in individual preferences – something that does not happen in standard neoclassical economics, where a person's preference is a primitive and depends on his own consumption. This, in turn, can help us understand the possibility of multiple equilibria in an economy: If very few people are on welfare in a society, then there is a lot of stigma cost to being on welfare; so very few people will want to be on welfare. In other words, they will accept worse jobs, just to stay out of the unemployment pool. If, on the other hand, lots of people draw on the unemployment dole, there is less stigma to doing so and more people may thereby be tempted to quit their low-paid jobs and instead go on the dole. A high and a low unemployment level can both be equilibria. This is formally established by Lindbeck, Nyberg and Weibull (1999), who then go on to examine a host of interesting policy questions and political equilibria that arise out of this basic model.

The above example clarifies the advantage of identifying social norms (in particular, preference-changing norms) and stigma costs as such. It is in principle possible to appropriate these under the single umbrella of a person's utility function. Yet to do so would be to blur our understanding of human behavior. One of the essential features of social norms and stigma is that they are dependent on what happens in society at large. Unlike the intensity of my preference for apples, which (at least according to textbook economics) does not depend on what others in society say or do, how bad I feel about being unemployed depends critically on what others do and say. Thus norms are socially embedded in a way that pure preferences need not be.

In reality, even our preferences are often endogenous, changing in response to what happens in society at large. In terms of mathematical structure, the model may be the same irrespective of whether our preferences are endogenous or whether they embody social norms and so are prone to changing as the norms change.[7] The upshot is that a person's preference may change as the social context changes. Once we allow for this, the path opens up for explaining a variety of social phenomena, such as herd behavior and fashion cascades (see Banerjee, 1992; Bikhchandani, Hirshleifer and Welch, 1992), reciprocity (Fehr and Gachter, 1997), inflation (Arce M, 1997) and even excess demand and supply (Basu, 1989). In Basu (1987, 1989), following a long tradition starting with Veblen (1899), I tried to formalize the human urge to choose one's "association" or sense

---

[7] Durlauf (1996) has shown how a diverse range of phenomena, where individual preference responds to the collective context, can be modeled as a form of statistical mechanics.

of belonging to certain groups. Akerlof and Kranton (1999) have recently formalized the more general idea of a person's "identity," which is mostly predefined (a person is a woman, or an Indian, or a Muslim) but can in some cases be chosen. Kuran (1988) has analyzed the process of "ethnification". These ideas challenge the standard neoclassical assumption of individual preferences being exogenous and fixed,[8] and is worth an incursion. Accordingly, the next section is devoted to sketching some of the implications of the human urge to seek association with certain groups.

Whether we are talking of preference-changing norms or association goods, one common difficulty arises from the fact that preferences are not primitives but may depend on the economy-wide output. Hence, in such a model, as an economy moves towards a general equilibrium, the preferences themselves will change, thereby making the search for the general equilibrium that much harder. Much of the literature gets around this by either making very restrictive assumptions or characterizing a partial equilibrium. The next section is no exception to this, with a comment on the general equilibrium being left to the very end.

4.3. A Digression on "Association"

There are many people who would be glad to pay (on the quiet) large sums of money in order to be knighted. There are persons who would happily give up the Nobel Prize money and even pay some in order to get the Nobel Prize. However, if the ones responsible for giving these awards and honors frequently sold them to the highest bidders, the awards would become devalued. Some government awards that invariably go to "loyalists" (that is, people who "pay" the government with their loyalty), instead of the most deserving, get so devalued that even the loyalists are not flattered when they get them.

This shows that the value to an individual of an award or a prize does not depend on merely its inherent value – for example, the gold in an Olympic medal, the money in a prize packet, or whatever it is that is used to confer a knighthood. It depends on the **allocation rule** itself that is used to decide who will receive the awards. If the awards are allocated by a rule that picks the "best" or most talented, they would have a certain value to

---

[8] It must be mentioned here that the literature on advertising has for long recognized the possibility of altering human preference through certain kinds of activities and expenditure (see, for instance, Dixit and Norman, 1978).

the recipients. If they are allocated via the price mechanism (that is, they are given to whomever is willing to pay most), they would have another value and, typically, a diminished one. This should caution us that turning the problem of allocation over to "the market" may not always be the right solution.

In Basu (1989) I studied a special class of such commodities (the word "commodities" being used generally enough to include services, memberships, awards and, of course, commodities), the utility from which depends on who its other recipients (or consumers) are. By acquiring such a commodity, a person tries to gain **association** with its other recipients in the eyes of fellow human beings.

The examples of people seeking association are many. Much of Veblen's (1899) classic work on the leisure class is on this subject. Anthropologists even have a name for the process by which members of lesser castes emulate the customs and rites of the Brahminic groups in order to impress upon fellow human beings their improving station in life. Following Srinivas (1955), they call it "Sanskritization" and, as a concept, we find its counterparts in most societies – both backward and advanced. As an essay in the *New York Times*, entitled "The Art of Selling to the Very Rich," notes, "Nobody buys one of Gerry Grinberg's watches to get unbeatedly accurate time. Mr. Grinberg admits it. You can get as good time on an $18 watch." As for the reason why they buy such watches, the essay quotes Mr. Grinberg: "People want to show their station in life."[9]

The subject of **association goods** is not new in the sense that it lies at the cross-section of many earlier themes: positional goods,[10] snob effects,[11] the theory of clubs, and status goods.[12] Nevertheless, the nature of the equilibrium that arises in the presence of such goods is ill-understood. Association goods can help us understand several real-life phenomena. Much of this

---

[9] And here is Veblen on the reason for some people's demand for alcohol and stimulants (1899: 70): "Drunkenness and the other pathological consequences of the free use of stimulants therefore tend in their turn to become honorific, as being a mark, at the second remove, of the superior status of those who are able to afford the indulgence."

[10] This influential concept was developed by Hirsch (1977), though he did not pursue its implications for market equilibria far enough. Similar ideas, albeit in more diluted form, can be traced further back in time to, in particular, Wicksteed (1910). A recent revival of this approach occurs in Frank (1985).

[11] The best-known work on this is that of Leibenstein (1950).

[12] See Basu (1987). Models in which individual choice is predicated on aggregate behavior are discussed in Granovetter and Soong (1983), Becker (1991), and Fershtman and Weiss (1998). For a novel approach to status consciousness, which results in social conformism, see Bernheim (1994). A very interesting inquiry into the widely observed phenomenon of "opinion conformism" of groups occurs in Sunstein (1999).

is discussed in Basu (1989). I will here illustrate, with the example of club membership, a point that seems to have been overlooked in this literature, namely that association goods can explain the existence of excess-demand and excess-supply equilibria.

A classic association good is the membership of clubs and societies, which restrict admission to social elites and distinguished persons. Such clubs may have some facilities, like swimming pools and libraries, but the real reason why people toil to become members is that there is status associated with being admitted.[13,14]

Consider a club that is run by a profit-maximizing entrepreneur. Before going into formal analysis, it may be useful to give an intuitive account. Suppose that there are two kinds of citizens: those who have much status but little money (type 1) and vice versa (type 2). Let us now consider the case where the club has many members of type 1 and a few (perhaps none) of type 2. In addition, there are many type-2 people wanting to be admitted as members and willing to pay more than the going membership fee in order to be admitted.

This is an excess-demand situation and at first sight it may appear that this cannot be a profit-maximizing equilibrium from the club entrepreneur's point of view. All he has to do is to take in some of these type-2 people at the higher charge that they are willing to pay (perhaps even replacing some type-1 people with type 2s) and the club's profit will rise. This, however, need not be so. Since the club membership is an association good, the act of admitting more type-2 people may change the status rating of the club and make everybody willing to pay less membership fee. Thus excess demand may exist in equilibrium with profit-maximizing agents. Any attempt on the part of the club to eliminate the excess demand by taking in more members or changing the composition of members may change the character of the club, make people less eager to join it, and thus lower the club's profits. It should be clear that since my purpose is to explain excess demand, my job would be easier if the club's objective was something other than profits. Thus my assumption that clubs are run by

---

[13] There may be reasons, quite unconnected with status, why people want to belong to certain clubs or communities. This could be because a sense of belonging is often an end in itself (this is discussed by Hirschman, 1985) or it is the basis of "well-being" (Rainwater, 1974). However, to the extent that people have preferences over belonging to different groups, the formal structure of my model would remain applicable.

[14] There is a large and interesting literature on clubs: see, for example, Ng (1973); and Sandler and Tschirhart (1980). But clubs that people join for reasons of association, namely the kind of clubs I am discussing here, have an extremely brief literature (see McGuire, 1972) but widespread existence in reality.

entrepreneurs who maximize *profits* is not made in the belief that this is so in reality, but simply to choose an assumption which is adverse from my point of view. With this, let us proceed to a formal analysis.

Let H be the set of all people and, for all i in H, let $H(i)$ be the set of all subsets of H that have i as an element. For all i in H, let v_i be a real-valued mapping on $H(i)$ such that for all $M \in H(i)$, $v_i(M)$ is the maximum amount that i would be willing to pay to be a member of a club in which M is the set of members.[15]

I shall, to start with, assume that the club cannot charge discriminatory fees from its members, and that admitting additional members does not entail any costs on the part of the club's entrepreneur. Hence, a club with a set M of members earns a profit of $(\#M)\min_{i \in M}v_i(M)$, where $\#M$ denotes the number of elements in M. The club's aim is to choose a subset M of H that maximizes profit. More formally, its aim is

$$\text{Max}_{M} \left[(\#M) \min_{i \in M} v_i(M) \right]. \tag{4.1}$$

Let M^* be a solution of (4.1). M^* may be described as an **equilibrium set** of members. The equilibrium membership fee (that is, the highest fee that can be charged without losing members) is given by

$$v^* = \min_{i \in M^*} v_i(M^*).$$

It is easy to show that there may be an excess demand for membership in equilibrium. We shall here say that there is an **excess demand** for membership if there exists a person j who does not belong to M^* and $v_j(M^* \cup \{j\}) > v^*$. In this case, j is a person who is willing to pay more than the membership fee to join the club but the club will not admit him.

The possibility of an excess-demand equilibrium may be illustrated with an example. Let $H = \{1, 2, 3\}$, and suppose

$$v_1(H) = v_1(\{1, 3\}) = v_1(\{1, 2\}) = 3$$

$$v_2(\{2, 3\}) = v_3(\{2, 3\}) = 2$$

$$v_2(H) = v_3(H) = v_2(\{2\}) = v_2(\{1, 2\})$$

$$= v_3(\{3\}) = v_3\{(1, 3)\} = v_1(\{1\}) = 0$$

---

[15] For someone like Groucho Marx, who said he would never pay to join a club that would have him as a member, $v_i(M) \le 0$ for all $M \in H(i)$.

We could think of individuals 2 and 3 as persons of status (the old nobility). Person 1 would pay a lot to join a club that has individuals 2 or 3 as a member. While person 1 (a *nouveau riche*) can pay a lot, he is not quite the coveted person. In fact his being in a club devalues its membership altogether for individuals 2 and 3. In this example, the equilibrium club is one that has individuals 2 and 3 as members and charges a fee of 2 units. Person 1 is denied membership even though he is willing to pay 3 units, which is more than the membership fee. This is a case of excess-demand equilibrium.

Several existing models of excess-demand or excess-supply equilibria make use of the assumption of nondiscriminatory prices – for example, the assumption that a firm cannot pay different wages to its workers. In the above model, I also use a similar assumption since it was supposed that all members have to be charged the same fee. However, the excess-demand result is more robust here in that it would survive a relaxation of the non-discrimination assumption.[16]

Let us consider now a club that is allowed to charge discriminatory fees. Its aim is to choose M (a subset of H) so as to maximize profit. Profit is now given by the aggregate of the maximum that each member is willing to pay. In this case there can be different ways of defining excess demand. Consider the following definition, which is the most adverse from my point of view. We shall say that **excess demand** exists if there is a person j who is not admitted to the club but who is willing to pay more than the highest-paying club member. That there can be excess demand in this sense even when a club can charge differential fees is clear from the above numerical example: person 1 would still be kept out even though he would be willing to pay a larger fee than is being paid by either of the two existing members.

Finally, it may appear that the club's ability to discriminate in its choice of members is crucial for the existence of excess-demand equilibria. This is, however, not so. Let us assume that a club is required to be nondiscriminatory in its selection of members in the sense that its proportions of different types of members must match the proportions of different types of people who want to be members. Even in this case it is possible to construct examples to show that there can be excess demand in equilibrium. But instead of dwelling on this, let me briefly comment on other possible areas of application – in particular, schools, prizes and the so-called Sanskritization.

---

[16] What constitutes "nondiscrimination" can have several formal interpretations, but here I take the simple meaning of "same fees from all."

Schools
Should schools be allowed to charge students discriminatory fees? In India, many schools and institutes (especially engineering and medical) have often charged special fees from some students. "Capitation fees," as these are usually called, have led to much criticism and, wherever possible, legislation preventing discriminatory fees. The implicit argument has been that this would lead schools to admit only richer students who are able to pay more. This argument ceases to be valid once we recognize that association effects are usually strong in the domain of schooling. In the presence of association effects, one can find parametric situations where discriminatory fees may be not just efficient but ethically desirable.[17]

The intuitive idea is this. Suppose that there are four kinds of potential students: clever and rich (cr), clever and poor (cp), mediocre and rich (mr), and mediocre and poor (mp). The term "clever" is used here simply to denote students who are able to absorb and make good use of education. The ethical concern is a limited one: we want to have a system in which cp students are not denied education. What I want to argue is that in the presence of association effects (i) there is no reason why allowing discriminatory fees will necessarily lead to cp students being denied admission and (ii) there are situations where permitting discriminatory fees may in fact mean that more cp students will be admitted.

The argument is based on the assumption that school labels help. A student from a college where the average student is brilliant stands a better chance of getting a good job than if the same student had been to an "ordinary" college. This is because firms and other employers use school labels as indices of quality. It is often too expensive to test each prospective employee and one uses one's knowledge of a school's general standing to judge its alumni.

Now suppose an entrepreneur (a profit maximizer) is setting up a school. If he is allowed to charge any and variable fees, would he admit only the rich at high fees? The answer is "no" because he will realize that the school's reputation – and consequently the fees that the rich are willing to pay – depends largely on the average quality of his students. Thus he will always have an eye on taking on good students, if necessary for no fees, because that will enable him to charge a higher fee from the rich. Having a law ensuring nondiscriminatory fees may lead him to abandon those who

---

[17] Given the obvious policy significance of the analysis that follows, it is worth clarifying that while it constitutes a case for allowing the private provision of education, it is not a case for the state to shrug off its responsibility to provide education to the poor.

cannot pay altogether. A formal model illustrating these propositions is developed in Basu (1989).

One could utilize the framework of this section to analyze other questions – in particular, the consequence of (A) fixing the fees (i.e., the case where the government not only prohibits discriminatory fees but actually fixes the fee at some level), and (B) setting an upper limit on the fees (i.e., discriminatory fees are allowed but they must not exceed a certain level). Instead of analyzing these formally, I shall make some brief comments drawing on the intuition already established in this section. Also, I tend to focus on how (A) and (B) could have effects that are unexpected and the opposite of what usually motivates the enactment of such laws.

The adverse effect of (A) on the poorest sections is obvious. In reality, unlike in our model, there are many levels of poverty. So no matter where the fees are fixed, the poorest sections would be unable to pay for their education.

Fortunately, (A) is unrealistic. No government would have such a policy, because presumably no government would prevent schools from giving scholarships and assistance to some chosen students. Now, a system of fixed fees with scholarships to some is effectively system (B), which sets an upper limit on students' fees. So let us turn to analyzing the consequence of (B). This is best done in two stages. First consider (A) and then analyze the effect of a switch to (B).

So let us begin with the case where the school fee is fixed (by law) at a level $\hat{f}$ that is very high. As just discussed, none of the poor will be admitted to school because they are unable to pay the school fees. Now suppose that the law is changed to type (B), with $\hat{f}$ being treated as an upper limit. That is, the government now allows the school to lower the fees for some students if it so wishes. So now the school can, in principle, reach out to the poorer students who were earlier priced out of the market. The question is, will it? Consider the reason why the school may want to lower the fees for some students. This could only be in order to admit some clever-and-poor students, which would improve the school's academic rating and thereby allow it (i) to charge higher fees from the rich students, or (ii), in case there were vacant seats in the original equilibrium, to admit more rich students at the ceiling fee. It is immediately clear that in the case where the seats are full when only one fee is allowed, the option of lowering the fees will not be exercised if the school is not allowed to *raise* anyone's fee. The maximum-fee law, by cutting off the school's option of raising the fees on the rich, cuts off its incentive to make concessions to students who are good but unable to pay their fees for reasons of poverty.

Prizes

Let me turn next to "prizes." There is now a considerable body of literature in economics on prizes (see, e.g., Lazear and Rosen, 1981; Nalebuff and Stiglitz, 1983). In this literature, a prize distinguishes itself from other systems of rewards, such as wages, by virtue of the fact that several people toil for it but only one (or perhaps a few) gets the award in the end, on the basis of *relative* performance; the others get nothing for their toil. This leads to many interesting questions, but those are not my concern here. What this literature does not consider is that a prize usually gives its recipient *recognition.* To that extent it belongs to the class of association goods, like club membership, jobs or schools. This immediately means, as is obvious from the models in the earlier sections, that the granting of prizes is a strategic variable in the hands of the prize-giver. The prize-giver can optimize his own profit, utility or whatever he is trying to maximize by suitably selecting the recipients and extracting payments in kind or as return favors out of them. This objective may not always coincide with that of selecting the most deserving people. However, the prize-giver does have the incentive not to deviate *too far* from selecting deserving people because that may diminish the worth of the prize, and once that happens he would no longer be able to "sell" the prize, that is, exchange it for whatever his objective is.

From the above remarks it is clear that prizes can be modeled much like the theory of clubs, discussed above. If we think of the prize-giver as the club entrepreneur and the group of prize-recipients as club members, the same kind of theorizing becomes possible. There is one interesting additional feature here, though. Prize-giving is usually a periodic affair (Olympic medals once every four years, Nobel prizes once each year, and so on) which means time is a more pronounced element in the activity of prize-giving than in a theory of clubs. This introduces some special elements. For instance, if the prize-giver is myopic in the sense of having a high time discount, then in any particular year he may be more inclined to selling the award to the highest bidder than giving to the most-deserving. Of course, this means that the following year's highest bidder will be willing to pay less (because the prize is a little devalued) and the process continues till the prize is totally devalued. The same would have a greater tendency to occur if each year a new selection committee chooses the recipients of the prize. The future value of the prize counts less in the decision-making process than it would in the case of a more permanent committee.

Sanskritization

Finally, a comment on Sanskritization, which is one of the purest manifestations of association activity. This, as already mentioned above, refers to rituals, customs, and behavior that the castes or classes at the lower end of a society's accepted hierarchy adopt in order to signal to others their improving station in life.

Sanskritization cannot be analyzed in the same way as we have analyzed clubs, jobs or schools, because an elite group or caste is not an entity whose membership is managed by an agent to achieve some objective. Nevertheless, it raises an interesting question in the light of our models. Clearly for the membership of some group to be an association good – that is, for others to want to join it – there must be costs involved in trying to join the group. If not, then outsiders would continue to rush in as long as there is value in joining the group. Its membership, in other words, would cease to be an association good in equilibrium.

The fact that Sanskritization exists at all raises the question as to what the costs of Sanskritization are. Though the "elites" of a society form a nebulous collection and no one charges an entry fee for joining them, there must exist hidden charges; and, indeed, there are. In the context of caste societies, these take the form of ridicule if one attempts Sanskritization and fails. Thus the cost is an *expected* cost but, sure enough, it is there. This is brought out very clearly in Srinivas's (1955) essay on a southern Indian village, where he says (p. 24): "Discrimination against the Smiths occurs everywhere in peninsular India, *possibly as a result of their attempts in the past to rise high in the caste hierarchy by means of a thorough Sanskritization of their customers*" (my italics). He goes on to make similar observations about the Kammálans of Tamil Nadu.

Using the theories of association developed here, it ought to be possible to formalize the concept of Sanskritization. Such a formalization in conjunction with Akerlof's model of customs could give us some insights into the dynamics of customs and more.

Caveat

One difficulty, as already noted, arises from the fact that people's preferences, in this model, depend on the society-wide allocation of goods; and, of course, what allocation of goods occurs in society depends on the preferences of the people. Hence, the search for an equilibrium can turn out to be a search for a fixed point in a rather complex space. A second and more conceptual difficulty stems from the fact that, for an association good, there need not be an initial endowment in the same way that endowments are assumed to exist for goods in standard economic theory. This is because association goods can, in reality, often be *created*. For instance, giving people certificates or giving them honorary titles are acts that, in principle, any agent can undertake and with virtually no resource being used. It is difficult to think of a *technological* or *resource-based* upper bound on the number of certificates that can be given in an economy. It is necessary to think of the bounds on certificates, honors and awards in very different terms from the bounds on guns, butter or even haircuts.

These are some of the open problems that this analysis brings to light. These problems may be conceptually difficult, but are worthwhile pursuits nevertheless.

It is time now to turn to the third kind of norm in the classification suggested in Section 4.1, namely the equilibrium-selection norm. This is arguably the most popular kind of norm in the economics literature. Section 4.4 illustrates the norm with a series of examples.

4.4. Equilibrium–Selection Norms

Madan Mitra Lane is a narrow, gently-winding by-lane in the overcrowded northern part of the city of Calcutta. The old houses with paint peeling off rub shoulders with one another and many sprout narrow verandahs where people sit, sipping tea and watching others do the same. In these homes live merchants, doctors, priests, the rebels, the orthodox, and the unemployed (this last explaining the high occupancy of the verandahs). Tucked away in the nooks and crannies of the street are little stores, printing presses, and even beauty parlors. It is the sort of setting to reach which one can imagine serious anthropologists leaving no stones unturned. In that sense I was lucky. I was born there and also spent the early years of my childhood there.

My father had seven brothers and four sisters, my mother had three brothers and two sisters. By the time I was born, all my uncles and aunts were married and many had children; and almost all of them lived in Calcutta – with most of the relatives on my father's side under the same roof in Madan Mitra Lane, thanks to the still-prevalent (though decaying) joint-family system. This vast network of relatives, with whom I have been very close, has been for me a Galapagos archipelago of social norms, many of which have existed for a long time but are now in the process of withering away.

Of special relevance to my current concern is the story of my father's youngest sister. She had an arranged marriage in 1936, when she was 17 years old, to a very eligible young man. By all accounts, it was a happy marriage; but tragedy struck soon. Her husband was diagnosed with a malignant brain tumor and died, and my aunt was left a widow at the age of 27. She had no children.

Indian social norms were harsh for the widow. She was forbidden from marrying again, had to wear white saris with, at most, a black border. She was expected to live the rest of her life hermitically in the house of her in-laws; to forgo eating fish, meat, eggs, garlic and onions; and to follow numerous other minor restrictions. These norms are currently in the process of breaking down, but it was different in 1936. My aunt followed the demanding regimen fastidiously all through her life, till she died at the age of 80, on May 13, 1999.

As a child I was very close to my aunt. My parents would often bring her over to our house for a couple of days at a time, to give her a break from everyday life. She was a very affectionate and warm person; and I spent long afternoons chatting with her. Unlike many other women in her shoes, she was lucky because her in-laws were kind. But, nevertheless, the social norms were cruel and, in those conversations we had, I could easily feel some of her pain.

What puzzled me was why she followed those norms. Under the law she was free to live life exactly as she wished. Why then did she not declare that she would not live by these harsh precepts? She professed to believe in an afterlife; so was her choice of lifestyle dictated by the hope of being compensated in the next life? Or did she have a bizarre utility function that made her prefer forgoing all the usual pleasures of life? She never answered these questions fully. Much of her plight she had rationalized as natural; cognitive dissonance ensured that she would do so. But from my many conversations with her, it was quite evident to me that the reason she followed those norms was the fear that if she violated them she would be ostracized and criticized by those close to her – essentially the network of our myriad relatives. So, given her expectation of the reaction of the other relatives, her choice was rational.

But that raises another question. If she did violate the norms and, for instance, got married again, why would these other relatives sanction her by criticizing and ostracizing her? I believe that the answer to this question is the same as the answer as to why my aunt in the first place followed the norms. Most of these relatives, if you asked them if they believed in these harsh norms, would say no. Why then would they criticize and ostracize my aunt? I believe the answer is fear – fear that if the aunt violated the norms and they did not sanction her, other relatives would sanction them. And what about these other 'other' relatives? The answer is again the same. . . .

In the end, all are caught in a web of self-reinforcing sanctions, which sustains the norm. We will see a formalization of this argument in the context of political power in Chapter 6. Akerlof's (1976) idea of a "caste equilibrium" is in essence the same. The caste norms may benefit no one but they nevertheless persist because, once they are there, it is in no individual's interest to violate them. Adherence to the norm is a Nash equilibrium.

The way I have described my aunt's adherence to social norms raises questions related to the well-known problem of backward induction since the world population is finite. I am not persuaded that this is something we should worry about, since backward induction gives rise to paradoxes (see Chapters 2 and 3) and conflicts so strongly with intuition. Moreover, there are ways of getting around this problem by describing a more elaborate game or by assuming i ostracizes j when i sees that j did not ostracize someone whom j should have, without having enough information to understand why j should have ostracized this other person. Instead of going by that route, let me here illustrate the idea of this kind of an equilibrium-selection norm with an even simpler example.

Consider a game in which each driver can either drive on the left of the road or the right. If they all stick to the same side, they do fine; but if they choose different sides there is chaos in the roads, there are accidents and everybody is worse off. Considering the case of only two drivers, we can write this as a game in which, if both choose L or both choose R, they get 5 utils each, and if one chooses L and the other R, they get 0 utils. Clearly, this game will have two (pure-strategy) Nash equilibria: (L, L) and (R, R). The equilibrium-selection norm to drive on the left (or, for that matter, right) is then nothing but a coordination device.[18] It helps players form beliefs about what to expect from other players and thereby enables them to go for the same Nash equilibrium, and avoid the dangers of mismatched expectations. An equilibrium-selection norm is similar in spirit to the idea of a "convention" developed by Lewis (1969).

Although in the driving story the two possible norms (Drive on the left or Drive on the right) are equivalent in utility terms, this need not always be the case. India's widowhood norm certainly gives rise to very different payoffs from what would happen in the absence of such a norm. Widows

---

[18] It is possible to tell more complicated stories for important real-life phenomena, which, in essence, has the same structure. See, for instance, Basu and Van's (1998) analysis of how sending children to work can be an equilibrium-selection norm; and Hoff and Sen's (1999) modeling of community quality or housing-ownership choices.

are certainly worse off and, in fact, everybody may be worse off. Consider the standard typewriter keyboard following the QWERTY pattern. It has been argued that this is not the most efficient keyboard. The presumed inefficiency of QWERTY has recently been questioned, but how that debate is resolved is not important for our argument, which simply asserts that a norm, once in place, has a tendency to survive even if it were not the most efficient norm. This establishes the important proposition that norms and institutions tend to be path-dependent (David, 1985; Ray, 1998: ch. 5).

In economics the dominant kind of norm that has been discussed – to the extent that any norm is discussed at all – is the equilibrium-selection norm. This must be because such norms fit quite comfortably into our standard models, causing a minimum of disruption. The idea is indeed very important, and is referred to repeatedly in our discussion of the state and laws in later chapters. In the context of more recent and sophisticated models, where games are construed quite differently (for instance, where the players are not fixed but are chosen randomly from a large population and, in addition, may not be fully rational), it can be shown that norms that evolve over time turn out to be Nash equilibria and are therefore, in a sense, the same as what I call equilibrium-selection norms.

Though in the remainder of this chapter we look at norms that do not necessarily constitute a Nash equilibrium, in later chapters, when there is a reference to a social norm, it should be taken to be an equilibrium-selection norm unless explicitly stated otherwise.

4.5. Hawk, Dove and Maynard's Cuckoo

This section and the next introduce the reader to some of the biological origins of modern economic ideas – in particular, the possibility of understanding social norms in terms of evolutionary games. The evolutionary game theory literature is very large and it has made interesting forays into understanding norms and behavior in terms of reproduction, imitation and learning.[19] My aim is not to cover this trodden ground. Instead, I want to pursue, in Section 4.6, the line of explaining how rationality-limiting norms may have an evolutionary basis. For this, it is necessary to go over some of the early ideas of evolutionary game theory, and the remaining pages of this section are devoted to this.

---

[19] See, for instance, Kandori, Mailath and Rob (1993), Weibull (1995), Blume and Easley (1995), Sethi and Somanathan (1996), Young (1998) and Harrington (1999).

The ground that I recapitulate here is associated with the work of John Maynard Smith. Maynard Smith, despite his name, is a biologist, who has done seminal work in reshaping and using the tools of game theory for understanding animal evolution. My aim here is to present his work – in particular that done jointly with George R. Price (Maynard Smith and Price, 1973; Maynard Smith, 1982) – and then to readapt it back to the *human* context.

To begin by giving an intuitive sketch of how evolution can explain rationality-limiting norms, I consider an example that I have discussed elsewhere (Basu, 1995a). It is an example that tries to reject what is often referred to as "functionalism" and replace it with what may be called "minimal functionalism."

It has been noted by anthropologists that in most primitive societies people have "possessory rights," that is, whoever first gets to possess a good has a right to it. Posner (1981: 182) has noted, however, that in primitive societies where investment is feasible, the investor is often protected by the grant of a non-possessory right. For instance, in a hunter-gatherer society, the trap-setter has the right to a trapped animal instead of the person who first finds the animal. Posner seems to be explaining with this example how societies choose institutions that are optimal for their life-styles. There are others who have adopted more extreme "functionalist" positions, arguing, for instance, that societies invariably choose laws and civil institutions that are functionally optimal or are ones for which benefits outweigh costs. Such naive transplanting of individual choice models on social domains has been rightly criticized by many. While it may be reasonable to assume that individuals choose what is in their own interest, this reasoning cannot be carried over to social norms and institutions. This is because norms and institutions are not chosen by any single person and, moreover, they typically evolve over long stretches of time and as a consequence of a multitude of opinions and decisions. So there is no reason to believe that the best institutions always get chosen (Bardhan, 1989; Ray, 1998: ch. 5).

It is, however, possible to argue that though such extreme functionalism is best jettisoned, a "minimal functionalism" can be defended by a very different route, namely evolution. If one finds that a society that has remained unchanged (and therefore survived) over a long stretch of history has certain norms, it is arguable that these norms cannot be too detrimental for the people. The fact that the people practicing this norm have survived for such a long time ensures this. Turning to the above example, suppose that there is a hunter-gatherer economy where the trap-setter does not have the right to the trapped animal, but the first person to lay his hands on the animal gets to keep it. In such an economy, people would either cease to set traps or, after setting a trap, wait there, forgoing all other activities (such as gathering). The productivity, or "fitness," of such an economy would be low, and it is possible that the economy would not survive for too many generations. Hence, hunter-gatherer economies that survive to be analyzed by anthropologists happen to be the ones that grant the trap-setter rights over the possessor. Thus, like the giraffe's long neck and the housefly's resistance to DDT, social groups have norms that serve minimal functions to ensure that they survive.

Unlike the color of my shirt or the structure of your house, the norms of a society cannot be explained in terms of human volition. Just as lions move in prides not because they choose to do so but because if they did not their hunting ability would fall drastically and they would not survive to be seen, hunter-gatherer societies may have the norms they do because these norms have survived natural selection.

Now let us move to formalism via the seminal work of Maynard Smith and Price (1973). The core of an evolutionary game is a two-person, normal-form game of the kind we encountered in Chapter 2. In this game each of the two players has the same set of strategies. We shall call these strategies $1, 2, \ldots, m$ and use S to denote the set of strategies; so $S = \{1, 2, \ldots, m\}$. The game is also symmetric. That is, we can describe both players' payoffs using a single payoff function, P, where $P(p, q)$ is the payoff earned by a player playing p when the other player plays q. Since S will throughout be held constant, this two-player game may be identified entirely with the payoff function, P; and so we may call the game itself P.

An **evolutionary game** is a symmetric, two-person game P, but it is played very differently from a usual normal-form game. In this game, players are preprogrammed to play a strategy. This is particularly appropriate for describing the animal kingdom. If we think of the strategies 1 to m as, for example, different degrees of aggressive behavior, 1 being the most aggressive and m the least, then a hawk is a player who always plays 1 and a dove is a player who always plays m. Hence, we may at times identify a player entirely with a strategy. Thus we could say a hawk *is* strategy 1; and, equivalently, we could talk in terms of a type-i player, meaning a player who always plays strategy i.

Now, think of a nation full of different types of players. In every period, players are randomly matched pairwise and made to play the game P. In evolutionary games the payoffs actually denote a player's fitness or survival chances or rate of reproduction. So if some player earns a higher payoff, it is expected that this type of player will procreate faster. With this interpretation in the background, Maynard Smith and Price's main equilibrium idea, that of "evolutionarily stable strategies," is now easy to grasp.

Consider a large population where all players are of the same type $p \in S$. We want to know whether or not this population is robust against the arrival of small members of mutants in their midst. For this, let us first define a strategy p to be *immune* to some other strategy q if

(1) $P(p, p) > P(q, p)$, or
(2) $P(p, p) = P(q, p)$ and $P(p, q) > P(q, q)$.

To appreciate this definition, recall that we are thinking of a large population of type-p players (where p is a strategy) with a few mutants of type q. Since players are matched at random and made to play game P, most of the time a player's opponent will be a type-p player. Now (1) says that p does better against p than q does against p. Since most of the time one will be playing against p, (1) suggests that a type-p player will have a higher payoff than a type-q player in this society; and, payoff being an index of fitness, type p's will overrun the population and gradually decimate the mutants q.

If, on the other hand, p and q do equally well against p, then how well they do in this society will depend on how well they do against q (their occasional game opponent) and if $P(p, q) > P(q, q)$, then q is again overrun by p. This is what line (2) says.

A strategy p is an **evolutionarily stable strategy (ESS)** if it is immune to all strategies q ($\neq p$).

Another closely related equilibrium concept is that of "neutral stability." If we change the strict inequality in (2) above to a weak inequality, $\geq$, then what we have is a definition of "*weak* immunity" (as opposed to "immunity"). A strategy p is a **neutral stable strategy** if it is weakly immune to every strategy q.

To illustrate how ESS works, I use a slight modification of Maynard Smith's well-known Hawk–Dove game (see Section 2.3). In Maynard Smith's game there are just two strategies open to each player: to be aggressive (be like a "Hawk," or H) or to be timid ("Dove," or D). To this I now add a strategy that denotes middling aggression, something that is between D and H. I shall denote this strategy by M, which is an abbreviation for "Maynard's Cuckoo." Maynard's Cuckoo is a bird that belongs to the Cuckoo family. It is a migratory bird that visits Florida to breed. Its aggression is between that of a hawk and a dove and its name, *Maynard's* Cuckoo, makes it a particularly apt choice for us.

	H	M	D
H	0, 0	3, 1	6, 2
M	1, 3	3, 3	5, 3
D	2, 6	3, 5	4, 4

Figure 4.1. Payoff matrix (Hawk–Dove–Maynard's Cuckoo)

The payoff function of the Hawk–Dove–Maynard's Cuckoo game is shown in Fig. 4.1. The payoff may be understood as follows. Suppose there is a resource of 8 units. If both players play D (Dove), they peacefully share the resource; hence the payoff (4, 4) in the above payoff matrix. If the row player is H (Hawk) and the other D, the hawk takes away most of the resource with no fight; so the payoff is (6, 2). When a hawk is matched against a hawk, they fight till the resource is destroyed; hence (0, 0). M (Maynard's Cuckoo), being less aggressive than H, does not manage to snatch quite as much from others and fights less as well. The remaining payoffs are easily justified keeping this in mind.

The question is: Which of these three strategies, if any, is evolutionarily stable? At first blush one may feel it is H, because its aggression should make it immune against all kinds of mutants. But no; instead the answer turns out to be M. The only evolutionarily stable strategy in the above game is M.

This is easy to check. Note that H is not immune against M or D (by criteria (1) and (2));[20] D is not immune against H or M. By criterion (2), M is immune against both H and D. In the long run, neither excessive aggression nor excessive timidity pays off.

4.6. Norms, Polyphiloprogenitive

In the model of Section 4.5 the type of player who comes to prevail in society may well exhibit rationality (it is easy to see that an ESS is always a Nash equilibrium) but it is important to recognize that though a player may *exhibit* rationality, a player *is* not rational. This is because players in

---

[20] To see that H is not immune against D, note that $P(H, H) = 0$ and $P(D, H) = 2$. Thus $P(H, H) < P(D, H)$ and so, by (1) and (2), H is not immune against D.

evolutionary games are programmed phenotypes. They have no choice. A player does not choose a strategy; he *is* a strategy. Standard game theory, on the other hand, gives players full freedom to choose from the set of strategies. In reality, human beings are somewhere in between. They choose and optimize over some strategies but also consider some strategies as out of bounds. These latter are determined by a person's inherited training and the norms of the society he lives in. Thus we may choose between several possible careers but may consider picking pockets as something we would not do, whatever the payoffs. There may be others who consider pickpocketing as a reasonable career – and I have first-hand evidence of the existence of such persons. Similarly, in some communities, children are taught to always pay their taxes when they grow up; whereas in others, children are taught that taxes ought to be paid if the expected penalty of not paying exceeds the amount of tax not paid. What we want to study is which of these norms will survive natural selection.

Let S be the set of all conceivable strategies open to a player. Taking a hint from the above discussion, I shall define a **rationality-limiting norm** (which will be here referred to in brief as a **civil norm**) as any nonempty subset T of S. If an agent adheres to civil norm T, it means that he *chooses* his optimal strategy from within T and does not even consider strategies in $S - T$. Norms, we shall assume, are inherited.

The idea of civil norms being a restriction on the set of alternatives from which a person can choose is an important idea both empirically and philosophically. The latter relates to the point made in Section 4.1. In reality, human beings have a huge choice. They can not only buy and sell goods but sing songs, commit murder, plagiarize, steal, plunder. . . . In fact, it is not even clear that the collection of alternatives from which a person chooses constitutes a set at all (a point elaborated on in Chapter 11). So economics, which is based so much on optimization over sets of alternatives, would have very little foundation if we really tried to start from *all* the things a person can do. In reality, the "set" from which a person chooses is, in the end, quite a restricted set for a variety of reasons but one of the most important is norms. A rural woman in India may choose to wear a red sari, but she does not choose to wear a sari. Non-sari clothes lie beyond the set she would even consider. Both an Indian and a Swede may not jump a queue; for an Indian this is typically a matter of choice, whereas for a Swede that is typically not so. He does not jump a queue not because of what others will do or say nor because of the remorse he will himself feel even if others said nothing; jumping a queue is just not in the set from which he chooses, and so it is not an alternative he even considers. None of these norms is immutable. In fact, after my first visit to Stockholm the example that I used to give of a civil norm is how Swedes do not cross roads except at pedestrian crossings. After my second visit to Stockholm I had to remove that example.

One of the reasons why, as European imperialism spread to Asia, Africa and South America, some otherwise advanced cultures succumbed so easily is that these cultures were not used to the kind of aggression that they were suddenly confronted with[21]; and, as a consequence, they had lost the use of certain kinds of defensive actions, just as antibodies disappear from a person's system if they are not used for a long time. One reason why it was so easy for the Europeans to establish control over large amounts of land was that establishing property rights over land that is not in one's immediate use was beyond the norms of some of these societies. They did not do it themselves and failed to anticipate that others might.

To move to a formal definition of evolutionarily stable norms, suppose that there is a planet (Earth) and people live in different nations. A mutant in one nation is like a migrant. With the notion of a planet and nations interpreted in abstract terms, one can see the importance of the mutant everywhere. A small trickle of migrants from one area to another has at times flourished in the region of their adoption, and at other times those migrants have perished. The Marwaris in Bengal, the Gujaratis in Maharashtra, the English in India in the eighteenth and nineteenth centuries, and the Indians in England today are the success stories. The stories where migrants have done poorly and have become negligible are equally numerous.

In these examples, who succeeds and who fails is not so much a matter of inherent traits of a community as a question of chemistry (see Goyal, 1996, for a model). X may do well in a population of Y's. The reason why this is at least *prima facie* possible is because every society has its civil norms. I shall call these gaps in utility maximization a society's **normative loopholes**. These are things that a person would not do (or would do) purely because they are a norm in his society and irrespective of their utility or payoff consequences. Not breaking queues is a normative loophole of, for instance, Finnish society. I call it a "loophole" because a mutant or a migrant from another society who does not have this norm can, as we discussed above, exploit this and do well for himself. I believe that the English took such easy control of India in the eighteenth and nineteenth centuries

---

[21] A dominant theme that occurs in Diamond's (1997: 79) account of the 1532 battle of Cajamarca in Peru is the naivete of the Incas. "It never occurred to Atahuallpa [the Inca monarch] that the Spaniards [. . .] would attack him without provocation. When the Spanish chief, Pizarro, offered to free him if he paid a ransom, Atahuallpa gave "history's largest ransom" in the "naive belief that the Spaniards would release him and depart." They killed him and his subjects. "He had no way of understanding that [the Spanish were] bent on permanent conquest, rather than an isolated raid."

because they exploited the normative loopholes of that India. The Spanish against the early American civilizations was a similar story. For some interesting contemporary examples of "intercultural encounters," see Hofstede (1991).

Consider a game P. As before, the set of strategies open to each player is given by $S = \{1, \ldots, m\}$. A civil norm is a non-empty subset of S. I define a **restricted game** of P as (X, Y) where X and Y are civil norms (i.e. $X, Y \subset S$). In this game the two players are restricted to strategies from X and Y respectively, but the payoffs are the same as in P.

Suppose a person with civil norm $X \subset S$ meets another person with civil norm $Y \subset S$. What is the expected outcome? I shall here stay out of the problem of informational asymmetries by assuming that the civil norms of the two players are common knowledge among the two players. If the two players are rational, it may be reasonable to suppose that a Nash equilibrium of the restricted game (X, Y) will occur. But if (X, Y) has more than one Nash equilibrium, which one should we expect? I shall get around this by assuming that this is *specified* as a primitive in the description of the "human evolutionary game" defined below.

There are, however, some restrictions on the Nash equilibrium that are specified for each restricted game (X, Y). First, the payoff of both players in the chosen Nash equilibrium of the restricted game must be the same if $X = Y$.[22] The payoff that player 1 earns in the chosen Nash equilibrium of (X, Y) must be the same as the payoff that player 2 earns in the chosen Nash equilibrium of (Y, X). The game P along with a specification of a Nash equilibrium for each restricted game (X, Y) of P is a **human evolutionary game.**[23]

Let $N(X, Y)$ be player 1's payoff in the chosen Nash equilibrium of the restricted game (X, Y). Following our earlier concept of (weak) immunity for strategies, we can now develop the idea of "immunity" for civil norms. Given a human evolutionary game, a civil norm T is *immune* against civil norm X if

(3) $N(T, T) > N(X, T)$; or

(4) $N(T, T) = N(X, T)$ and $N(T, X) \geq N(X, X)$.

We can now define a civil norm to be an **evolutionarily stable norm (ESN)** if it is immune to all civil norms X. The idea is the same as in Maynard Smith and Price's model. We are looking for norms that are fitter

---

[22] There can be one technical problem with this. If we do not allow for mixed strategies, such a Nash equilibrium may not exist. We avoid this problem here by choosing our examples carefully so as to ensure that they do have pure-strategy Nash equilibria.

[23] A formal definition of this occurs in Basu (1995a).

than their mutants. A player endowed with such a norm gets a higher payoff and therefore replicates faster. It is **polyphiloprogenitive**. This strange word was created by T. S. Eliot's embellishing of the word philoprogenitive[24] to capture the concept of rapid proliferation or multiplication, rather aptly for our use.

ESN is an interesting equilibrium concept. It can explain why some norms can survive that on the face of it seem disadvantaged. Consider two distinct norms X and Y such that $X \subset Y$. Thus Y could consist of X plus the strategy of cheating people. At first sight it may seem that norm Y (immoral though it may be) is more robust than X because a person endowed with Y has a wider range of options that he can choose from compared with a person endowed with civil norm X only. What can be demonstrated is that long-run evolutionary survival does not (fortunately) follow this logic.[25] Further, ESN can explain how some non-Nash strategies can survive the sieve of natural selection.

I will illustrate these properties with an example – a game that is a more elaborate version of the Prisoner's Dilemma. I shall call it the Sophisticated Prisoner's Dilemma (SPD, in brief). It is a game that illustrates how traits such as trust and honesty help a society to prosper in the long run. The game is as follows. Each individual has to decide whether to do business or to abstain (action a) and, if he opts for business, whether to cooperate (action c) with his business partner or to betray (action b) him. In other words, each individual can choose among a, b and c.

Suppose two individuals meet who have both chosen to go into business; it will be assumed that they get locked into a Prisoner's Dilemma. If both play c, they get 1 unit each. If you cooperate while the other betrays, you get −2 while the other gets 2. If you both betray, you get −1 each. Hence, the payoff matrix is as set out in Fig. 4.2.

If, on the other hand, you choose to abstain from business, you get a payoff of zero no matter what the other person does. Also, if the other person chooses to abstain, you get a zero payoff no matter what you choose,

	b	c
b	−1, −1	2, −2
c	−2, 2	1, 1

Figure 4.2. Payoff matrix (Prisoner's Dilemma)

[24] In his poem "Mr. Eliot's Sunday Morning Service."
[25] A special case of this is discussed by Banerjee and Weibull (1995).

because it is assumed that, to get a business started, you need two persons. The upshot is that the payoff matrix for the full game, SPD, is as shown in Fig. 4.3. Note that the Prisoner's Dilemma described above and shown in Fig. 4.2 is embedded inside this game. In other words, what we have is a Prisoner's Dilemma with an option to stay out of it (by choosing a).

	a	b	c
a	0, 0	0, 0	0, 0
b	0, 0	−1, −1	2, −2
c	0, 0	−2, 2	1, 1

Figure 4.3. Payoff matrix (Sophisticated Prisoner's Dilemma)

If we think of the payoffs as profit from business, then the payoffs are reasonable. If even one player refuses to go into business, the business does not start and both earn zero profit. If both go into business and one player cooperates while his partner betrays, the former makes a loss of 2. And so on.

The Nash equilibrium payoff of this game is (0, 0). Hence, standard game theory would predict that at least one player would choose to abstain and so the business would not take off. It can be checked that recourse to the first ideas in evolutionary games does not help very much in predicting the outcome because this game does not have an ESS, or a neutrally stable strategy.

Once we turn to the concept of ESN, more interesting results begin to emerge. It is easy to check that this game does have an ESN.[26] This is given by the civil norm {a, c}; and in such a society each person gets a utility of 1, which is the cooperative outcome.

One way of checking this, formally, is to describe a full human evolutionary game based on the SPD. This is shown by the 7 × 7 matrix in Fig. 4.4. This is how the matrix is to be interpreted. The rows and columns show different civil norms. Thus a represents the civil norm {a}; ab denotes the civil norm {a, b}; and so on. The payoff in each box is the payoff earned

---

[26] Before locating an ESN we need to define a human evolutionary game based on the game shown in Fig. 4.3. There is a natural way of doing this for this game, which involves choosing the Pareto-dominant Nash equilibrium in each restricted game.

	a	b	c	ab	ac	bc	abc
a	0	0	0	0	0	0	0
b	0	-1	2	0	0	-1	0
c	0	-2	1	-2	1	2	2
ab	0	0	2	0	0	0	0
ac	0	0	1	0	1	0	0
bc	0	-1	-2	0	0	-1	1
abc	0	0	-2	0	0	1	0

Figure 4.4. Payoff matrix (civil norms)

by the row player in the relevant restricted game. Consider, for instance, the entry denoted by (bc, bc). This denotes a game where the row player has to choose between strategies b and c; and the column player has to do the same. By looking at the game in Fig. 4.2 it is clear that this restricted game is the Prisoner's Dilemma (as shown in the payoff matrix). In this restricted game there is only one Nash equilibrium (b, b). Hence there is no problem in specifying the Nash equilibrium that will occur. The row player we know earns a payoff of −1. Hence the entry of −1 is the box (bc, bc).

Fortunately, in this case very few restricted games have multiple Nash equilibria; an example is ({a, c}, {a, c}). The human evolutionary game described above simply specifies the Pareto-superior Nash equilibrium in each of these cases.

To check that {a, c} is an ESN, note {a, c} is immune against all mutants except {c} by rule (3) in the definition of immunity. This is obvious by looking at the column of payoffs under ac. Next, by looking at the column under c, it is clear that {a, c} does as well against {c} as {c} does against {c}. Therefore, {a, c} is immune against {c}, by (4). Note that c is not a Nash equilibrium of the Sophisticated Prisoner's Dilemma. Yet its use survives the process of natural selection.

In other words, we can conceive of a society where citizens are taught the norm not to betray others. So they may choose to go into business and cooperate or to abstain from business. What is interesting is that this norm is evolutionarily stable. It is immune to invasion from people with other norms. The intuition is easy to see. When these people meet a mutant who does not mind betraying, they choose to abstain from going into business with the mutant. So mutants do badly. This suggests why adherence to honesty and trustworthiness may be a useful norm, and nations that practice this may benefit in the long run. This model may thus be viewed as a confirmation of the informal idea that links trust with economic progress (games Coleman, 1990, Chs. 8 and 12; Fukuyama, 1996; Dasgupta, 1997).

In the literature on development, much has been written on the role of economic factors in ushering in technical progress. We have learnt of the role of credit availability, extension services, the terms of trade between sectors, and macroeconomic stability. What has, however, been seldom studied – though we do pay frequent lip service to it – is the role of social norms, civil institutions and trust. In some societies, hard work is a cause of embarrassment; in others, it is a source of pride. In some societies, honesty is an ingrained habit; in others, honesty is practiced only when this is to one's advantage (in other words, honesty is not, in itself, of any value).

The purpose of this section has been to develop a model for studying the strengths and weaknesses of civil norms. The model provides a bridge between the optimality claims of some schools of thought and its total neglect in others.

There are several directions that can be fruitfully pursued from here. Zoologists have drawn our attention to the phenomenon of "stotting" among gazelles, which gazelles indulge in when they perceive danger, thereby helping other gazelles in the group to get alerted. Dawkins (1976: 11) has written: "This vigorous and conspicuous leaping in front of a predator . . . seems to warn companions of danger while apparently calling the predator's attention to the stotter himself." The question is: Can we explain such individual irrationality as stotting by invoking evolution?

This line of thinking has been of sustained interest in diverse fields (see, for instance, Maynard Smith, 1964; Basu, 1996; Ensminger, 1998) under the label of "group selection," the classic work being that of Wynne-Edwards (1962). Maynard Smith (1964: 1145) observes: "If groups of relatives stay together wholly or partially isolated from other members of the species, then group selection can occur." He goes on to observe that "if all members of a group acquire some characteristic which, although individually disadvantageous, increases the fitness of the group," then such groups may survive natural selection. Maynard Smith also talks of how successful groups can multiply by splitting or sending out "propagules." It is not obvious whether this has a counterpart in economics. If, however, we assume that groups form through some arbitrary process but the less fit ones perish, we could establish an argument for group selection in economics.

There are some difficulties *en route*. As Dawkins (1976: 8) points out, if a selfish mutant emerges within a group of altruistic agents, he may be able to destroy the group. If in one group of gazelles, a few "non-stotters" appear, their population will soon increase since they will have the protection of the stotters without being exposed to the risk themselves. In due course the group will have only non-stotters and be more vulnerable and perish. So what happens ultimately may depend on whether the mutation occurs at the level of groups or individuals and, if both, on which mutation occurs faster. Hence, "group selection" is not easy to formalize, but the ideas developed in this section may give us some cues for future research.

4.7. Beliefs

Just as social norms play a crucial role in determining how an individual or a group fares in life and whether a nation prospers or stagnates, so can the beliefs of people. But beliefs have received even less attention than norms in the economics literature.[27] This is a serious omission, because the beliefs of people, both about how an economy works and about what is fair and unfair, influence their behavior and the behavior of the agents with whom they interact, and beliefs are therefore an important ingredient determining an economy's efficiency and pace of development (Basu, 1993; Denzau and North, 1994).

Where do beliefs come from? Which beliefs survive and which ones perish? While full answers to these questions are difficult to formulate, some partial answers can be given using the same kind of analysis that I used for modeling social norms. But before going to that it is useful to construct a brief taxonomy of human beliefs.

First, it is useful to draw a distinction between what I will call "positive beliefs" and "normative beliefs." **Positive beliefs** are beliefs about the way the world works. They take the form of positive statements. Here are some examples of positive beliefs:

> If I blockade his ships, he will bomb my cities.
> Hard work leads to prosperity.
> Two plus two make five.

---

[27] I make this claim using the term "belief" in the broad sense in which it is used in everyday language, because belief, in the sense of expectations about one another's strategy in games, has a large literature. For a discussion of how beliefs translate into action in the domain of politics, see Goldstein and Keohane (1993).

The first one is pretty much the kind of belief used by players in games. The third belief is false. The second one may be controversial. But all these are beliefs about the way the world is.

Normative beliefs are beliefs about what is fair or unfair, about what is commendable and what is not. Goldstein and Keohane (1993) call them "principled beliefs." They take the form of normative statements.[28] Here are some examples of such beliefs:

> For a widow to remarry is wrong.
> Shopkeepers who charge a higher price than the state-owned supermarket are unethical.
> It is shameful to live on unemployment benefit.

It is clear that normative beliefs are closely related to social norms. They often play the role of buttressing social norms by creating stigma or social approval for certain actions. The first and the third normative beliefs above help prop up the norm preventing widow remarriage and making unemployment costly to the unemployed. If we think of "shamefulness" to be a well-defined property based on what others think of you, then the last proposition may be thought of as a positive belief – it is a statement about how society views unemployment. I am, however, here thinking of "shameful" as a value judgment on the part of the person possessing that belief.

Social norms *can* of course exist without beliefs. A person may decide not to eat pork simply because that is not done, and other people's normative beliefs on this matter are then irrelevant. But to the extent that being approved of is a common human trait, certain widely held normative beliefs can have important effects on norms and preferences and, through them, on behavior.[29]

From the point of view of the economic performance of nations or groups of people, a useful classification of beliefs is between those that

[28] The reader may find it useful to refer to the Appendix, where there is a discussion of the general ideas of positive and normative statements. Several examples of normative beliefs with citations to the literature occur in Cozzi (1998).

[29] I suspect that, even while doing pure abstract reasoning, people find it difficult not to let their normative beliefs interfere. Hence, people find it easier to reason over mathematical objects like numbers and symbols (or words and sentences without any significance) than over issues that have emotive content. I put this to the test in 1995 by asking 89 students in Delhi to answer (in a limited time) a set of logic problems, in which every problem came in a pair, once using categories that had no emotional content and once in terms of emotive matter. The test was not scientifically designed (I had conducted it for my own curiosity), but I was impressed by how the subjects, systematically, did worse while reasoning over emotive matters. Here is an example of a pair of questions I had asked: In each of these questions the subject was asked to assume that the first two statements (A and B) were true and, from that, deduce whether the third statement (C) was true or false.

are "economically advantageous," "economically disadvantageous" and "economically neutral." Interestingly, these may have nothing to do with whether they are true or false, appealing or unappealing, or positive or normative.

Consider the belief that "those who are rich are deservedly so" or, more restrictedly, "those who are rich through their own work (that is, not through, for instance, inheritance) are deservedly so." Let me call this the "deserving-rich belief." Treating the word "deserve" as one of commendation, this is a normative belief (see discussion in the Appendix to this book).

Since this is a normative belief, one can, without being right or wrong, take differing views on it. To me, the deserving-rich belief seems quite unappealing. There are too many society-based factors that determine what kinds of talent will be rewarded and so who will be rich. In a hunter-gatherer society a person's physical strength may be the most important determinant of prosperity; but in today's world that matters little. Moreover, even if hard work is a universally useful trait for economic success, who will be hard-working and who not depends a lot on one's genetic makeup and upbringing, over which one has little or no control.

However, even though I and many others like me may reject this belief, it seems entirely possible that this is an economically advantageous belief. That is, a society, that has this belief is more likely to succeed. In such a society, the rich will be more universally admired and more people will strive to be rich and, it is arguable that that will help the society as a whole to progress economically. Conversely, a society that rejects this belief may be disadvantaged.

In Calcutta in the late 1960s and early 1970s, when anger against the rich was pervasive and led to a series of attacks on the wealthy, including acts of theft and burglary, much of this was prompted not so much by the direct desire to acquire another's money and goods but as a kind of moral reprisal against those who had made it from among a seething mass of humanity living in abject poverty. Indeed, many of these "thieves" were

Question 1:   A. Every Sunday it rains.
              B. Whenever it rains my dog barks.
              C. Every winter Sunday my dog barks.
Question 2:   A. All women are grey-haired.
              B. All grey-haired human beings are fit to do only housework.
              C. All Indian women are fit to do only housework.

These questions were not asked consecutively but mixed up among other questions. Question 1 was meant to be the question without emotive content. It turned out that 77% of my subjects did the deduction right for Question 1, whereas only 59% did it right for Question 2.

quite conversant with the contemporary radical literature. Among the middle class and the rich, and even among many of the poorer people, such acts were widely criticized. Those who had earned more money had done so through their hard work and intelligence; so no one had the right to deprive them of their property – so went the argument from those who adhered to the deserving-rich belief.

If one can, however, take a detached view of this, that is, abstracting from one's own position in society, it is not difficult to reach the conclusion that such a belief is not necessarily valid or invalid. It is not outrageously wrong to maintain the normative belief that the beggar has the right to snatch the pastry packet from the hands of the society lady, since she has had lots of such pastries whereas he has had none; and, moreover, if it were all right for her to have amassed wealth by the rules of her society, it may also be right for the beggar boy to try to acquire some of that wealth by the rules of *his* society.

The cardinal mistake that was made in the debate that occurred in the schools and colleges of Calcutta in the early seventies was to take the view that if a belief was not invalid, then holding it could not be bad for society. That made people miss the point that the deserving-rich belief is probably good for the economy. In its absence, people did not feel secure about their property, and this insecurity meant that they invested and saved less and made less of an effort to improve their lot. In many areas in rural India, it is standard practice for the rich landowners growing mangoes or bananas to pluck them before they are fully ripe because of the risk of burglary, much of it committed by members of political parties that rejected the deserving-rich belief. Such behavior on the part of the landlords means a net loss to society and this is the outcome of the belief that the deserving-rich view is wrong. Hence, though one may not subscribe to the deserving-rich belief, one should not blind oneself to the possibility that societies that adhere to this belief are more likely to prosper.

Another such example comes from the multistorey housing complex in east Delhi, where I used to live for some time. An enterprising shopkeeper set up a shop very close to the multistorey houses and started charging a premium of around 10 percent on virtually all items. This caused much anger and resentment among the residents. It was considered immoral profiteering. The criticism was so severe that the shop was on the verge of closing down. In this case, fortunately, it did not because it soon became one of the most frequented shops in the area, as the residents often found it worthwhile saving themselves the long walk to the cheaper shops by paying a small premium. If the belief of immoral profiteering had gathered more force and had the shop actually closed, all would be worse off. Hence, such a belief, *whether valid or not*, is economically disadvantageous.[30]

In India, speculators and hoarders are considered to be evil people. This must handicap speculative activities, which could otherwise smooth out prices. In Russia, "profit-maximizer" is still considered a pejorative term. Such a belief is surely a handicap for a society trying to develop a market economy.

Given that so much depends on beliefs, the question must arise as to how we come to have the beliefs we do and which are the beliefs that survive. Though we can give no definitive answers, thanks to modern methods of analysis we can at least give some partial answers. To begin with, one can take a textbook view of individuals and assume that they are perfectly rational and can elicit the correct information from the world around them. In that case, the positive beliefs that people have must be accurate depictions of reality. In other words, we would never see the belief that two plus two makes five, and we would encounter the view that hard work leads to prosperity only if that were true. Even this excessively rationalistic view of beliefs can give us some interesting insights. In some situations where the belief influences the world, there may be different possible beliefs – even contradictory beliefs – that may come into existence. This is because a belief can be self-fulfilling.

Consider the beliefs, mentioned above, of hoarders and speculators being evil or obnoxious (widely held in India) or that of profit-makers being evil or obnoxious (widely held in Russia). Let me here interpret these as part-positive and part-normative beliefs, in the sense of taking "obnoxious" to be some objective definition of unappealing moral traits, and, further, of taking the description of someone as obnoxious as an expression of disapproval.

We argued above that these beliefs are likely to be economically disadvantageous. In addition, I have the impression, based on casual empiricism, that hoarders and speculators in India are actually pretty unpalatable people. At first glance, this is puzzling, because, as we argued above and know objectively as economists, hoarding and speculation can be valuable activities, like any act of commerce or trade that generates welfare for the people. Why then are hoarders and speculators more likely to be obnoxious? The reason can be that the belief that they are obnoxious is a self-fulfilling belief. This can be so for several reasons. Here is one. Suppose that

---

[30] For an example of how normative beliefs influence not just individual action but government policy, see Katzenstein (1993). He shows how Germany and Japan deal differently with terrorism because of their beliefs and how this has implications not just for Germany and Japan but for other nations as well.

people vary in their zeal for making money. And those who have this zeal too strongly are willing to bend the rules, cut corners and perhaps even cheat friends. We will agree that such persons are obnoxious. We also argued above that most people like to be liked. Now suppose that we are considering a society in which it is a widely held view that speculators are obnoxious. In such a society, it is possible that only those whose love of money is sufficiently strong will be willing to incur the social opprobrium of being thought of as obnoxious. However, that will in turn make true the belief that speculators are obnoxious. This is the reason why in different societies different categories of people may be thought of as obnoxious and in each case the beliefs may turn out to be true.

There is, however, enough evidence in the world of people holding on to beliefs which are patently false. Where these beliefs come from may be difficult to explain, but we can use evolutionary arguments of the kind seen above to get a sense of which beliefs – positive or normative – are likely to survive. In particular, one could argue that beliefs that are very harmful to the people who subscribe to them will not be seen in a stable society. This is because a person who adheres to such a view is likely not to survive for too long. Now, if beliefs are transmitted from one generation to another – and it is undeniable that, to a certain extent, they are – then the really self-destructive beliefs will not be seen, because their carriers and the progeny of the carriers will cease to exist, which is the essence of an evolutionary argument.

Given that beliefs can influence the world (and we will see more of this in the next four chapters) and that a variety of beliefs can be held by human beings, there may be gains to be made by trying to influence beliefs. There are people and agencies that try to influence human beliefs. Governments often try to persuade people that it is noble to be patriotic. Parents try to endow children with beliefs that they feel will help them lead better or happier lives. Much of this happens at an intuitive level. Once the crucial role of beliefs is fully appreciated, there may be scope for a more scientific approach to the subject.

While a fully rigorous understanding of beliefs will remain a distant dream, we will in the next four chapters, on several occasions, encounter the role of beliefs in the formation and sustenance of government, the law, and even political oppression.

Part III. THE STATE

5. Law and Economics

5.1. The Law According to Social Science

The understanding of law is crucial to our understanding of the state and government. Not surprisingly, some of the shortcomings of the social scientist's understanding of government is rooted in his or her flawed notion of the role of law. This chapter lays the foundations of a revised and a more inclusive view of government. The next three chapters constitute an attempt to construct a view of the state and government that follows the logic of the view of law espoused in the present chapter. What these four chapters provide is not a final model of this inclusive conception of the state but, rather, different perspectives of such a model. But let us begin by recapitulating the orthodoxy.

In economics and related social sciences, the standard view of law is of something that changes the set of alternatives open to an individual or the returns to certain courses of action that an individual receives. More formally and using the language of game theory, a law is taken to be an instrument that either changes the sets of strategies open to individuals or the payoff functions of individuals. If the law declares that a road on which traffic was previously allowed in both directions will henceforth have only a "one-way" traffic flow, we may well take this to change (in this case, shrink) the set of strategies open to an individual in the given society, because the strategy of traveling in the "wrong" direction is no longer per-mitted. If the law requires me to pay fines for emitting pollutants into the atmosphere, then my payoff function does seem to change, because now the payoff that I expect when I build a factory that emits pollutants into the atmosphere will be different from the payoff I would expect from the factory if the pollution-control law was not there. In the former case, in addition to the profits from sales, I would have to calculate the probability of being caught and fined and adjust that against my expected profit in order to get to the expected net payoff.

This view is predicated on a conception of the economy as a game. In other words, each individual in the economy is supposed to have a feasible set of strategies or actions open to him or her. As seen in Chapter 2, the payoff that each individual, or "player," receives depends on the strategies chosen by all the players – often referred to as an "n-tuple of strategies."

The payoff is a number that expresses the net utility that a player receives from the state of the world that emerges when every player has picked a strategy from his or her set of strategies. The "payoff function" of a player, as may be recalled, is a rule that summarizes the payoff received by that player for every possible tuple of strategies that can occur in the game.

This is the view taken, implicitly or explicitly, in virtually all works of law and economics and, arguably, in all social science. The idea is often associated with Pigou and referred to as the **Pigovian view** (*see* Buchanan, 1973). This is explicitly the approach taken by Baird, Gertner and Picker (1995) in their treatise on law and game theory (*see also* Benoit and Kornhauser, 1996). It is possible to contest this view of the economy as a game, but that is not my purpose here; indeed, it seems to me to be an adequate model for many purposes.[1] What I want to focus on is the role of law in such an economy.

To some commentators, it has seemed that we need not take the law to be changing a player's set of strategies but just the player's payoff function. Baird, Gertner and Picker (1995) take this line. This is quite harmless, since a restriction on a player's strategy set can always be equivalently expressed by saying that some strategies give the player a huge negative utility – one so large that it is never worthwhile for a player to adopt any of these strategies. So not having access to some strategy can equivalently be modeled (for all practical purposes) by saying that the strategy is available but it gives such a disastrous outcome that no one will adopt it. There is no real difference between modeling the role of law in terms of strategies *and* payoff functions (as in the two above paragraphs) and modeling it in terms of *just* payoff functions (as in this paragraph); and so I shall take both these to be expressions of the traditional view.

Since a "game," as explained in Chapter 2, is identified by the strategy sets open to, and the payoff functions of, the players, we may summarize the traditional view of law as something that changes the **economy game**. Thus Baird, Gertner and Picker (1995: 15) observe: "We can capture the change in the legal rules by changing the payoffs. . . ." And, given that the payoffs are an integral part of a game, a law is treated as something that changes the game.

This approach has immediate appeal. Consider a new law that raises the income tax rate. The payoff that one now expects to earn from eight hours

---

[1] Dixit (1996), in his recent work on the political process in an economy, also views the interaction between agents as a game. While not going into such a formal construction, O'Flaherty and Bhagwati (1997) nevertheless adopt a game-theoretic approach in which individuals who constitute government are also players with their own objective functions.

of work will be less than what one would have earned from the same action or strategy earlier. Likewise with the examples of the pollution law or the one-way traffic rule above. Not surprisingly, virtually all traditional models of law in the social sciences are based on this approach.

I shall, however, argue that, while this ubiquitous view of law serves well for some limited purposes, it is fundamentally flawed. The law needs to be understood very differently if we are to get a better grip on reality while building models of economics, politics and society. It will, in particular, be shown that the law has similarities with (equilibrium-selection) norms, discussed in the previous chapter, that are more fundamental than has been recognized.

5.2. Law and Economics: A New Approach

The standard view of the role of law in an economy, summarized above, would be accurate if it were the case that the economy game was played only by the "non-governmental" individuals in society. That is, if the police, the tax collectors, and the judges were agents exogenous to the game, who mechanically went about doing what the law required them to do, then indeed for the *other people* in the society – that is, for the players of the game – a law would be something that determined the game by fixing the payoff functions; and so a change in the legal regime would amount to a change of the game.

In reality, however, those who work for government – the police, the district judge, the tax collector, the bureaucrat, the individuals in the pollution-control department and, more generally, the "sapient sutlers" of the law – are also individuals with their own motivations, dreams, striving and cunning. Hence, they are also players and should not be treated as exogenous to the economy game. This fact, in itself, is now recognized in the new literature on economics and government (see, e.g., Bhagwati, Brecher and Srinivasan, 1984; Friedman, 1994; Dixit, 1996; Basu, 1997).[2]

What is not always recognized is that this throws a wrench in the traditional models of law and economics. Morever, even those economists who recognize the significance of endogenizing the "law enforcer" balk at

---

[2] These writings may be viewed as belonging to the larger literature on modeling institutions: see, for instance, Schotter (1981), Ostrom (1990), Eggertson (1990), North (1990), Putnam (1993), Rutherford (1994), Calvert (1995), Williamson (1985), Aoki (1999) and Zambrano (1999). An interesting attempt to apply some of these theoretical ideas to political events and phenomena occurs in Bates and Weingast (1996). An institution-sensitive approach to development is outlined in Hoff and Stiglitz (2000).

taking this idea all the way to its natural conclusion; and they tend to err on the side of the traditional approach in their instinctive moments.

Note that, whether a particular law is there or not, the policeman's, the tax collector's and the judge's sets of *available* strategies remain the same. Now, if *everybody* chooses the action that he or she would have chosen if the law were not there, then, even if the law happened to be there, everybody must get the same payoff as he or she would have got in the absence of the law. Hence, the law cannot change the payoff function.

Consider, for example, the case of an antipollution law. *Whether or not the law is there*, the strategies open to a policeman include (a) arrest a person who emits pollutants and (b) not arrest a person who emits pollutants; the strategies open to the judge include (1) punish the policeman who arrests a person who pollutes the atmosphere, and (2) punish the policeman who does not arrest a person who pollutes the atmosphere.[3] Now if, whether or not the law is there, the person, the policeman and the judge behave the same way, then the person, the policeman and the judge will get the same payoff. Hence, the game played by all the individuals in the economy is unaffected by the law.

If the enforcers of the law or the agents of the state mechanically enforce the law like automatons, then a new law affects the payoff function and therefore the game *played by the rest of the citizens*. But once everybody, including the enforcers of the law, are included in the game – as they should be – a law is nothing but some ink on paper. There being or not being such ink on paper cannot alter the game.

To digress for a moment, consider the new literature on rights and liberty, which expresses rights as game-forms (see, for example, Gaertner, Pattanaik and Suzumura, 1992; Sen, 1992; and Deb, 1994). There has been much controversy about whether this is the correct way to describe rights. My criticism of this conception of rights is that it asserts that a change in the structure of rights changes the sets of actions open to individuals, and therefore changes the game. But it is not clear why a new rights assignment will change what I *can* do, even though it may well change what I *will* do. I argue that granting a person i a right to do something (call it x), must mean that if i does x then another person j will not have the right to do something (for instance, punch i's nose). Of course, j's not having the right to do something in turn must mean that if j does do that thing then others will acquire the rights to certain actions (typically punitive actions against

---

[3] The game, properly defined, would require specifying what the remaining strategies are, the sequence of moves, and other such details; but since I do not aim to analyze the game in any detail, it is all right to leave the description at this level of generality.

j) to which they otherwise would not have had a right.[4] Rights, according to this formulation (discussed in Basu, 1998a: Appendix B), do not change the game.

The subject of rights will be taken up in earnest in Chapter 10. For now, returning to the subject of law, note that the above discussion may give the impression that law does not have any effect on society; it is a chimera. Such an impression is wrong. One of the central theses of this monograph is this: The law does not affect the payoff functions of the individuals nor the game, but it can and often does influence the *outcome* of the game.

It does so by creating focal points, and by giving rise to beliefs and expectations in the minds of the individuals. Thus, in the above example, the policeman can choose between (a) and (b) and the judge from among (1) and (2), but the policeman may *believe* that the judge will choose (1) if there is no antipollution law in the state and (2) if there is an antipollution law in effect. Hence, this may prompt the policeman to choose (a) if and only if the law is there. This in turn may mean that no one will pollute the atmosphere if and only if there is an antipollution law in effect. Hence, the outcome of the game may well get influenced by the law. Note that the law works here entirely through its influence on people's beliefs and opinions. It is a central thesis of this book that law's empire, tangible and all-encompassing as it may seem, is founded on little else than beliefs.

Of course, it will need to be checked whether a particular outcome is self-enforcing (that is, an equilibrium solution) or not before we can say that that will occur given the law. But the important point is that a law *can* affect the outcome; and that in the final analysis the law and the state are simply a self-supporting structure of beliefs and opinions. Hence, the order that one finds in very different kinds of collectivities, ranging from the total-itarian state to what anthropologists in their zoological moments call the acephalous society, are *self-enforcing* outcomes.

What is a self-enforcing outcome or a reasonable equilibrium solution for a game is itself a controversial question. Over the last two decades, solution concepts have proliferated rapidly. It would be a mistake to get drawn into that debate here. Hence, without further justification, I shall treat the set of Nash equilibrium outcomes[5] as the **self-enforcing**

---

[4] More formally, a **rights structure** is simply a specification of a subset of actions at each information set from among all the actions open to the relevant player at that information set. The interpretation is that the player has a **right** to choose an action only from the specified subset.

[5] Recall from Chapter 2 that a Nash equilibrium outcome of a game is a choice of strategy by each player (that is, an *n*-tuple of strategies) such that no individual can do better by *unilaterally* deviating to some other strategy. Thus, once a Nash equilibrium outcome is expected by all players, the outcome becomes self-enforcing.

set.[6] So in this chapter a reference to an "equilibrium" outcome is always to a Nash equilibrium. When we discuss sequential (or extensive-form) games, as we will in later chapters, we will often equate "equilibrium" with a special kind of Nash equilibrium, namely a subgame perfect equilibrium.

Many games have the problem of there being too many Nash equilibria. Consider a game in which you and another player will each have to choose one number (without letting the other player see what you are choosing) from among 3, 7, 9 and 100. If both of you choose the same number, each of you gets $1000. If you choose different numbers, both of you get nothing. In this game, the following pairs of choices are the only Nash equilibria: (3, 3), (7, 7), (9, 9) and (100, 100).[7] If you were playing this game, your essential problem would be to try to guess what the other player will do. What complicates the guess is that what the other player does will depend on what she guesses you will do. One way of guessing is to try to see whether a particular strategy is salient, or "focal," and to go for it in the expectation that the other player will do the same. If such a salient outcome exists, it is called a **focal point** (see Schelling, 1960) and predicting a focal outcome often turns out to be a good prediction. This method has no rigorous explanation but works through human psychology. In the above game, for instance, most human beings would choose 100: it is a large number, it is well-rounded and somehow it stands out.

Nebulous though this method is, it works fairly well and has been used to great effect. At Heathrow airport, London, there is an arbitrary place with a large sign above it saying MEETING POINT. If you plan to meet a friend at Heathrow airport and fail to decide in advance where to wait for the friend, then in this game there are millions of Nash equilibria. As long as both of you choose the same place you have a Nash equilibrium. It does not matter where that place is. The value of the sign, MEETING POINT, is that it creates a focal point among all the possible Nash equilibria. You would typically choose to wait under the sign and so will your friend. There is no hard reason why you should do that, but each of you expect the other player to do so; and that becomes reason enough. It works. Putting up the

---

[6] Left to myself, I would prefer to use the coarser solution concept of "rationalizability" or at least a "curb set" (Basu and Weibull, 1991), but for the present purpose it is simpler to rely on the much more widely used solution of Nash equilibrium. It is worth being aware that in some situations, despite there being a rationalizable equilibrium and a Nash equilibrium and these being unique, there may be no reasonable way of predicting the outcome (Basu, 1990) based on individual rationality, where "rationality" is defined as a primitive set of qualities. One can catch a hint of this problem from the Traveler's Dilemma discussed in Chapter 3.

[7] In each pair, the first number denotes your choice and the second number the other player's choice.

hoarding, MEETING POINT, does not change the game that you and your friend are forced to play by virtue of having forgotten to decide where you will meet, but it nevertheless influences the outcome. The writing on paper that constitutes a nation's law is like the signboard in Heathrow. In itself, it is quite a vacuous thing, but it creates expectations in the minds of individuals as to what the others will do, it creates focal points, and thereby influences the outcome.

Suppose now that the airport authority at Heathrow, in trying to be helpful and not have people walk too far, puts up twenty signboards saying MEETING POINT at different places in the airport. You may then decide that it is futile to wait under one of these (since it is not clear which one you should wait under), and remembering that your friend is a bookworm and he knows that you know that he is a bookworm, and you know that he knows that you know that he is a bookworm, and so on, you may go to the store, Books Etc, and wait for him there. In anticipation of this, he too may choose to go to the bookstall. Whether he does so or not, in this case the well-meaning signboards fail to influence behavior and the outcome of the game. This can happen with the law as well. Poorly drafted legislation or legislation that takes inadequate cognizance of individual incentives can fail to have effect on people's behavior or can have unintended effects by actually causing confusion.[8] To avoid such poor-quality legislation, we have to first understand how and when the law works in the first place. For that, we have to cast aside the widespread view that law changes the payoff functions and, hence, the game.

A little more formally, the entire **set of laws** of a nation should be thought of as a specification of actions or strategies that are **legal** (and, therefore, also of actions that are not legal, or **illegal**) in the economy game.[9] In itself,

---

[8] For a more general and a different kind of argument, which pins down some of the legal failures in developing countries to the transplanting of a Western conception of a law, *see* Trubek (1972).

[9] The meaning of a particular law need not, however, be limited to what it literally says. As Sunstein (1996) has argued in a well-known and provocative paper, any utterance can have meanings that go beyond the literal. This is best understood by considering (nonspeech) actions. By definition, they say nothing. Yet actions can be "expressive" and can carry meanings. The fact of a banker's wearing jeans to work can amount to making a statement. Of course such a statement can be misread by others – for instance, a banker who has just migrated from another country or is genuinely naive may not wish to say what others take him to be saying by his choice of clothing. Just as a nonspeech act can have meanings, speech or a written statement can have meanings other than the literal one. Granting a minority a special right may amount to a recognition of its larger rights. Likewise having a law that is not enforced by the state may nevertheless result in its being upheld because of the recognition among citizens at large of the law. Cooter (1998) gives the example of smoking prohibition and pooper-scooper laws. In developing countries, giving women certain rights or share tenants certain protection can result in some adherence to them even when the state's enforcement machinery is nonexistent.

this is a pure definition – a set of dicta, written in bulky books (usually in painfully archaic English, in the name of precision). Next, note that the law, or the set of laws, could be thought of as being **implementable** if every individual finds that, if he believes that others will use only legal strategies, it is best for him to confine himself to a legal strategy. In other words, if the law is implementable it has a chance of being implemented. It can create a focal point such that everybody will follow the law. Hence, the nation's laws are in themselves some definitions and beliefs, which *can* translate into action if the laws are self-enforcing and if people somehow believe that the law will be followed. In nations in which general anarchy prevails, even if a law is implementable it may not be implemented because people do not expect others to live by the law.

Recall, from Chapter 4, that equilibrium-selection social norms[10] are also simply an instrument for players to coordinate onto an equilibrium (or some outcome within a certain set of equilibria). It follows that actions and behavior (and therefore outcomes) that are enforceable by the law are also enforceable by social norms. Since an outcome that is enforceable by the law is an equilibrium, we can always imagine norms (which lead to beliefs) that sustain the same actions, behavior and outcome.

To take an example, consider a society in which the law allows you to drive on any side of the road but the norm is to drive on the left. Since we have seen that if such a law were in existence it would be enforceable, it follows that this norm is also enforceable. This is an easy example because it is empirically transparent – in some remote parts of India, the hand of the law is so weak that it is indeed the case that, in effect, there is no law about which side of the road to drive. Yet people do drive on the left because, once the norm is in place,[11] there is no reason for one to violate it.

For another example, consider a country where there is no antipollution law but there is a social norm that, if someone pollutes the atmosphere, then you ostracize that person; and if someone who does not ostracize someone who pollutes the atmosphere, then you ostracize that person, and so on. In that case it is possible that every person will adhere to the norm and no one will pollute the atmosphere. This is essentially Akerlof's (1976) idea of a caste equilibrium and also the idea behind an equilibrium-selection norm.

In the following chapter, we shall see that obedience to a tyrant is also best explained along these lines, since no one really fears the hurt the tyrant can *himself* bring upon one. The subordinate's fear of the tyrant,

---

[10] All reference to norms, from now till the end of this chapter, is to *equilibrium-selection* norms.
[11] In this case the norm is imported from the cities where it is the law and is enforced.

based on what the subordinate expects other subordinates to do to him, should he disobey the tyrant, is the usual basis of obedience and that is what Hume (1758: p. 34 of the 1987 edition) was talking about when he wrote: "No man would have any reason to *fear* the fury of a tyrant, if he had no authority over any but from fear; since, as a single man, his bodily force can reach but a small way, and all the farther power he posseses *must be found on our own opinion, or on the presumed opinion of others.*" (The second set of italics is mine.)

This brings me to the central proposition of this chapter, which is christened the **core theorem of law and economics.**

Core Theorem: *Whatever behavior and outcomes in society are legally enforceable are also enforceable through social norms.*

In discussing the theorem it is useful to break it up into the two following corollaries, which are equivalent to the core theorem.

First Corollary: *What can be achieved through the law can, in principle, also be achieved without the law.*

Second Corollary: *If a certain outcome is not an equilibrium of the economy, then no law can implement it.*

Let us begin with the first corollary and, in particular, with some examples. As discussed in the previous chapter, in India, till fairly recent times and, in some parts, even now, a widow was expected to lead a life of general abstinence after her husband had died – eat vegetarian food, wear black and white clothes, avoid close relationships with men, and so on. This social norm used to be adhered to very strictly in many parts of India. To an outside observer, unfamiliar with India, this would appear to be a practice enforced by law, just as in some Islamic states women are required by law to wear a *chador*. But this appearance would be deceptive because there is no law that achieved this remarkable conformity in India. The conformity was achieved entirely through a system of sanctions and threats of ostracism, the threats themselves being given by individuals who feared that, if they did not give such threats, they themselves would be ostracized. So this is an example of behavior that we would expect to be caused by the law but is actually the result of social norms.[12] The rules of caste are another

---

[12] An interesting case of a hybrid is "customary international law." It is unsupported by any centralized law maker, or the equivalent of the state; it very often blatantly reflects the interests of the more powerful nations. On the other hand, national courts frequently refer to them and nations go to war to uphold what they believe are customary laws. For an interesting game-theoretic study of customary international law, *see* Goldsmith and Posner (1999).

example of the same. The core theorem and in particular the first corollary, challenges the myth that norms are somehow spontaneous and natural while laws are intrusive and unnatural. The collection of *rangdari* tax in India, discussed in the opening chapter, and the protection and punishment regimes of the mafia (Gambetta, 1993), though not supported by the law, function *as if they were*, and illustrate this point.

E. P. Thompson, in his classic essay on the morality of the crowd (reprinted in Thompson, 1993), gives several examples from eighteenth-century Britain of how, even in riotous situations, informal control can mimic the law. In 1766, perambulating crowds in the Thames Valley, threatening land-owners who they thought were profiteering excessively and enforcing price ceilings, called themselves "the regulators." Thompson (1993: 242) notes: "Such pressures as these, in anticipation of riot, may have been more effective than has been proposed: in getting corn to market, in restraining prices; and in intimidating certain kinds of profiteering. . . ." Reflecting the power of social control, one Mr. Toogood (the name, contrary to the impres-sion it creates, is not concocted by me, to protect his identity or otherwise) of Dorset, wrote in his diary to his sons not to get into trouble with the heavy hand of the crowd: "If the like Circumstances [that is, riotous condi-tions] happen hereafter in your Time and either of you are engaged in Farmering Business, let not a covetous Eye tempt you to be foremost in advancing the Price of corn but rather let your behaviour shew some Compassion and Charity towards the condition of the Poor. . . ." At a more micro level, Black (1983) has written persuasively on how crime is so often thought of as a moral act by the criminal.[13]

Turning to a different setting, consider a researcher who is given the task of finding out the extent to which the press is free in different countries. The typical step that this person will take is to find out what kinds of legal restrictions each country places on its scribes. She may also check on more general laws and statutes, such as the First Amendment to the US Con-stitution, which guarantees freedom of speech to individuals and therefore also to the press. It has been found that in some countries the state per-secutes its critics even when the law does not disallow criticism; and so this researcher may go a step further and check the record of state persecution of journalists and television commentators. She would then somehow combine all this information to decide in which nations the press is the

---

[13] There is now a growing literature in economics on the private provision of certain basic rights, such as property rights (Skaperdas, 1992; de Meza and Gould, 1992), and also a literature on pre-dation and the use of force to seize other people's property (Grossman, 1991; Gambetta, 1993). But these continue to be developments on the fringe.

most free and in which nations the least. To most of us, at least at first sight, this seems like a reasonable procedure.

However, in the light of the core theorem it turns out that this method of research can yield seriously flawed results, because the method presumes that the only curb on press freedom can come from the nation's law and the state. But the theorem tells us that exactly what the state can do, individual citizens, going about their daily chores, can achieve. So it is not enough to observe the law and state or governmental action.

One may try to rebut this criticism by arguing that that is asking for too much. There are practical limits to what we can study; so when we look for whether certain freedoms are guaranteed in a certain nation, it is only natural to study the nation's law and governmental behavior. Suppose we agree to this rebuttal. Then of course we have to use this criterion for all studies of a similar nature. Now suppose the researcher were asked to study the amount of freedom that a widow has in different nations. She would then have to say that the Indian widow is no less free than widows elsewhere in the world because she faces no legal or governmental restrictions on her behavior. This would then also be true of India several decades ago, when in some parts of the country the widow was expected to commit *sati* – burn herself in her dead husband's pyre. Most of us would agree that the woman climbing on to the pyre was not, typically, committing a voluntary act. The voluntary-act conclusion is evidently a folly stemming from the erroneous presumption that it is only the state that can curb individual voluntariness.

Let us turn back to the example of press freedom. Newspapers and magazines come under all kinds of social, and in particular nongovernmental, pressures. If a newspaper criticizes a wealthy business lobby, it can face debilitating cuts in advertisements; and so it may feel compelled not to criticize the lobby. If it criticizes its government during an international crisis and the people of that nation are sufficiently nationalistic, it may face a boycott by general readers; and, fearing this, it may decide not to criticize the government. Once these extra-legal constraints are taken into account, certain rankings become ambiguous. Between, for instance, China and the United States, it may be relatively easy to conclude that the latter has a freer press even without studying social control because the state is "so much more" repressive in China;[14] but between the United States and

[14] This brings to mind Tom Stoppard's simultaneously funny and chilling description of informal control of the media in his play *Day and Night*. The President of a fictitious African nation asserts his belief in a "relatively free press;" and when asked what he means by that, he clarifies: "I mean a free press which is edited by one of my relatives."

India the answer is less obvious. In terms of *legal* restrictions, the mass media may be more free in the US than in India; but the social and business sanctions seem to be considerable on US newspapers and television channels. This is not just because of the pressures of political correctness, but there seems to be a wide recognition among corporations, lobbies and power brokers that the control of opinion and information is an important ingredient for profit and survival; and so they have tried to use such control. Even if my empirical conjecture is false, it still remains true that just studying legal controls may be inadequate, not just for determining press freedom but the freedom of the widow or the low caste.[15]

It is true that, in the light of the core theorem, individual freedoms become vastly more difficult to compute. But that cannot be reason enough to confine our attention to the law and the behavior of *government* when studying individual freedom.

Let us now turn to the second corollary of law and economics. According to this, if we have a law, the adherence to which entails out-of-equilibrium behavior on the part of some individual, then such a law is doomed to failure; it can never be enforced. This is because, as we have earlier argued, law cannot alter the payoff functions of players; and so it cannot create new equilibria. By influencing beliefs and creating focal points, it can only direct society to some existing equilibrium. A law cannot induce a non-equilibrium outcome.[16] Attempts to induce such an outcome would either result in the law being inconsequential or have unintended effects on the economy. Ellickson's (1991) claim that there can be "order without law" is now easy to understand, but so is the converse of that claim – the possibility of disorder despite law.

One can think of a variety of laws that are routinely ignored and situations where anarchy prevails despite the law. There are easy examples that one can think of where the law has had a negligible effect on society, or not the kind of effect that the law was intended to have. India's main antitrust

---

[15] Bernstein's (1992) engaging study of the diamond industry makes it amply clear that the advice carries over even to the more microeconomic domain of specific industries and markets. Informal control and "home-grown" rules are important instruments of control. The same point gets reinforced by McMillan and Woodruff's (1999) study of how firms in Vietnam enter into contracts in the absence of the law (*see also* Ellickson, 1991; and Fafchamps, 1992).

[16] Following Leibnitz, Steiner (1994: 2–3) has argued that, for a set of rights to be implementable it is necessary that the rights be "compossible;" that is, the set of social outcomes or states where each of these rights is satisfied must be nonempty. By the same argument, he would no doubt reason that for a set of laws to be implementable a necessary condition is that they be compossible. Viewed in this light, the second corollary can be thought of as simply taking this argument further and claiming that, for a set of laws to be implementable, the intersection of the set of outcomes that satisfy these laws and the solution set of the economy game must be nonempty.

legislation according to several observers falls into this category (Chandra, 1977). The same is true of legislation meant to keep child laborers out of hazardous industries. Ellickson (1991) has talked about how the ranchers of Shasta County live by their own rules, oblivious of the law. When, on June 23, 1832, Michael Thomas Sadler, Esq., in preparing his report for the regulation of child labor, asked Peter Smart, a former child laborer, whether the children were kept bonded "by law," Smart's answer was: "By law? I cannot say by law; but they were compelled by the master; I never saw any law used there but the law of their own hands."[17]

Before moving on, it is useful to make one remark clarifying further the core theorem. It has been noted in the literature that certain laws get implemented even without state enforcement (see footnote 9 of this chapter), because once the law is in existence then social norms develop and people take it upon themselves to enforce the law. All of us have seen civilians enforcing smoking prohibitions by pointing out to an errant smoker a no-smoking sign (which could then result in shame or self-enforcement leading to stubbing out the cigarette). When the core theorem says that every law that can be implemented by the state can be implemented by social norms, it is not being asserted that this kind of social enforcement, where ordinary citizens enforce the law, is feasible. It of course may be, as Cooter (1998) persuasively shows. But what the theorem asserts is different, namely that, if there is a law that can be implemented by the agents of the state (the police, the judge and the jailor), then, even in the absence of such a law, there must exist an equilibrium in which it is in the interest of *each of these same agents* to behave as they did when the law existed.

In the light of the core theorem, the question must arise as to in what way the law is *different* from norms,[18] since up to now we have shown how, in certain important respects (in particular, their consequences) they look very similar. To answer this we have to recognize that the economy, described as a game, ignores a lot of information concerning prior beliefs and histories, which is a part of any real economy. In the world as we know it, even before a specific law is enacted there exists a predefined set of roles for various players concerning the way they should relate to the law, *whatever the law is*. Of course, the players are free to violate these rules, but they are nonetheless there. Thus the traffic policeman is supposed to follow the rule that

---

[17] See page 339 of the British Parliamentary Papers (1968). An engaging historical account of the consequences of switching from a norms-based institution to one based on the law occurs in Kranton and Swamy (1999).

[18] For discussions of this question, *see* Fuller (1969), Knight (1998), and Cao (1999).

he should stop drivers who violate the traffic laws. This instruction to the traffic police remains in force *no matter what the traffic laws are*. The ordinary citizen is supposed to follow the rule that he or she respects the orders of the traffic police.[19] The judge is supposed to follow the rule that she should punish the person who violates the law and this remains valid no matter what the law is. Even if the speed limit is changed, the judge's rule remains the same.

I shall refer to these prior rules and institutions as **anterior laws** or **preexisting laws**. Though anterior laws are also laws, some of them may not have any bite on their own. The rule that the policeman should stop a car that breaks the speed limit is of no operational consequence till the speed limit is specified. But once the speed limit law is specified, the anterior law comes to life. The speed-limit law thrown in with the anterior law is much more than a law that simply says that a driver must not exceed 65 m.p.h. It is a law (or a set of laws, if we want to emphasize its reach) that specifies behavior rules for various people – the driver, of course, but also the policeman, the magistrate and, frequently, the ordinary citizen (who, for instance, may not obstruct a policeman carrying out his duty). The role of anterior laws or preexisting laws is illustrated with an example in Section 5.4. The role of law and the state also gets an interesting twist when we think of an economy explicitly as a *sequential* game. This is discussed in Chapter 8.

Given that all modern societies have predefined rules for people to follow with respect to the law, which are independent of what the actual law is, this means that when new laws are enacted, the set of supporting activities and behavior by the various citizens do not have to be specified separately each time. It is this preexisting structure of rules and instructions, along with the expectations in people's minds that these will be adhered to as long as they are not against the adherer's self-interest, that makes it possible for new laws to be implemented. For any law, the full ramification, in terms of what it implies for individual behavior, is enormous.

Suppose the US state of Montana enacts new speed-limit legislation. This asks not just drivers to behave in a certain way but traffic wardens to

---

[19] It is interesting to ask oneself why we would not stop driving if an ordinary civilian – let us say a vagabond – pretending to be a traffic warden asks us to stop. The reason is not what we expect this person to do to us. Neither the traffic warden nor the civilian would do anything directly to us; moreover, both may report our license plate number to the police department. The difference is not in that. The difference is in how we expect *others* to react to this person. When the license plate number is reported to the police department, we expect very different kinds of actions on the part of the policemen, depending on who the report comes from – a traffic warden or a vagabond.

behave in a certain way, judges to behave in a certain way and so on.[20] The existence of preexisting rules (and, therefore, expectations) for laws is one of the ways in which a law is different from a norm. If the Montana speed limit were to be introduced as a *norm*, all these supporting behaviors by the various agents would have to be specified, since the norms may not (and often do not) have the advantage of preexisting rules and expectations coming automatically with them. So, although for each implementable law there is also a norm that would yield the same outcome, the full statement of that norm would be enormously complicated. The statement of the full law is also complicated, in principle; but, at any point of time, the statement is easy because the standing orders are already there; so the full new law, which includes the anterior laws, does not have to be stated fully each time a new piece of legislation is enacted.

The histories of norms and laws are also different. Usually (though not always), social norms appear through long processes of evolution. Similar acts repeated over time can become a norm. Moreover, the process of emergence of a norm can witness mutations, disruption and long periods of stagnation followed by rapid change.[21] Even some very sharply defined social norms and customs, such as the caste system or eating habits of different peoples, have such distant and diffused origins that there may be no agreement among historians as to where they came from. The law, on the other hand, is normally a product of deliberate choice, with dates of enactment commonly known. Of course, there are exceptions. The laws that certain tribes follow often merge into what we think of as norms; even in modern societies there are laws that have emerged from common customs. This is true, for instance, of English Common Law, and also much of US law, because of its practice of relying on interpretive principles and judicial rulings (Ferejohn, 1995; Basu, 1998b). Conversely, there are some norms that are deliberate decisions.

There is another difference of significance. Since, in the end, both norms and laws have their impact on outcomes by influencing people's belief

---

[20] Some of these preexisting rules may not even have the status of anterior *laws*. They may be more in the nature of *norms*. Thus for the successful implementation of a law it may be valuable for the law to be embedded in a certain structure of norms. Cooter's (1999: 2) claim that "state law builds upon pre-existing social norms," though based on a different kind of argument, has some parallels to the position being taken here.

[21] To quote Ullmann-Margalit (1977: 8): "Norms as a rule do not come into existence at a definite point in time, nor are they the result of a manageable number of identifiable acts. They are, rather, the resultant of complex patterns of behavior of a large number of people over a protracted period of time". For a micro study of the formation of norms in particular economies, *see* Boyd and Richerson (1994), and Hayami (1998).

about how other people will behave, if a country has a reputation for efficient implementation of its laws, a new law makes people expect that it will be implemented and, as long as the outcome of the law happens to be an equilibrium outcome, it gets implemented. Hence, in a nation with the reputation for laws being implemented effectively, a new law can quickly become effective. And so, even though for whatever can be achieved by the law there exist norms that can achieve the same, there may be no easy way to will the right norms into existence.

For the above reasons, norms are difficult to change, since norms do not have the paraphernalia of preexisting rules, which can be used to usher in a new norm. On the other hand, norms may well be more robust than the law because, just as most norms were not deliberately instituted, it is difficult to deliberately relinquish them.

5.3. Law and Enforcement: A Model

This section illustrates formally some of the principles discussed in Section 5.2. I proceed here entirely through an example.

For most games that economists talk about, it is possible to define a larger game by adding on to it the possibility of punitive actions after the end of the main game. Thus chess is a game; but at the end of a game of chess I can sock my opponent on his nose; he can sock me back; I can sock him again; and so on. Thus for every game G we can define an "expanded game" G_E that appends to G a string of punitive actions.

I shall consider a very simple game G. This game consists of one player, called player 1, who has to choose any action (or strategy) from the interval [0, 1]. His payoff function is as follows. If he chooses an action x from this interval, then he gets a payoff of x. We could think of the action as the amount of pollution generated by him, taking a value between 0 and 1. The more he pollutes, the more profit he earns. If this was all there was to it, player 1 would pollute up to level 1.

Now consider the expanded game G_E, which consists of two players, the above player (that is player 1) and another player, called player 2. In period 0 of G_E, player 1 plays the above game G. In period 1, player 2 can choose between P (punish the other player) and N (not punish the other player). In period 2, player 1 chooses between P and N; in period 3 player 2 chooses between P and N; and so on *ad infinitum*. Suppose in period t (≥ 1), player i has to move. Then if i plays P, player j ($\neq i$) earns $-B$ (where $B > 0$) in that period and i earns 0; and if i plays N, both earn 0. In other words, punishment hurts and inflicting a punishment is costless and joyless. Both players have a discount factor of $\delta \in (0, 1)$.

It is possible to generalize and say that punishing someone also has a small cost (punching someone can hurt the puncher's knuckles), say D. As long as this is sufficiently small, in particular $D < \delta B$, our analysis remains unchanged. For simplicity, we are assuming $D = 0$.

What we are interested in checking is how much pollution can be controlled through legislation. To keep the analysis simple, we shall assume that there is the following pre-existing or anterior law. This is simply a contingent definition: At any time period $t \geq 1$, agent i's chosen action will be called "illegal" if he chooses P (i.e. punishes player j) even though player j's move at time $t - 1$ was legal (i.e. not illegal), or if he chooses N even though j's move at $t - 1$ was illegal. In words: (a) It is illegal to punish someone who has done nothing illegal; and (b) it is illegal to not punish someone who has violated the law. We can think of other kinds of anterior laws. We can, for instance, think of dropping (b).

This pre-existing anterior law is just a definition and has no bite till we specify a law regarding what constitutes an illegal move in game G, and that is the reason I refer to it as "anterior" law. Consider a possible law, which I will call "the pollution law": In period 0, if player 1 chooses any action greater than α, where α is a given number in $[0, 1)$, then 1's action is "illegal."

The pollution law coupled with the anterior law is a well-defined law – let us call it "the set of laws." This allows us to classify every action in every play of the game as either legal or illegal. Given a play of the game, a person is described as law-abiding if he or she makes no illegal moves. Note that the set of laws that we are considering is parameterized by α. We want to investigate for which α's the legal system is enforceable in the sense that there exists a Nash equilibrium outcome where everybody is law-abiding.

Observe that a new pollution law, or for that matter a new set of laws, leaves the strategy sets and payoff functions (and therefore the game) unchanged. As discussed in Section 5.2, the law *can* nevertheless influence behavior – in particular, whether everybody abides by it – by affecting everybody's expectation about everybody else's behavior. This is so as long as it is enforceable.

To check this, suppose both players are law-abiding. In particular, let us suppose that player 1 decides to play α in period 0 (i.e. the highest possible legal move) and be law-abiding throughout. To check whether this is an equilibrium position, we have to verify that no one stands to benefit by deviating unilaterally. If both are law-abiding, player 1 gets a payoff of α

and player 2 gets a payoff of zero. Clearly, player 2 cannot do better through any deviation since zero is the highest she can earn in this game. Consider player 1's strategy if he decides to deviate from being law-abiding. It is easy to see that the best deviation is to play 1 in period 0 and from then on to make only legal moves. That will, of course, invite punishment from player 2 in period 1 (since she is law abiding). After that it is not worthwhile for player 1 to play P because that and only that will prompt player 2 to play P in the following period. Hence, if player 1 deviates from being law-abiding, his highest possible payoff is $1 - \delta B$. Thus player 1 will not deviate if and only if $\alpha \geq 1 - \delta B$.

It follows that the only pollution laws that are enforceable are ones that permit people to pollute up to some level at least as high as $1 - \delta B$. If $1 - \delta B > 0$ and the pollution law sets $\alpha \in [0, 1 - \delta B)$, then a behavior in conformity with the law cannot be enforced in any way. Since the law cannot change the game, a pollution level below $1 - \delta B$ is impossible to have in this society. No amount of legislation can do it.

5.4. A Digression on Freedom of Speech

Contemporary popular opinion, especially among intellectuals, favors a commitment without exception to the freedom of speech of the individual. This proclamation of commitment is treated as so much of a signal of all that we cherish as decent and desirable that reasonable people hesitate to express an opinion to the contrary.[22]

The aim of this section is to challenge this sacred commitment of the intelligentsia. Let us begin by considering a person – one who believes in the total freedom of speech without exception – pondering Salman Rushdie's *The Satanic Verses*. She does not really need to read the book to reach the conclusion that it must not be banned. Publishing a book is, after all, an exercise in one's freedom to say what one wishes.

The trouble with her taking such an absolute position is that she cannot be against the *fatwa* of the Ayatollah Khomeini either. The Ayatollah could rightly claim that he was not himself hurting Salman Rushdie at all; he

---

[22] When I was visiting Oxford many years ago, I was told by one person after another how the architecture of Nuffield College was ugly. It happened so many times that it was impossible not to have one's anthropological antennae go up. And on further investigation I indeed was convinced that finding Nuffield College ugly was a Veblenesque signal of one's station in life. No one could express an opinion to the contrary and expect others to believe that one had intellectual sensitivity or "class."

was just exercising *his* freedom of speech. Indeed, to make this even more reasonable, the Ayatollah, instead of giving out the *fatwa* in words, could have published a thin book (I am sure he could have commandeered a publisher, and even get the requisite prepublication commendations on the back cover) that contained the *fatwa*. If our ponderer believes that no book should be banned, she cannot ask for a ban on the Ayatollah's *fatwa* either.

One possibility for her, as a believer in the total freedom of speech, is to go along with this and say that she will allow the Ayatollah to *issue* the *fatwa* and only punish the person who *carries it out*, since giving the *fatwa* is speech, while carrying it out is (a non-speech) action. If the intellectual takes this desperate line, which she logically can, we can drive her into a more difficult corner. By the same token of her own argument, if a mugger writes a short book, which says inside, "Give me your wallet, or else I will kill you," and opens the book and shows it to a person on a lonely street, he cannot be arrested because he can say that he was simply exercising his freedom of speech; he never actually intended to have blood on his hand and he certainly *does not have* blood on his hand. Indeed, he cannot be arrested even if he manages to get the wallet by this act, since he can correctly point out that he did not take any hurtful action. In other words, taken to its very end, a total commitment to freedom of speech would allow us to intervene only *after* the crime has been committed – for instance, if the passerby refused to give the wallet and got killed. Surely, no one will take this position and so, once we have thought through what it really entails, there will be no one with a commitment to free speech without exception.

Indeed, what is surprising about the intelligentsia's stand on freedom of speech is that it is so extreme. No one says that people should have individual freedom to undertake any *action*. Why then do we take this polar stance on speech? It is true that actions can have negative externalities – i's action can hurt j. But the same is true of speech. The speech of person i can hurt j, not just indirectly by stirring others into action but even directly. Speech can, as we know, be used to wound, lacerate and scar people's minds. So one has to argue that there is something special about speech such that, even though it does often have externalities, it is not worth giving governments the power to regulate speech. This can be because, once the state has this power, it is difficult to draw a line where it should stop; and so, we may argue that while giving the state some power to restrain speech would be fine, that would amount to risking the breakdown of democracy. In other words, our commitment to the freedom of speech may be justified as "rule optimization" for society, in the sense in which this expression was used in Chapter 3. It is akin to us telling children not to go into deep water, when we know that what is ideal is that they remain in the shallow area but also know that, once they enter the water, they will not be able to restrain themselves.[23]

This argument is not good enough, because as we saw with the Rushdie example, this extreme position, that government should give individuals total freedom of speech, is not something that anybody would wish – nor, indeed, is it practiced in any country. So we have already violated the rule. In the United States, where the First Amendment to the Constitution enshrines this principle more directly than in virtually any other country, there are a variety of ways in which the state nevertheless restrains individual freedom of speech. This is so, not just in arresting a mugger who *says* that he will kill if he does not get the wallet, or the prankster who shouts "Fire" in a crowded cinema, but in more substantial ways. An elegant commentary on this is the essay by Fish (1994: chapter 8). He argues that it may be good to place restrictions on certain kinds of hate speech, such as anti-Semitic or other racist speech, or speech that humiliates women, and retorts that (p. 111) "And when someone warns about the slippery slope and predicts mournfully that if you restrict one form of speech you never know what would be restricted next, one could reply, 'Some form of speech is always restricted, else there could be no meaningful assertion; we have always and already slid down the slippery slope . . .'."[24]

---

[23] Another example of how the meaning of "freedom" can quickly become complicated occurs in the context of labor markets. Most people feel that slavery is coercion but modern labor markets are voluntary. Those who study developing societies agree that bonded labor is unfree but wage labor is voluntary. But once one goes beyond contemporary and industrialized societies to consider examples of labor markets from primitive societies or bygone eras (Engerman, 1992), the dividing line between what is free and what is not becomes unclear, as one encounters institutions that appear strange to the modern observer. Moreover, on returning to contemporary markets after such a journey, the dividing lines that had earlier seemed obvious also appear less sharp, as must have been Darwin's experience after his return from the Galapagos Islands.

[24] While I agree with much of Fish's conclusions, it must be remarked that there is one logical error, which flaws a part of his argument. He points out, rightly, how no one would ask for a law that gives individuals total freedom of action. From this he goes on to argue (p. 105): "If the First Amendment is to make any sense, have any bite, speech must be declared not to be a species of action, or to be a special form of action lacking the aspects of action that cause it to be an object of regulation." This is not a valid conclusion. Our belief that action needs to be regulated, does not mean that *all* action needs to be regulated but that there exist actions that need to be regulated. The belief that some action needs to be regulated is logically compatible with the view that no speech–action ought to be regulated, which is in fact an extreme interpretation of the First Amendment. In other words, maintaining that speech is a form of action does not in itself destroy the meaningfulness of the First Amendment. Hence, though Fish reaches very similar conclusions to those reached in this chapter – that speech may need to be restricted, depending on the context and the content of the speech – the bases of our analysis are not the same.

James Keegstra was a high school teacher in Alberta, Canada, who "systematically denigrated Jews in his classes," holding them responsible for "depression, anarchy, chaos, . . ." (Fish, 1994: 104). Should the expression of such opinion be stopped by law? The answer is "yes". A great deal of violence in society, including large-scale racial carnage, has its origins in speech, pamphleteering, radio broadcasts and books. To tie the hands of the state by taking a position of principle not to halt *any* such activity is like refusing to arrest a mugger until the mugger actually carries out a threat.

It is true that states, even in democracies, do often intervene in such speech, but since this is done while professing a commitment to total freedom of speech, not only does that amount to hypocrisy but it distorts the manner of intervention.

Once we make the minimal concession, as we ought to, that certain kinds of speech should be regulated, many new questions crop up. Note that, till now, when speaking of the freedom of speech, we have restricted our attention to actions of the state (meaning the actions of the agents of the state). But the state is not the only institution that can restrict individual freedom. Suppose you say that you believe that "individuals should have the freedom to say what they want or what they believe in." If by the above declaration you mean that the set of feasible actions available to an individual should include his ability to make different speeches, then your commitment to free speech is pretty meaningless. It is based on the same flawed view of an economy that underlies some of the literature on rights. Having a freedom or a right must be interpreted as other people not having certain freedoms or rights after you have exercised that freedom. And unless it is made at least partly clear what restriction one is willing to put on other people's freedom when guaranteeing a certain freedom to one person, the declaration that you believe in that freedom remains fairly meaningless.

Now, just as an individual's freedom of speech can be curbed by the state, it can also be curbed by the voluntary, atomistic actions of ordinary citizens (Loury, 1994). Some societies are temperamentally more prone to sanctioning one another's speech and behavior, of being less tolerant of what one considers to be deviancy. In such societies, individual freedom of speech can be severely curbed without the state having to lift a finger. It was argued in Section 5.2 that the United States displayed some of this dichotomy, by allowing for enormous freedoms of speech under the law but lots of social, norms-based restrictions. Given the above argument that certain kinds of speech are undesirable and can make minorities feel insecure, these informal restrictions and system of sanctions can have their advantages; and, in the case of the United States, they have contributed enormously to the openness of society and to the preservation of civil society. On the other hand, to the extent that these informal restrictions prevent open discourse and can result in certain undesirable controls, they can be a disadvantage.

But let us, for now, go along with the simple assumption that we want to maximize the total amount of free speech, taking for granted that this can somehow be measured. If we are committed to maximizing the freedom of speech and recognize that such freedom is not just a matter of law and government but also social norms and individual citizens, who are not part of government, we must allow for the possibility that government placing some restrictions on some speech may result in a society where the total freedom is maximized. This dilemma of freedom versus freedom is a subject matter of Fiss's provocative monograph (1996). As he puts it so eloquently, "Sometimes we must lower the voices of some in order to hear the voices of others" (p. 18). It is the recognition of this possibility that gives rise to the dilemma that his book addresses. He contrasts between the "libertarian" and the "democratic" interpretations of the First Amendment. In the language of the present book, the former is a deontological interpretation (see Sect. 10.1), concerned with preventing the state from curbing anybody's freedom to say anything; while the latter is a more consequentialist interpretation, whereby the state is entrusted with the task of maximizing the total amount of free speech in society, and which entails some curbs to be placed by the state.

In summary, most commendations to guarantee the freedom of speech in popular discourse take the form of disarming the state from being able to place curbs on speech and enact laws that curb freedom of speech. But once it is recognized that the state is not the only agency that can control speech – big corporations, religious organizations, schools and universities can all restrict speech – and that one person's freedom can lead to another person's restriction, it is clear that if we want to maximize the total amount of free speech we may need to recognize that the state may have to place some restrictions on individual freedom of speech. Morever, it is not anyway clear why we should maximize the total amount of free speech, given that speech can hurt as much as action. And to the argument that, even if this is right in principle, once we allow the state to curb individual freedom of speech there may be no stopping the slide, the counter-argument is that we have already allowed the state to curb individual freedoms of speech in a variety of ways. In brief, when it comes to the freedom of speech, the best stopping place is the slippery slope.

5.5. Concluding Remarks

In this chapter we discussed how to correctly model the role of law in an economy. There are, however, situations where we may wilfully choose to reject the correct method, just as economists often do a *partial* equilibrium analysis of some problem even when they know that, strictly speaking, they should be doing a *general* equilibrium analysis. They do it for reasons of simplicity and keep their fingers crossed. Indeed, one way of viewing the standard literature on law and economics is like partial equilibrium analysis. It *presumes* law-abiding behavior on the part of the law-enforcement officers. Even in more sophisticated models, which allow for bribery and other kinds of lapses, ultimately (and often implicitly) there is a layer of enforcement that is assumed to be automatic.[25] This can work within limits because those who are assumed to do the job automatically may actually find it in their interest to do so, or may have a commitment to rationality-limiting norms that make them do their job unquestioningly. For instance, in the model of Section 5.3, suppose the economist simply assumes that whatever is the law will be followed, considers a law that prohibits emitting pollution above a level α, and then goes on to analyze the economy-wide ramification of such a law. His analysis will be valid as long as he chooses an α that happens to be at least as large as $1 - \delta B$. But, surely, instead of working with models that run on remaining within some parameters, which can often be very restrictive, it would be better to approach modeling law and economics as suggested in this chapter.

If one adopts this approach to law and economics, it will have implications for several related areas of research, notably the study of government and the state. In general, economists have been quite cavalier in their modeling of government. It has usually been treated as a receptacle of exogenous variables or as an agent exogenous to the system but ready to carry out the advice of economists. Even when economists have gone beyond this, they have usually taken a simplistic and mechanical view of government (Hardin, 1997).

This chapter drew our attention to the fact that both the enforcers of the law and, for want of a better word, the "enforcees" need to be modeled together, as strategic agents having volition and choice. Some of these ramifications are studied in the chapters that follow, but there is much that will remain for the future.

---

[25] For an exception see Basu, Bhattacharya and Mishra (1992).

6. Power and Coercion

6.1. Of Dyads and Triads

The subject of power has received an enormous amount of attention from sociologists and political theorists; but it is too important a subject to be left to their charge alone. The treatment of power and coercion has always been peripheral in economics. One reason for this is that these are very difficult ideas to formalize and, given the importance attached to formalization in economics, the only effective option has been to ignore them. One unfortunate consequence of this is that, having omitted the ideas of power and coercion from our discourse, we have deluded ourselves into believing that they are unimportant in reality or at least redundant for understanding the functioning of an economy. As the uninitiated know, this is delusion indeed; and when we go beyond the humdrum of demand and supply to larger questions of economic success and failure, inequality and overall growth, the inability to incorporate power into our models becomes a major handicap.

The objective of the present chapter is to do some groundwork for rectifying this. Its aim is the modest one of enquiring into the nature and consequences of one kind of power – that which works through "triadic" relationships and which allows rulers and the institution of state to exercise control over the lives of ordinary people. The equilibrium idea discussed here has similarities to the concept of equilibrium-selection norms discussed in Chapter 4 and the idea of law-abiding equilibria examined in Chapter 5. This concept of power fits nicely into the agenda of endogenizing government, discussed in the previous chapter and to be discussed further in Chapter 8.

Let me begin with the standard economist's assumption, namely that all individuals are selfish utility maximizers (to the extent that they are so in traditional neoclassical theory). I do not do this to defend this axiom but to demonstrate that even without relaxing this axiom we can accommodate in our models concepts and results that have generally been left to the charge of other social scientists. The point of departure with standard economic theory lies in permitting the relation between two agents to be affected by, and to affect, each of their relations with others.

The significance of going from two-person to three-person relationships – that is, from the "dyad" to the "triad"[1] – has been discussed in sociological writings, and most emphatically in the works of George Simmel (Simmel, 1950; *see also* Caplow, 1968). Simmel argued that as soon as the direct relation between two individuals is appended by an indirect one, operating via a third person, there occurs a qualitative change from a formal sociological standpoint. Adapting somewhat to the context of *economic* analysis, the term **dyad** will be used here to describe models where whether or not i agrees to trade with j does not affect i's relation with k. Hence, a dyad is not a two-person society but a society where individuals *interact pairwise*. The term **triad** will be reserved for models that allow triangular and, more generally, multiple relations.

"In previous models current transactions (so long as they are legal) do not result in changed relations with uninvolved parties in subsequent transactions," argues Akerlof (1976: 609) in setting out to construct his extremely insightful model of caste relations, which is, in essence, triadic. He goes on: "On the contrary, in a caste society any transaction that breaks the caste taboos changes the subsequent behavior of uninvolved parties towards the caste-breakers." Once triadic relations are allowed, we are able to explain many interesting social concepts within the bounds of our models. Caste is one of them. Power is the other.

Are models in economics dyadic? In general equilibrium models, for instance, what happens to person i may be influenced profoundly by what happens in parts of the economy with which i has no direct dealings. So, in this sense, much of traditional economics is not dyadic. But there is another sense in which it is so. What transpires in the social relation between i and j (for instance, whether i talks to j in a manner that is respectful to j) is treated implicitly as irrelevant to what happens between i and k. And this is what Akerlof is referring to. Formally, game-theoretic models have the catholicity to accommodate even these kinds of triadic interactions, and they often do so. But in modeling power, ostracism and caste, and to see how these can influence economic outcomes, "triadic interaction" deserves the primacy that is only rarely given to it.

The first model in this chapter (Section 6.2) is a formalization of some intuitive ideas of Václav Havel. It gives us insight into how the state, even when it is fully endogenous, can be powerful; and it also helps us understand a certain kind of totalitarianism.

---

[1] These are the popular English translations for Simmel's *zweierverbindung* and *verbindung zu dreien*.

The second model (Section 6.3), which is more explicitly triadic, demonstrates how an agent may agree to an exchange from which he gets negative utility, that is, he loses out. In doing so, it takes us some distance toward formalizing the idea of coercion, a theme that is directly addressed in Section 6.3. It is argued that what appears to be a voluntary exchange may be indirectly coercive. I have used this to explain certain kinds of oppressive relationships in backward agrarian relations and in international relations. Section 6.4 is a digression on some further implications of coercion, and is a deviation from the rest of the chapter in being a conventional dyadic model. Section 6.5, which is an extension of the triadic model, is an attempt to explain the *modus operandi* of the so-called "man of influence."[2]

Before going on to build models, it is useful to see why power has proved so hard to formalize. This is a subject that has drawn in some of the most eminent thinkers and social scientists – Max Weber, Bertrand Russell, Gaetano Mosca, Friedrich Hayek, John Kenneth Galbraith and Steven Lukes, to name a few. All agree that power is, broadly speaking, the ability of one person to get another person to do something that is of advantage to the former but not in the latter's interest. It proves, however, very hard to go beyond this. Even in this chapter, with the advantage of modern game theory, all I will do is construct some examples that are indicative rather than definitive.

The difficulty may be appreciated by considering Galbraith's (1983) classification of the three channels of power: condign, compensatory and conditioned. **Condign power** wins submission by the threat to punish or hurt, whereas **compensatory power** wins submission by offering rewards. In both of these cases, the one who submits to power is aware of it. There are, however, also situations where the oppressed are so habituated to their situation that they are unaware of being oppressed. It is almost as if their preferences are in conformity with what they are expected to do for the oppressor. This latter Galbraith called **conditioned power**. It is similar to what Lukes (1974) has called the "three-dimensional view of power."

First, note that it is not always possible to distinguish between condign and compensatory power. Suppose a feudal landlord tells his serf to do something that is against the latter's wishes – for instance, to hit another person (action H) – and adds: "If you do not do H, I will not give you any food to eat." At first sight this is a threat, and if, upon learning it, the serf does commit H, this would seem like a case of condign power. However, the

---

[2] This chapter draws on my earlier paper (Basu, 1986).

landlord could have said the same thing as above but phrased it differently: "If you do H, I will reward you by giving you food." And this would make it look like compensatory power. There seems to be a deep ambiguity here because a punishment is often the denial of a reward, just as a reward can be the remission of punishment.[3] It is true that there are cases where we can intuitively differentiate between punishment and the denial of a reward, but a formal distinction between the two is by no means easy. Moreover, even in basing our judgment on intuition, we encounter a rather broad "grey zone" where classification seems hard. In distinguishing between these, we need a prior notion of what is normal, what is expected, and a prior sense of rights. It is interesting to note that Dixit and Nalebuff (1991) have discussed very similar categories and met with the same problem of a blurred line of distinction.

Another difficulty is that, in the case of compensatory power and, by extension, often for condign power, it is not clear who exercises power over whom. Suppose a certain politician, who happens to be rich (call her person R), offers to compensate another politician (person P) financially if he will vote in parliament against a motion that he, left to himself, wanted to support. Suppose P votes against the motion and collects the money. Presumably this is the kind of case where one would say that R has exercised compensatory power over P. Indeed we can think of R as going home and boasting to her husband how she has managed to exercise power over P by making him vote in a way that is against his innate preference. But by the same token we can imagine P telling his wife how he has exercised power over R and got "the miser R to part with her money, which is against her innate preference, by offering to compensate her with my altered vote." The trouble is that getting something by making a compensation has an important element of symmetry in it, and it is therefore not a convenient instrument for defining power, which, by its very nature, is asymmetric.[4]

[3] One must be careful not to make the mistake that economists often make, namely that of dismissing even a conceptual distinction between giving a punishment and denying reward. What is punishment and what is denial of reward should depend on what we consider to be a person's status quo, or normal state. To the extent that this is ambiguous, the dividing line between punishment and denial of reward will be inherently ambiguous. But that does not mean that it does not exist.

[4] This problem was noted by Hayek (1960: chapter 9). However, Hayek uses this to construct an argument about how transactions affected through the market cannot be coercive, because in markets people have the choice of taking an option or leaving it. He tried to make an exception for monopolies, but one gets the inescapable feeling in reading Hayek that his conclusions are priors in his mind and therefore the process of reasoning, which does not at all clearly reach his conclusions, *seems to him* to do so.

Galbraith's idea of conditioned power is extremely important and perhaps the most pervasive form of power that one encounters in society.
The trouble with this is that it is as yet too broad an idea to be formalizable.
Yet, the story that I am about to tell comes closer to this third kind of power
than the other two. While it is true that conditioning often results in the
alteration of the preference of the oppressed, I do not go into that here.
The power I describe is conditioned in the sense that it permeates through
society; the oppressor does not have to do anything special to obtain
compliance.

6.2. Political Power, Havel's Allegory, and McCarthyism

History has seen dictatorships where the rulers and the ruled have been
"two socially defined and separate communities,"[5] with the former controlling and, perhaps, even tyrannizing the latter. In such "classical dictatorships," power is concentrated on one side – on the side of the rulers, who
devise methods of rewards and retributions to dominate the majority and
sustain their regime. Such a dictatorship can be tyrannical, but it is com-
prehensible: everyone can see who keeps it going. In some ways, more
frightening is what Václav Havel calls a "post-totalitarian system." It may
be more tyrannical or less; that is not its distinguishing mark. Its distinguishing mark is that it is faceless. In it, power is diffused through society.
The line that divides *society* in a classical dictatorship, "runs through *each
person*" in a post-totalitarian system, in which "everyone is, in his own
way, both a victim and a supporter of the system."

I will return to the work of Havel later. I argue that Havel's idea of a
diffused dictatorship is a coherent concept that can be interpreted very
precisely in terms of equilibrium notions.

Let us begin with a simple case of a **classical dictatorship**. Consider
an unwanted ruler (or a ruling class[6]) who punishes whoever does not
cooperate with him. Suppose that the agony of punishment is greater than
the benefits a person gets from *individually* not cooperating. Then, even if
it were true that *if everybody chose* noncooperation the ruler would get
overthrown and everybody would be happier, *no individual would choose*

---

[5] This and the following quotes in this section are from Havel's (1986) essay.

[6] In his classic essay, Mosca (1939) had argued that power never resides in an individual but in
a ruling *class*. He had also argued that neither can it reside in the whole community. Both claims
can be and have been contested, the latter – as we shall just see – for an interesting and intricate
reason.

noncooperation and the ruler would survive, to the misfortune of all. This is the standard "coordination problem" and is the popular conception of political power.[7]

For a first sketch of a post-totalitarian system, I begin with a very simple characterization and then follow it up with a more sophisticated treatment. We begin by talking about a king, who is in a sense exogenous to the "game" and, as will be transparent later, the equilibrium can survive even without such a king. So the outcome that I will describe implies a conception of the state that is fully endogenous, as suggested in Chapter 5.

Consider a model in which the direct punishment for disloyalty to the king is small (causing k units of disutility to its recipient) and, in particular, smaller than the benefit an individual gets by choosing noncooperation (say, n units), i.e. $k < n$. Then the above straightforward argument as to why citizens cooperate with the government no longer holds true. However, given the following definition and two assumptions, the sustenance of the unwanted ruler is guaranteed. (Here, as above, I assume that there is a definite behavior called "noncooperation." What exactly that entails is not immediately relevant to us and, so, is left unspecified.)

Definition: A person is considered **disloyal** to the king or the regime if either he does not cooperate or he maintains relations with someone who is disloyal.[8]

Assumption 1: Everybody believes that no one else would be disloyal.

Assumption 2: $n - k - d < 0$, where d is the cost to an individual of being ostracized.

Consider an individual contemplating noncooperation. This will give him a joy of n units, a punishment of k units and, given his "conjecture" about others (embodied in Assumption 1) he expects an additional cost of d units. These, given Assumption 2, add up to a negative number and so noncooperation is not worthwhile. Everybody reasons in this manner and the regime persists.

Note that Assumption 2 *could* be valid even with $k = 0$. This means that even if the direct punishment meted out by the ruler is nonexistent, individuals would cooperate with the regime and thereby help its sustenance.

---

[7] This is what Crozier (1969) has in mind in his chapter, "Power through Terror." Russell (1938) discusses several examples in his chapter 6. A context-specific and, as a consequence, more formal discussion of power occurs in Desai (1984).

[8] This simple statement has a small risk of causing a misunderstanding of the term "loyalty." But I leave it like this because a more elaborate and risk-free statement occurs shortly.

The regime persists because of mutual suspicion between people. Each person is worried about what the others will do to him, and so he or she cooperates. And, of course, as a moment's contemplation will show, there need not even exist a ruler in the system. "Cooperation" could merely be the name of a certain mode of behavior (which no one likes) or act of obeisance to some institution. The power that sustains this regime pervades the entire society. And everyone is – as Havel describes – "both a victim and a supporter of the system."

We shall now give the model more sophistication by describing an exchange economy and by deriving some of the parameters treated as primitives above. To do this properly, let us begin from scratch.

Consider an economy with a set, N, of individuals or citizens. We assume that there are n citizens; that is, N has n members, and $n > 1$. The number of goods is also n. Every individual i has an endowment of e (which is assumed to be greater than 1) units of good i and no other goods.[9] Every citizen i has the same utility function given by:

$$U^i = \sqrt{x_1^i} + \sqrt{x_2^i} + \ldots + \sqrt{x_n^i}, \tag{6.1}$$

where x_j^i is the amount of good j consumed by person i.

The general equilibrium of this exchange economy occurs at the price vector $p^* = [1, \ldots, 1]$. Essentially, what this means is that at this price the demand for each good is equal to supply. This is easy to check. Given that the economy is symmetric, all prices must be the same; and setting price equal to 1 is a matter of normalization.[10] More formally, given the price vector, p^*, the usual consumer maximization yields

$$x_j^i = e/n, \text{ for all } i \text{ and } j.$$

That is, person i's demand for good j is equal to e/n units. Hence, aggregate demand for good j equals e (since there are n individuals each demanding e/n), which is also the aggregate supply of good j. Hence, p^* is an equilibrium price vector.

Note that, at equilibrium, each person gets $n\sqrt{(e/n)}$ utils. This equilibrium will be referred to simply as the **Walras equilibrium**.

Now consider the same economy again, this time with a dictator or a king added to it. He does no good for the economy but charges from every individual one unit of his endowment. This the dictator uses for his own

---

[9] This identification of each commodity with a person, whereby Mr. Apple sells apples, is purely for mathematical convenience.

[10] The analysis would actually be unchanged if, instead of taking all prices to be 1, we set it at some other arbitrary (positive) number p.

merriment and protection. The two essential elements in this model are a definition and a conjecture. These are as follows:

Definition 1: In this economy a person is described as **disloyal** (to the king) if (a) he does not give the king one unit or (b) he trades with someone who is disloyal.

Conjecture: Every citizen conjectures that no other citizen j wants to be disloyal.[11]

A clarification concerning the definition of loyalty is worthwhile here. The definition given above, although it generally conveys the right meaning, is not quite accurate since we can define arbitrary sets of people who are "disloyal." This definition should be treated as a quick reminder of a more precise definition, which is stated as Definition 3, below, but for which we first need to define "k-disloyalty" recursively:

Definition 2: A person is k-disloyal if he trades with a $(k - 1)$-disloyal person. A person is 1-disloyal if he does not give the king 1 unit.

Definition 3: A person is **disloyal** if there exists k such that he is k-disloyal.

The conjecture described above may, at first sight, convey the impression that i believes that others would be loyal under *all* circumstances. This need not be. It is possible and more interesting to suppose that behind the formal and brief statement of the conjecture above is the following: i conjectures that no j would be disloyal unless assured of general disloyalty, and i also conjectures that each j lacks such assurance.

We shall suppose that whoever is disloyal incurs the king's displeasure. This, in turn, could take any form. For instance, it could mean being debarred from the annual royal ball or being whipped. It is not necessary to specify this. We simply need to assume that everybody knows what "incurring the king's displeasure" entails. Let k_i (≥ 0) be the disutility to person i of incurring such displeasure. In other words, k_i is the direct cost to person i of being disloyal.

In this economy, the same price vector as before (that is, p^*), with everybody paying the king one unit, can be an *equilibrium*, in the sense that, given their conjectures, no one expects to do better by altering his or her strategy. Let us check that this is an equilibrium in this sense. If person i pays the king 1 unit, his disposable endowment is $e - 1$, and usual

---

[11] On some occasions we will use a slightly more elaborate conjecture: "Every $i \in N$ conjectures that no $j \in N\backslash\{i\}$ who is currently loyal would want to be disloyal in other situations."

consumer-utility maximization shows that his demand for good j will be given by $(e - 1)/n$. That is,

$$x_j^i = (e - 1)/n \text{ , for all } i \text{ and } j.$$

Hence the aggregate demand for good j is $e - 1$, which is also the aggregate supply to the market. Hence, demand equals supply for each good.

What remains to be checked is that no individual expects to do better by not giving the king 1 unit. If i gives the king 1 unit, he buys $(e - 1)/n$ units of each good and so gets a total utility of $n\sqrt{(e - 1)/n}$. Suppose i does not give the king 1 unit. Then anybody who trades with him will be considered disloyal to the king. Hence i, given his conjecture, will not expect anybody to trade with him. Therefore, his utility from consumption of goods will be $\sqrt{e}$. In addition, there is the direct cost of the king's displeasure, that is, k_i. So his total expected utility from this strategy is $\sqrt{e} - k_i$. If

$$n\sqrt{\left(\frac{e - 1}{n}\right)} > \sqrt{e} - k_i, \quad \text{for all } i,$$

then it is not worthwhile for any i to deny the king 1 unit. Hence, if this condition holds, then for each person to give the king 1 unit is part of an equilibrium.[12]

Assume for a moment that $k_i = 0$. The above condition becomes (by squaring both sides)

$$n(e - 1) > e \tag{6.2}$$

Clearly this can be true. If, for instance, n is large then (6.2) is likely to be satisfied. In other words, if one lives in a large interactive society, the threat of ostracism is likely to be a good deterrent. The same threat would not work on the Unabomber living in the forests of Montana.

Assume from now on that (6.2) is true.

What is interesting is that even if individuals did not mind at all incurring the king's displeasure, that is k_i were zero (for instance, because they

---

[12] One question that may be raised is: Could the *king* do better? What I have implicitly assumed here is that a king is not a "rational agent" in the conventional sense (an assumption that cannot be faulted for gross unrealism) and that his behavior is exogenously given. An alternative strategy would be to exploit the fact that, as it stands, there is no *obvious* way for the king to improve his condition. (For instance, if he tried raising the 1 unit demand to 2 units, this could disturb the conjectures, so that, some might start believing that, given the larger cost of loyalty now, others might not mind being disloyal; and this could end up with no one paying the king anything.) By bringing in some extra assumptions, it may be possible to show that the king in fact cannot improve his welfare. An alternative line of enquiry is to see how much a king would be able to expropriate in models of this kind, if he were rational.

are bold and hate to curry favor, or because the displeasure takes the form of a mild snub from the king), they would continue to show loyalty and thereby help sustain the evil regime. And what is more, there need not even be a king. The act of loyalty could merely be a self-sustaining "ritual" of wasting 1 unit of endowment. Individuals are not worried about what the king will do to them but what the others will do to them. And it is this interpersonal suspicion which sustains the suboptimal equilibrium in this chillingly Kafkaesque world. This is a sketch of Havel's "post-totalitarian system" with its "blind automatism." No individual is at the helm; it is a "dictatorship of the ritual."[13]

The fact that the equilibrium survives (and the ritual of giving the king 1 unit persists) even when all k_i's are zero (that is, there is no direct punishment that the king delivers) answers a problem that Malinowski had raised in a paper that he had published, uncharacteristically, in an economics journal (Malinowski, 1921). Plainly, he was directing the question at economists. Trobriand Islanders, living on a coral archipelago off the coast of New Guinea, have, as with all tribal societies, an elaborate organization of hierarchy, with each district being headed by a tribal chief or the *guya'u*, and elaborate customs of gift exchange. Where the chief is involved, however, seemingly the gifts go one way, from the ordinary tribal members to the chief. By Malinowski's (p. 8) own calculation, "by various channels . . . about 30 per cent of the whole food production of his district finds its way into the large, finely-decorated yam houses of the chief." The chief then exchanges some of this food for other forms of wealth – ceremonial axe-blades, necklaces of red shell discs – and displays them proudly. But why do the members of the tribe give the chief so much of their produce? These are clearly not in direct exchange for anything. Malinowski does mention that the chief has his henchmen, but that in itself does not explain people's compliance (and, moreover, raises the question of why the henchmen do what they are supposed to do). The answer in all likelihood lies in the kind of reasoning that the above model exemplifies, where the same people who pay the chief his "due" end up monitoring one another.[14]

There is now quite a substantial body of literature on oligopoly equilibria based on "conjectures" of agents. An important question that has arisen in this context is whether the conjectures postulated in a model are

[13] As Joseph K wonders in Kafka's *The Trial*, just before the death sentence is carried out on him, "Where was the judge whom he had never seen? Where was the High Court, to which he had never penetrated?"

[14] For a discussion of some similar forms of monitoring in fishing communities in India, *see* Platteau and Abraham (1987). *See also* Basu, Jones and Schlicht (1987).

consistent or not? There are some game-theoretic difficulties with the concept of consistency and, moreover, the model and equilibrium just described are not founded in game theory, and so there is no need to delve deeper into this subject. Suffice it to note that if $n > 2$, then (even if $k_i = 0$) the above equilibrium turns out to have "consistent conjectures" in the sense of Bresnahan (1981). A **consistent conjecture equilibrium** is basically an equilibrium where the conjectures of individuals would, *given a chance*, be borne out.

Let us spell out the conjecture in our model. What is relevant in the equilibrium is that i conjectures that if he does not give the king 1 unit then others will refuse to trade with him. We want to check whether this conjecture would actually be true. Without loss of generality, suppose that person 1 does not give the king his due, and let us see what person 2 will do. If person 2 trades with person 1, then, given 2's conjecture, he will expect no one else[15], i.e. 3, 4, . . . , to trade with him. Hence person 2's expected utility would be $2\sqrt{e/2}$ units. (Recall that $k_2 = 0$; if he trades only with person 1, he will spend half his income on the two goods he consumes; and given that he is anyway labeled disloyal, he has no reason to give the king 1 unit.) If he does not trade with person 1, his utility – it is easy to see – will be equal to $(n-1)\sqrt{(e-1)/(n-1)}$. This is greater than $\sqrt{e/2}$. Hence, he will not trade with person 1, and therefore 1's conjecture is valid.[16] There is a problem of pushing this reasoning to higher orders of punishment, because when there is only one person left, the argument can begin to unwind through a process of backward induction. But it seems fair to ignore this problem, because this model is not that of a formal game and because, even in games, the logic of backward induction (see Chapters 2 and 3) is not confirmed by our intuition or experimental evidence. Moreover, there are ways of rewriting the model (see p. 88) to avoid the backward-induction problem.

This model raises an interesting ethical question. Normally, we castigate individuals who, by currying favor with an unwanted leadership, help to sustain the regime. This model shows that people who do so may be entirely a victim of their "situation." This can be elaborated by supposing that the economy has two provinces: the inner and the outer. The inner province is exactly like the economy described above. The outer province has a set M

---

[15] This may be clearer if we think of the conjecture in a more elaborate manner, via the concept of "k-disloyalty."

[16] What this establishes is a kind of "first-order" consistency of conjectures, because we are not showing that person 2's conjecture (about what others will do to him if he trades with person 1, who has refused to pay the king his due) would be true under perturbation.

(whose member of elements = *m*) of individuals, numbered $n + 1$, $n + 2$, ..., $n + m$. Every person *i* in *M* has an endowment of *e* units of good *i* and his utility function is given by:

$$u^i = \sqrt{x^i_{n+1}} + \ldots + \sqrt{x^i_{n+m}}.$$

The only difference between the two provinces is that the people want to consume different kinds of goods. Let disloyal be defined in the same way as above, and let the conjecture be the same. It is now easy to construct an equilibrium where every individual in *N* gives the king 1 unit, and all those in *M* refuse to give the king anything. At this equilibrium, the set *N* will soon get to be labeled the "caucus" around the king who through their fawning and show of loyalty help sustain the regime, whereas the people of the outer province would allegedly be the "courageous ones" refusing to comply with the king's unfair demands. But, of course, what is clear to us from a distance is that the members of the caucus and the members of *M* could be identical human beings in terms of their attitude to the king, but merely those caught in different "situations." It is interesting to note that the k_i's for the elements of *N* could in fact be lower than the k_i's of the members of *M*. That is, the members of *N* could be the ones who actually care less for the king's favors.

Finally, let us take a look at the role of coalitions, which Akerlof (1976) showed could break the grip of caste. Return to the original equilibrium. Clearly, if all *n* members decided to form a coalition and not to pay the king, they could establish the Pareto-superior Walras equilibrium. Why do they not do this? There are, of course, the standard arguments in terms of trans-actions or organization cost. There is, however, a more natural reason here. It seems reasonable to suppose that the definition of disloyalty, above, should include a third category: (c) he tries to form a breakaway coalition. Now, if we assume that to have a breakaway coalition somebody has to make the first move, and that individuals conjecture that the probability of others joining in is below a certain level, then a breakaway coalition would never get formed.

Václav Havel's (1986) allegorical account of dictatorship in Eastern Europe of the 1970s and 1980s is a real-life counterpart of the above abstract model. He argues that the system there was not a "classical" dicta-torship but a "faceless" one where society cannot be partitioned between the rulers and the ruled. He labeled it a "post-totalitarian system," where totalitarianism permeates society. In it, the same people who are strangled by power are the ones who constitute power. Havel's beautiful writing and surreal description are reminiscent of the austere prose of one of his countrymen. In Kafka's *The Trial*, Joseph K, an ordinary bank official, is suddenly put under arrest, though for what crime it is never made clear. As a frustrated and nervous K fights this charge, which he does not fully comprehend, he is drawn into a labyrinthine bureaucracy and legal system, where everybody is a minion. There is no one *in charge of* the situation; there is no one he can turn to for pardon or to let his anger out. It is this facelessness that makes it so hopeless for Joseph K. Whomever he encounters in this surreal world is a cog in the wheel.[17] Havel brings this same idea out sharply in his perceptive account of a typical greengrocer in a post-totalitarian state.

> "The manager of a fruit and vegetable shop places in his window, among the onions and carrots, the slogan: 'Workers of the world unite.'
>
> "Why does he do it? . . . Is he genuinely enthusiastic about the idea of unity among the workers of the world?"

Havel argues that the answer to that is "no." The greengrocer does it because everybody does it. The poster was delivered to him "from the enterprise headquarters along with the onions and the carrots. . . . If he were to refuse, there could be trouble. . . . someone might even accuse him of disloyalty." He would then be persecuted and "his superiors will harass him."

That such things happen, we all know. Where Havel shows his insight is not in his analysis of the greengrocer but in his analysis of the superiors – those who harass the dissenting greengrocers. Why would they harass a greengrocer if he refused to put up the poster? Is it because they are, unlike the grocer, committed to the government? The answer once again is "no," for the superiors are, in turn, exactly like the greengrocer. "Most of those who administer these sanctions, however, will not do so from any authentic inner conviction, but simply under pressure from 'conditions,' the same conditions that had once pressured the greengrocer to display the official slogans. . . . The executors, therefore, essentially behave just like everyone else, to a greater or lesser degree: as components of the post-totalitarian system, as agents of its automatism, as petty instruments of the social auto-totality." Such is the web of interpersonal conjectures that no individual would try to deviate from the "rules of the game" if he does not "want to be excluded" and to "fall into isolation."

---

[17] Analysts have read into *The Trial* the power of guilt, the pervasive sense of sin that human beings have to contend with, homoeroticism and expressionism, mirroring the age of anxiety in art that was about to begin in Europe. But *The Trial* is also social science. As Sussman (1993: 9) rightly observes, "Through the image of the Court, Kafka exemplifies the encompassing and bewildering potentials of twentieth-century organizations."

Economists encountering this argument will question why the "victims" do not collusively overthrow such an oppressive regime or, in case there is such a well-identified person, the oppressor. This misses the point, as noted above, that for a collusive protest to begin, typically, someone or some few need to stand up and initiate it. And the first person who does so has to take a risk (may be unbearably high for most ordinary mortals) that the protest will not take off and he or she will be isolated, ostracized and punished. One recalls Erich Maria Remarque's chilling account from *The Night in Lisbon* (New York: Harcourt, 1964, p. 91):

> "The SS men cast furious, challenging glances at me as they passed, and the prisoner stared at me out of paralyzed eyes, making a gesture that seemed to be a plea for help. . . . It was a scene as old as humankind: the minions of power, the victim, the eternal third, the onlooker, who doesn't raise a finger in defense of the victim, who makes no attempt to set him free, because he fears for his own safety, which for that very reason is always in danger."

In Havel's system, no individual is to blame. From the head of the state to the greengrocer, everybody is a "victim" of a situation. There is something almost metaphysical in this kind of power, where the enemy cannot be identified. Individuals, innocently going about their daily chores, in their totality give rise to this power, which then transcends them and acquires its own *raison d'être*.

Reality, of course, is always more complicated; and there were no doubt some individuals who stood to gain from the totalitarianism. What is of interest to us is that there *need* be no such persons, as our model showed. It is not impossible to have dictatorships with no dictators. And the first step in controlling this latent (or not so latent) power in societies must be to recognize it and demystify it. That is precisely what the model in this section has tried to do.

One does not have to search too hard to find oppression of this kind. Peer pressure among school children, the pressure to conform to unpleasant caste norms in traditional Indian societies, and McCarthyism in the United States in the 1950s are all examples of this.[18] McCarthyism, understood as a general term describing a period in the United States of persecution of people believed to be Communists, or sympathetic to Communists, or sympathetic to those sympathetic to Communists, . . . , began well before Senator Joseph McCarthy came into the picture and, in weakening form, persisted after his fall from prominence in 1954. Some of its roots were

---

[18] Eric Posner's (1998) insightful analysis of why symbolic laws, such as those against flag burning, find so much support is based on a very similar argument. *See*, specifically, his pp. 131–3.

undoubtedly external. With the rise of the Soviet Union and the ruthless expansionism of Stalin, there were some genuine fears in the United States. McCarthy, beginning with his speech on February 9, 1950, to the Women's Republican Club of Wheeling, West Virginia, where he claimed that he had an actual list of Communist agents in the state department, fueled this fear. It is true that quasi-official mechanisms were used to carry out some of this persecution. In 1938 the House Un-American Activities Committee (HUAC) was set up and this played an important role in the spread of McCarthyism in the fifties. There were during the McCarthy purges also the occasional references to the Taft–Hartley Act of 1947, which prohibited trade union leaders from professing "belief in" and "association with" Communism. But none of this would have worked, as Schrecker (1994: 76) reminds us, "had they not been reinforced by the private sector." Very often, all that existed were lists of people believed to have un-American or pro-Communist sympathies, and it was left to others to use the list as they wished. The trouble with this vague charge of "un-American activities" was that to defend someone against this charge was to risk yourself being categorized as un-American. So, like disloyalty in our model, un-Americanism was infectious. One risked contracting the label if one tried to defend someone already charged of it. Not surprisingly, the initial lists had second- and third-order effects, which are crucial for the above kind of equilibrium to persist. Thus, liberal governors tried to cleanse the government of those charged as above for fear that they themselves would otherwise be vulnerable to similar charges.

As is well known, the blacklists spread from state department, through trade unions to even the entertainment industry. In 1950 American Business Consultants published *Red Channels*, which consisted of a list of 151 actors, writers, musicians and directors with *alleged* Communist sympathies.[19] As Schrecker (p. 80) notes, the list – despite having no force of law behind it – had a devastating effect. "By 1951, the television networks and their sponsors no longer hired anyone whose name was in the book, and *the prohibition soon spread to anyone who seemed controversial.*"[20]

What is striking in all these examples is the extent to which the atmosphere of persecution ran on its own steam. Eric Posner (1998: 782) is right

---

[19] Leonard Bernstein, Aaron Copland, Zero Mostel and Orson Welles figured on the list. Humphrey Bogart, who had defended some of the persons in Hollywood charged of pro-Communist sympathies, narrowly escaped the list by agreeing to publish an article in a fan magazine confessing: "I am no Communist," just an "American dope."

[20] On this, *see* – using the word literally for a change – the film *The Front* (1976, Devon Co.), in which Woody Allen, a quasi-literate bartender, agrees to pretend to be a screenplay writer for actual writers who are ostracized by the entertainment industry, thereby giving rise to situations that are both comic and sinister.

when he observes that "one of the most striking aspects of McCarthyism was that this campaign resulted from McCarthy's entrepreneurial modification of focal points, not from changes in the law." Just as I discussed in Chapter 5 how my widowed aunt did not dare depart from the norms of her society for fear not of the state but of being ostracized by society at large, and Akerlof (1976) has written about how in caste societies people do not deviate from caste norms for fear of being labeled an "outcaste," during the McCarthy period "there is a fear of being labeled a 'subversive' if one departs from the orthodox party line. That charge – if leveled against a young man or young woman – may have profound effects. It may ruin a youngster's business or professional career." These words are of the US Supreme Court Justice, William O. Douglas, one of the most courageous critics of McCarthyism ("The Black Silence of Fear," *New York Times Magazine*, January 13, 1952). He began the essay by noting that if a person left the country and went away to "the back regions of the world" and returned after several months, "he will be shocked at the . . . intolerance of great segments of the American press . . . and many leaders in public office . . . He will find that thought is being standardized." And he ended with the words: "Our weakness grows when we become intolerant of opposing ideas, depart from our standards of civil liberties, and borrow the policeman's philosophy from the enemy we detest." It is evident from his essay that the enemy he was referring to was the same kind of totalitarian state that is the subject of Havel's attack.

6.3. Triadic Markets and Coercion

In this section I turn to another kind of triadic relation – a more explicit one that occurs in small groups, where the agents involved know one another. As sociologists have noted, a person can on occasions benefit from being "seen with" some other person, who happens to be powerful or famous or rich.[21] Here the gain comes from what happens to the person's interaction with *others* by virtue of being seen with the "powerful" person.

  Turning this around note that, when this is so, the "powerful" person will be in a position to exercise special powers over the person who benefits from being seen with her, because by threatening to cut off connections with him, she can imperil his relationship with the uninvolved others. This kind of interaction is not an imaginary construct but quite common inside

---

[21] This is related to the discussion of "association goods" in Section 4.3.

organizations, bureaucracies and village societies, and in dealings between nations. In Basu (1986) I tried to model this kind of triadic expropriation in the context of feudal, village societies. That model was, however, not strictly game-theoretic.[22] In the remainder of this section, I want to develop a formal game model to illustrate triadic expropriation. It is sufficiently abstract for it to be applicable beyond rural markets. In fact, it will be argued that to analyze a certain class of international sanctions it is essential to construct triadic models.

Consider the use of sanctions in international relations. There is an enormous volume of literature on this (*see, for instance*, Eaton and Engers, 1992), but most of this treats the problem of sanctions in dyadic terms, as a problem involving a sender and a target.[23] In reality, sanctions are often triadic, such as the US threat to cut off certain trade links with any nation that trades with or invests in Cuba. Plainly, these are not just sanctions against a country – Cuba in this case – but explicitly involve third parties, namely the trading partners of Cuba. I am referring here to the United States' Helms–Burton Act of 1996. It is meant to penalize companies or nations doing business in Cuba. Its aim is to bring pressure on Cuba but its strategy is to involve companies and nations which may otherwise have nothing to do with Cuban–American relations. The law has, for instance, been used to warn Sherritt, a Canadian company, and also some Italian companies.

There are many important questions that a triadic model should be able to answer. Do triadic sanctions have greater effect than direct sanctions? Is a nation that is more open economically more prone to triadic expropriation? What will happen to wages and interest rates if a rural market has triadic links? But these are not questions for me to go into here. I am here interested in the more general issue of whether triadic markets can shed light on coercion and liberty. Suppose that individuals can only make take-it-or-leave-it offers to one another, as they do in market economies. At first sight it appears that there can be no coercion in such a model, because

---

[22] An attempted formalization occurs in Naqvi and Wemhoner (1995) (see also Janakarajan and Subramanian, 1992; Deshpande, 1999; Villanger, 1999; and Hatlebakk, 2000). Another recent formalization occurs in Chambers and Quiggin (1998) though their interest is not in the gaming aspect of the relation. Instead, they question the realism of the conventional assumption that the reservation utility of the exploited agent is exogenous, and formally model the case in which the exploiter is able to influence the reservation utility level.

[23] An interesting recent paper on which I am, as yet, unable to comment at any length is by Maggi (1999). He models the case of a set of countries that interact bilaterally, and he shows the role that a multilateral organization such as the World Trade Organisation (WTO) can play even when it has no power to directly enforce agreements.

agents need not accept an offer unless it benefits them. What the model demonstrates is that the answer may be more complicated.[24]

In order to keep the model very simple, I will develop it through an example. Suppose there is a landlord (agent 1), a laborer (agent 2) and a merchant or a moneylender (agent 3), the triangle in Fig. 6.1 depicting their possible links.

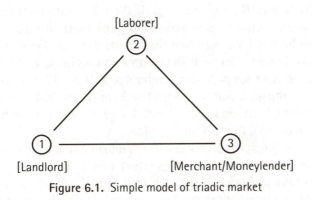

Figure 6.1. Simple model of triadic market

The landlord has a plot of land and needs the laborer's labor in order to be able to produce goods. Let the production function be $X = X(L)$, where X is the output and L the amount of labor applied to the land. This entire labor has to come from agent 2, the laborer. This could be because the village norms do not permit the landlord or the merchant to work. If the landlord pays the worker a wage of w, the landlord's profit π is given by:

$$\pi(w, L) = X(L) - wL$$

The landlord in this model has to choose w and L (we denote the choice as a pair (w, L)) and make a take-it-or-leave it offer to the worker. How badly agent 1 can squeeze agent 2 depends on the latter's reservation utility. The essential interest in triadic markets comes from the fact that agent 1 may be able to threaten 2 that if she rejects 1's offer, then not only will she lose out on the interaction with 1 but agent 1 will make sure that her relation (trade, exchange or whatever it is) with agent 3, the merchant, will be broken. How does agent 1 achieve this? By giving the following *threat*:

---

[24] For a model of power based on a very similar setting, but pursuing a different line of argument, see Bowles and Gintis (1992). Bardhan (1992) provides a lucid account of alternative notions of *economic* power.

If agent 2 turns down my offer, then I will not cooperate with anybody who does business with agent 2.[25]

What will be shown is that there are circumstances where such threats have bite. That is, it will not be in the interest of agent 3 to do business with agent 2 if 2 rejects 1's offer. To show this as simply as possible, suppose that 2 and 3 normally do some business with each other (the merchant may be giving the laborer credit or selling goods), from which agents 2 and 3 earn, respectively, B_2 and B_3, where $B_i > 0$. If there is no trade, they both earn zero. Moreover, if either agent refuses to participate in trade, there is no trade. It will be assumed here that the laborer's (leisure) cost of providing each unit of labor is c. Hence, if the laborer accepts (w, L) and earns X from her interaction with agent 3, the laborer's payoff or utility is given by $wL - cL + X$. Of course, X will turn out to be B_2 or 0 depending on whether or not there is trade between agents 2 and 3. Agent 2 will choose her strategy in order to maximize this payoff function.

For agent 1's threat to be credible, there must be scope for multiple equilibria in the interaction between agents 1 and 3. In most relationships, between nations or between the rich in a feudal village, it is natural to suppose that the interaction can have several equilibria. Indeed, for most nations, once a threat is given publicly and the occasion arises for carrying it out, it is in the interest of the nation giving the threat to carry it out. At times, the nation can tie its own hands by making the threat into a law. An example of this is the US Helms–Burton Act referred to above. It is because such laws are binding and the United States wanted to have *some* flexibility that in this case it was explicitly built into the law that the President could waive it.

Continuing with our example, all we need to say about the game between 1 and 3 is that there be at least two equilibria in it, one that is good for both and another that is bad. Any model that accommodates this will do. What follows is the description of the simple game with these properties. I have chosen this game for simplicity, and because it is clear that it does not have to be *this* game. Let us suppose that the landlord and the merchant own some common property, for instance, a pond. Each one of them can use a simple net to catch fish (strategy C) or use some modern machinery

---

[25] With a little more trouble, this threat can be made infectious like the definition of disloyalty in the previous section. All that agent 1 has to say is that he will not trade with anybody who trades with anybody who trades with . . . anybody who trades with a person who turns down his offer. In a three-agent world, this threat is indistinguishable from the threat we are considering, but in an n-agent world it will make a difference, and it will be interesting to analyze the power of these two kinds of threats. As one would expect from the above discussion, the threat can also be couched as an incentive (*see* Janakarajan and Subramanian, 1992).

(strategy D). The modern machine is costly, but once one has it one can catch all the fish, depriving the other of any when the other uses the net. Given this assumption, the game between agents 2 and 3 can be characterized as in the payoff matrix shown in Fig. 6.2.

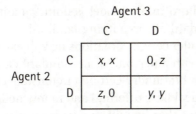

Agent 3

		C	D
Agent 2	C	x, x	0, z
	D	z, 0	y, y

Figure 6.2. Payoff matrix (fishing game)

In this game, $x > z > y > 0$. Hence, if the other person goes for the high technology, you would be best advised to do the same, but both would be better off if both stayed with fishing nets – and, indeed, in that case nobody would have an interest in changing his or her strategy. Hence, this game has two Nash equilibria: (C, C) and (D, D). Given that $x > y$, we can think of strategy C as the cooperative strategy and D as the strategy of defection or noncooperation.

Now think of the full game as follows. In period 1 agent 1 chooses (w, L). In period 2, agent 2 accepts or rejects the offer (w, L). In period 3, agent 3 decides whether to trade with agent 2 or not. In period 4, agents 1 and 3 play the single-shot game described above. Depending on the values of x, y and B_3, it is possible to have an equilibrium where agent 1's *threat* works. Assume

$$x - y > B_3. \tag{6.3}$$

That is, agent 3 has more at stake in his relation with agent 1 than in his relation with agent 2.

The Mexican cement company Cemex that used to do business with Cuba has decided to pull out of Cuba, because it calculates it has more to lose if the United States decides to sanction it under the Helms–Burton Act. In the case of Cemex, a condition like (6.3) must be valid. Suppose it is common knowledge that (D, D) will occur in period 4 if and only if agent 2 rejects agent 1's offer and agent 3 chooses to trade with agent 1. Now, it will be evident to 2 that if 2 turns down 1's offer, 2 will end up being ostracized by 3 as well. Note that if 2 had no dealings with 1 but traded with 3, 2's payoff or income would be B_2. If agent 2 has no dealings with either of them, her income is zero. Hence, if (6.3) holds, the landlord will choose (w, L) in order to maximize $\pi(w, L)$ subject to $wL - cL + B_2 \geq 0$. It is evident that, in equilibrium,[26] agent 2 will have a payoff of 0. This is because in equilibrium $(wL - cL)$ will be equal to $-B_2$. Hence, the totality of what she gets from agent 1 and from the trade with agent 3 will add up to zero.

Note that the landlord in my model is doing qualitatively nothing different from the standard all-or-nothing landlord. In both cases he simply makes it clear that under certain situations he will exercise his freedom not to trade or transact with a person. In the standard case he tells agent 2 he would not trade with him under certain circumstances (namely, if 2 turns down the particular deal he is offering) and in my model he tells 2 the same and in addition tells 3 that he will not trade cooperatively with 3 under certain circumstances. It is also worth pointing out that, as in the standard all-or-nothing monopsony case, it is not necessary to assume that the *threat* is actually announced, but simply that it is simply known.

So, the equilibrium that we have just encountered is, at one level, like a standard market equilibrium. No one holds anybody at gunpoint; they just make offers that others can take or not take, and they also exercise their right not to transact with anybody if they so wish. It may therefore appear that, though agent 2 does very badly in the equilibrium, this is not a case of coercion.

This is an important matter because many economists subscribe to the view that, as long as all choices were voluntary, the market outcome is acceptable. And voluntariness being the opposite of coercion, how we interpret this observation about market outcomes depends on our view of what constitutes coercion (Friedman and Friedman, 1980).

Unfortunately coercion, like power, turns out to be very difficult to define formally.[27] Nevertheless, as with many concepts, we may be able to *recognize* certain cases of coercion and voluntariness as such even without being able to define those terms. And that is the method that I use here. No formal definition is provided; I proceed instead by appealing to the reader's intuition.

Though I say that we can often recognize coercion intuitively when we see it, this does not mean that the intuition is always right. By looking at the same story in different ways and cogitating, our *considered* view often turns out to be different from our first reaction. I would in fact argue

---

[26] The equilibrium, it is not hard to verify, is subgame perfect.

[27] And, as in the case of power, one can find lots of examples of flawed efforts by distinguished people. A serious look at the subject occurs in Nozick (1972), but it illustrates more the shortcomings of standard and legalistic approaches than giving us new ways to formalize it.

that, in the above example, although the transactions between the three individuals is of the standard market kind, and therefore appears to be voluntary, on further thought this is no longer so evident.

Note first of all that if person 2 had *no* interaction with person 1, 2's level of payoff would be B_2, namely, whatever she earns from her trading relation with person 3. Hence, the fact of meeting 1 (and listening to the offer made by 1, with full freedom to take the offer or leave it) lands her with a payoff of 0, that is, a net loss of B_2. So here is a case of exchange where the returns are negative. On the basis of this it is arguable that this is a case of coercion; and it illustrates that just the freedom of individuals to transact or not transact with persons can result in someone being coerced. Ordinary market transactions, which on the face of it look all voluntary, can be coercive.

Since this is not a matter of proof but persuasion, my readers may disagree with me by arguing that the laborer's negative return is after all an outcome of her free choice. This is so because, thanks to the landlord's use of triangular threat, the laborer does not face a choice between (i) trading with the landlord and (ii) not trading with the landlord. Her choice is between (i) trading with the landlord and (iii): not trading with anyone. And given this choice, she opts for (i). Hence her choice seems to be "voluntary." One way of showing that this reasoning is flawed is to consider another more stark example.

A is walking down a dark alley when he comes across B, who pulls out a revolver and offers: "Either give me your watch or I kill you." Confronted with this easy choice, A parts with his watch. Is this transaction voluntary or not? It definitely is a utility-maximizing act and if we look at A's choice *from after the point he is accosted by B*, it is a voluntary act. But of course, if we describe this exchange as voluntary, coercion becomes almost an impossibility. And, fortunately, almost all social scientists who have examined similar situations agree that this is a case of coercion.[28] One important element that makes this a case of involuntary exchange is that once A has met B he can no longer return to his normal state. Let us suppose that A's normal level of happiness – that is, with his life *and* watch intact – is 100. Without the watch this would be 90 and, alternatively, without life this would be zero. As soon as B confronts A, the possibility of 100 vanishes

---

[28] Sociologists distinguish between the exercise of physical force and the threat of such an exercise. Thus a large man who ties up a lone walker and then snatches his watch, all without a word, exercises physical force, while our mugger, who also ends up with the watch in his pocket, merely uses the *threat* of physical force. However, there seems to be general agreement that both cases engage a person in an involuntary act (*see, e.g.* Simmel, 1971: 96–8; Lively, 1976; Blau, 1964: chapter 5).

from A's feasible set: he can only choose between 90 and 0. And it is in this sense that a transaction at Marks and Spencers is voluntary: if you wish, you can walk out to your normal state. It is not the case that once you enter the shop you are suddenly compelled to pay a fine if you do not make a purchase.

Turn back to the model. Suppose that the three agents live on three different islands and although the merchant trades with both 1 and 2, 1 and 2 have not met each other. In this case 2's utility level is B_2. As soon as 2 meets 1, 2's options change and she emerges in the end with a payoff of 0, which is less than B_2. *After the encounter* she makes a voluntary choice alright, but the exchange in its entirety is involuntary *by analogy with the above example*, since in that example we would agree that the mugged person parted with his watch involuntarily (or was coerced into parting with it) and, in terms of essentials, the mugging example seems to be the same as the landlord–labor–merchant example.

Why, then, do we not immediately recognize the landlord–labor exchange as one of coercion, as we do in the watch-mugging case? This is because, in the landlord–labor model, the landlord is taken to have always known the laborer, whereas to establish the analogy fully we need to go through the hypothetical exercise of what it would have been like if they did not know each other and compare it with what is actually postulated to happen. But surely that difference in the two examples is not a significant one. The fact that someone is always coerced (for instance, a person born into slavery) and never experiences the change from freedom to unfreedom does not make him a free agent.[29]

There are many examples of civilized human beings having got wonderful bargains from tribal peoples, for instance, the aborigines in Australia or the Mayans in Central America. They have effected exchanges through which they have got to buy the land and restrict the rights of the native people. What the above discussion makes us aware of is that, even when this did not happen through the use of brute force but only through take-it-or-leave-it offers, it is not evident that the transactions can all be described as voluntary. This is also true of many "trades" and exchanges in today's world. Because we view so much of the "economic" world through neoclassical lenses, this latent coercion goes unnoticed. But once we begin

[29] Another reason why the coercion is not so obvious is because, if we think of this problem in bargaining-theoretic terms, there is an ambiguity about what constitutes the threat point. If the "bargain" between agents 1 and 2 fails, how much utility does agent 2 get? If we take the breakdown in 2's relation with agent 3 into account, we have one answer; and if we ignore that, we have another. In the former case the bargaining solution will always vector-dominate the threat point, whereas in the latter case it need not.

to look at data with these kinds of triadic models in mind, my guess is that we will begin to see the true scope of coercion and immiserizing exchange.

Friedman and Friedman (1980) treat "acting according to one's self-interest" and "voluntary exchange" as two sides of the same coin. The above model demonstrates that that need not be so, because the model illustrated a case where every agent maximizes his own utility but nevertheless there is coercion. Moreover, the concept of "voluntary action" is by no means an obvious one. Friedman and Friedman (1980: 13) claim that the basic argument for *laissez-faire* is "misleadingly simple:" "if an exchange between two parties is voluntary, it will not take place unless both believe they will benefit from it." I have tried to demonstrate that this proposition is not "misleadingly simple" but misleading.

6.4. A Digression on Sexual Harassment

In this section I want to pursue the line of argument developed in the previous section in a normative direction. Since this book is almost entirely concerned with positive social science and this is especially so for this part of the book that is concerned with endogenizing institutions, the present section is best viewed as a digression into some finer issues concerning coercion.

Economists have often argued that *voluntary contracts between two adults, which do not have any adverse effect on others, ought not to be banned*, with some going further and arguing that government ought to help to enforce such contracts. Let us call this italicized normative proposition the **principle of free contract**. In some form or other, this has been advocated by prominent economists and social scientists from the eighteenth century. They have been right to do so because governments too often restrict free contract or specify the terms of contracts irrespective of the needs of the contracting parties. Economic progress and the ability of the market to function efficiently depend, to a large extent, on the ability of individuals to choose contracts freely. And, by its converse, many a nation has suffered prolonged backwardness by virtue of a misguided denial of this principle. I stress this because I am about to discuss a possible exception to the principle; and want to warn against the risk of treating the exception as a justification for the wanton thwarting of free contracts.

When there is coercion, either through the use of brute force or, more subtly, as in the previous section, most of us would argue in favor of stopping such transactions. Even a "conservative" thinker like Friedrich

Hayek[30] would presumably agree with this – he would certainly do so in the case of brute-force coercion. But even when there is no coercion of the kind in the previous section, there may be cases where the principle of free contract has to be violated. To focus on this, let me assume that we are in a realm of economic transactions where acts of exchange between two agents confer positive benefits on both – or at least non-negative benefits on both and positive benefit on at least one. So coercion of the kind discussed in Section 6.3 does not occur.

Hayek (1960) had argued that when there is monopoly control of some essential good and the monopolist extracts large benefits by offering the good to consumers, this is also a case of coercion. His reasoning is not too persuasive on this, but to stay clear of all easy cases of coercion let me assume that the market we are considering has no monopolistic elements.

My example is concerned with sexual harassment in the workplace.[31] Ought this to be allowed? Most of us would instinctively say "no." But that is because most of us, when we think of sexual harassment, think of extra-contractual harassment, that is, the case of an employer who gives no indication, at the time of employment, of the fact that there will be harassment but nevertheless proceeds to sexually harass the worker after she (or he) joins the firm. But in such a case it is arguable that there is *violation* of a contract, even if only implicit, and so there is no question of this being defended under the principle of free contract. But think now of sexual harassment that is contractual – for instance, of a firm that posts a sign saying that it will pay higher wages than other firms but the employer will reserve the right to sexually harass the worker. Now, if a worker joins this firm, under the principle of free contract there should be no interference by the agents of the state. It must be that the worker considers the benefit of the higher wage as more than compensating for the pain of harassment. In other words, this transaction is Pareto-improving.[32]

Is there a case for banning sexual harassment of such contractual kinds? One may, of course, decide on a certain ban as an end in itself, that is,

---

[30]   In describing him as a conservative, I am going along with convention. He himself (Hayek, 1960: 397–411) vehemently opposed such a characterization.

[31]   I am here taking for granted that it is known to all what an act of harassment is. In reality, there are ample grey areas here. For an insightful account of what constitutes sexual harassment, see Hadfield (1995). For useful discussions on the principle of free contract, see Ellerman (1992) and Trebilcock (1993).

[32]   A work contract that is combined with sexual favors may be thought of as equivalent to a work contract and a separate prostitution contract. While this is true, it will be argued that the fact of the two contracts being joint may create a case for a ban that would not be there for an independent contract for sexual favors in exchange for money.

without giving any reason. But that is a dangerous route to policy, as it can end up justifying whimsical interventions, and in any case that is not my question here. I want to investigate if there is *reason* for such a ban. I believe there is. Indeed what I will argue is that allowing contractual sexual harassment may result in a form of coercion, which is even more subtle than the coercion that occurred in the story in the previous section.

Note first that under normal circumstances the following is true: If harassment is allowed, then those workers who are especially strongly averse to harassment will be worse off because the market wage that they will be able to command will be lower than what it would be if no harassment were allowed by law. I call this the **harassment lemma**, and give here a short proof following Basu (1999).

Suppose that we have a market with two kinds of workers, with type-1 workers having a stronger aversion to sexual harassment than type-2 workers. For reasons of algebraic ease, let us assume that type 1's distaste for harassment is infinite (so such a person would rather be unemployed than face harassment), while type 2's distaste is zero. If the wage rate is w and there is no harassment, let the aggregate supply of labor by type-i workers be $f_i(w)$. As usual, $f_i'(w)$ is assumed to be positive.

This is a competitive model; so workers and employers are wage-takers. Let me, for simplicity, assume that there is only one employer and he gets a satisfaction of $\theta\,(>0)$ from harassing each worker. The production function of the employer is given by

$$x = x(n), \; x' > 0, \; x'' < 0,$$

where n is the number of workers and x the total output.

Let w_H denote the wage given to those workers who sign the with-harassment contract (H-contract) and w_N be the wage given to those who sign the no-harassment contract (N-contract). If the employer hires n_H workers under the H-contract and n_N workers under the N-contract, his total utility Π (which is the aggregate of his profit and satisfaction from harassment) is given by:

$$\Pi = x(n_H + n_N) - n_H w_H - n_N w_N + \theta n_H.$$

The first-order conditions from maximizing this can be rearranged and written as follows:

$$x'(n_H + n_N) = w_N; \tag{6.4}$$

$$w_H = w_N + \theta. \tag{6.5}$$

Clearly, type-1 workers will sign N-contracts and type-2 workers will sign H-contracts. Hence, the total supply of workers for N-contracts will be $f_1(w_N)$ and the total supply for H-contracts will be $f_2(w_H)$. Therefore, using (6.4) and (6.5), we can say that w_N^* and w_H^* is an equilibrium if $w_H^* = w_N^* + \theta$ and

$$x'(f_1(w_N^*) + f_2(w_N^* + \theta)) = w_N^*.$$

Consider now a legal regime where harassment is never allowed. Hence, there is only one wage in the market, w. The employer maximizes $x(n) - nw$. The total supply of labor is given by $f_1(w) + f_2(w)$. Clearly, w^* is an equilibrium wage if

$$x'(f_1(w^*) + f_2(w^*)) = w^*.$$

Since $f_2' > 0$ and $x'' < 0$, it follows that $w_N^* < w^*$. This completes the proof of the harassment lemma.

Given this harassment lemma, the principle of free contract has a somewhat quizzical normative implication. It implies that, if we adhere to the principle of free contract, then even though we may have no reason for stopping *any* pair of individuals (an employer and an employee) from getting into harassment contracts, there may be reason for adopting the *rule* that no harassment contracts should be allowed in the workplace. This happens because in a competitive market, such as the labor market described above, the aggregate effect is not simply the sum of the effects of atomistic acts taken individually. This is another manifestation of what we have already encountered in Chapter 3: conflict can exist between the recommendations that emerge from act optimization and from rule optimization.

Note that the harassment lemma does not provide *sufficient* reason for banning harassment, but simply shows that allowing contractual harassment cannot (though even this is so with some ambiguity, as explained in the attached footnote[33]) be justified *on grounds of* the principle of free

---

[33] The ambiguity in the use of the principle of free contract occurs because the principle of free contract, as stated above, says that if *one* freely chosen contract between two persons has no negative fallout, then it must not be banned. If we were to replace the italicized "*one*" with "a set of" and made the necessary grammatical changes in the statement of the principle, for most standard examples this would make no difference, because if each freely chosen contract has no negative fallout then a set of such freely chosen contracts cannot have a negative fallout. In our example of a competitive market, this is, however, not so. A set of contracts can have a very different fallout from each of its components (and to formalize this strictly we need a continuum of possible contracts). So, if the principle of free contract is interpreted exactly as stated, then harassment contracts must not be banned. If, however, by "*one*" we mean "*a set of*", then we get the proposition that I am discussing here, namely that while there is no case for banning any *one* harassment contract, there may well be a case for banning harassment contracts in general.

contract. This is because allowing harassment will mean that some laborers will sign contracts in which they submit to sexual harassment, and (though none of these contracts individually has a negative fallout) the totality of these contracts has a negative externality on uninvolved individuals – in particular, the individuals who are strongly averse to sexual harassment.[34] However, the principle of free contract does not say that, whenever a contract (or a set of contracts) has a negative fallout, that contract (or those contracts) should not be allowed. It simply says that if there is no negative fallout, it (or they) must be allowed. Hence, what I have established is not a sufficient reason for banning harassment contracts but simply established that not banning cannot be deduced from the principle of free contract.

From here to establish a sufficiency criterion, we need to go beyond economics and identify human preferences, which are "fundamental" in the sense that no one should have to pay a price for having such a preference. I shall call such preferences "inalienable" (not to be confused with inalienable *rights*). Any list of inalienable preferences is likely to be controversial at the edges but very few people will deny that there are such preferences, and also that not all preferences are inalienable. Most of us would agree that it is fine for a person to have the preference not to work four days a week, but it is also all right if he has to pay *some* price for having such a preference. Likewise we may consider it all right for someone to insist on wearing a huge red hat to work, while recognizing that he may have to sacrifice some wages or career advancement because of this preference. On the other hand, we may consider a person's preference for adhering to some of her religious rites, such as praying at a certain time of the day, to be inalienable in the sense that not only does she have the right to have such a preference but, in addition, she should not have to pay a price for having such a preference.

In most societies the preference not to be sexually harassed would be considered inalienable. It is the harassment lemma coupled with the recognition that the preference not to be sexually harassed is inalienable that clinches the case for a ban on sexual harassment. Of course, this argument can be extended to other markets, such as the trade in body parts[35] (though

---

[34] In the context of bonded labor, Genicot (1998) has argued that even though particular laborers may benefit by signing bonded labor contracts (that could, for instance, enable them to escape extreme poverty), having the *institution* of bonded labor may leave all workers worse off. In her model, even having the *option* of bonded labor contracts leaves workers worse off by worsening conditions in the credit market.

[35] For a thought-provoking discussion of trade and rights in body parts see Munzer (1994).

I am personally not convinced that this is a market that ought to be banned). Instead of leaving the decision to ban certain kinds of trade to hunch, the above discussion suggests a moral criterion for taking such a decision.

Finally, turning away from the normative question, note also that some people may argue that permitting sexual harassment contracts results in coercion. This is because allowing such contracts lowers the utility that some individuals can attain and, more starkly, may result in some people submitting to harassment, because now (that is, with such contracts allowed) the cost of refusing to submit may be too high. Somewhat informally, we could append to the above model a third kind of laborer whose cost of harassment is between 0 and θ, such that, faced with a choice between being harassed and getting a wage of w_H^* and not being harassed and getting a wage of w_N^*, she chooses the former, but she is worse off now than she would be if she was not harassed and got a wage of w^*, as would be the case if no harassment was allowed. This is, however, not caused by the choice of an agent in the model; so it is not quite analogous to the example in the previous section. Here the loss in welfare occurs in one *institutional* setting in relation to another – one where certain kinds of contracts are permitted and one where they are not. It is for this reason that I am inclined to leave it as a somewhat open question whether such a person can reasonably be described as subject to coercion.

6.5. On the "Man of Influence"

Once the axiom of dyadic relations is eschewed and triadic and, more generally, multiple relations are allowed for, we are better able to understand the *modus operandi* of the so-called "man of influence" and also the reasons for his or her existence.

The concept of "influence" has been subject to considerable sociological examination – at times as a notion indistinguishable from power (Dahl, 1957) and at times as a distinct category (Parsons, 1963). I will treat influence as a specific kind of power. For the limited purpose of this exercise, let us take a man of influence to be a person who, if he so wishes, can get people to do him favors; that is, he can get things done out of turn. This will be made more precise as we go along.

In most less developed economies – and even in many advanced countries – where bureaucratic norms are sluggish, there emerges in society the person of influence (P). If you need a new telephone connection and do not want to wait for too long, your best strategy would be to persuade P to do it for you. He can simply phone the chief of the telephone department and get it done for you. He can also get you railway tickets out of turn during rush seasons, get your daughter admitted to a good school, get you a good job, and so on. There are many people who have the reputation for being able to get such things done. They are popularly known as men of influence.

The question that will be briefly examined here is: What is the source of such a person's power? Why do bureaucrats *agree* to do him "favors"? In the light of the discussions in the earlier sections, the answer is straight-forward. Every individual bureaucrat complies with P's request because he conjectures that P is a person of influence and by complying with P's request he will in the long-run benefit. When every bureaucrat makes this same conjecture, the conjecture becomes a self-fulfilling prophecy.

It is useful to formalize this a little bit before examining the phenomenon more closely. I will construct here a very specific model to illustrate the main argument. Suppose there are k (≥ 3) bureaucrats in k different ministries and another person P, the man of influence. Each bureaucrat has the authority to dispose of a certain number of licenses of a distinct type. In particular, bureaucrat j can dispose of n_j licenses of type j. "Licenses" is a general term being used here to connote bureaucratic permissions: permission to buy train tickets under some special quota, to get a telephone connection, to get admission in a government school, and so on. Strictly speaking, the bureaucrats are not supposed to trade these licenses for their own benefit and it will be assumed that they are honest to the extent that they would not do so "directly," that is, for a bribe.

Assume that, for all $j \in \{1, \ldots, k\}$,[36] bureaucrat j needs one license of type $j + 1$ for his personal use, from which he gets a utility of ϕ units. He needs no other license. Every time j gives out a license of type j to a friend or as a "favor" to someone (basically, giving it not strictly in accordance with the rules in the government's rule book), he feels a little guilty and this amounts to d units of disutility. It will be assumed that

$3d > \phi > 2d.$

P gets a positive utility from one license each of type j belonging to a non-empty set $S \subset \{1, \ldots, k\}$.

---

[36] If $j = k$, then $j + 1$ should be treated as equal to 1. In mathematics this would be described by saying that j belongs to a modular number system with mod k. Clocks are an example of modular numbers being used in everyday life. – The same digits recur after 12 or 24.

"To ask a person for a favor" will be taken to mean "asking the person to get you a license." An individual can ask anybody for any favor: he could ask bureaucrat j to get him a license of type t. It is just that he will be wasting his effort if he asks a person who has no power or no wish to comply.

Now suppose individuals $1, \ldots, k$ and P have the following conjectures. Every $j \in \{1, \ldots, k\}$ conjectures that P is a person of influence and P can and will do j any favor j asks for, as long as j gives P what P asks for. P conjectures that every j will give him (or to whomever P tells him to give to) a maximum of two licenses as long as P gives j what j asks for.

In this model, an equilibrium exists and it is as follows. At equilibrium, every j will ask P to get him a license of type $j + 1$. P will ask every $j + 1$ to give a license of type $j + 1$ to person j. In addition, he will ask every j belonging to S to give him a license of type j. Every j will comply with P's request. It is easy to check that through these exchanges every individual $1, \ldots, k$ and P, is better off[37] and, more importantly, *given their conjectures*, no one expects to do better by altering his strategy (i.e., for example, no j would expect to be better off by not giving P the license he asks for). Hence, this is an equilibrium situation.

In reality, these exchanges will not occur simultaneously but will be scattered over time. And it is this that allows each individual to believe that he is doing someone else a favor, while what he is actually doing is performing an extended exchange. In this model, P is the man of influence. Whenever he asks j to do a favor for i, j complies. It is now easy to see why j complies: precisely because j believes that P is a person of influence. What is interesting is that though P has no initial endowment (unlike the bureaucrats, who can dole out licenses), he ends up collecting whatever license he needs for himself (i.e. one of each type in S). In this model P plays the role of money; he facilitates exchange. And just like money, he succeeds because everybody believes he will succeed.[38]

One should be clear that this is a model that merely describes an equilibrium. How this equilibrium comes about, that is, how a particular person

[37] Every $j \in S$ gets a utility of $\phi - 2d$. Every $j \in \{1, \ldots, k\} \backslash S$ gets $\phi - d$. P gets the total utility of having one of each license of types belonging to S.

[38] In our example, if one bureaucrat refuses to comply then the whole chain breaks and P loses his influence. In reality, instead of there being one large circle there will generally be several little interconnected ones – like, e.g., the symbol eight or the olympic logo – and if one bureaucrat pulls out, one circle would collapse but not the entire system. These ideas are closely related to the concept of "the middleman" and "network externalities" in sociology (see Breiger, 1990; Burt, 1992).

establishes himself as a man of influence, is a much more complex question, for which the present analysis offers no answer.

Some interesting insights can be gained by studying the conditions in which the man of influence would have no scope and, therefore, would not exist.

First, consider the case where there are no rules or social reasons not to dispose of licenses as the bureaucrat wishes. In this case, the licenses would come to have prices and would be traded against money, like any other good. Money having entered, its surrogate – the man of influence – would have no role. Note that money, unlike the man of influence, does not in the process of exchange pocket some of the gains from trade. Hence, if both money and the influential person are there to perform a role, there would be a tendency for the former to displace the latter.

This has two corollaries. (1) Suppose there are rules (licenses for school admission should go to the poor, licenses to buy train tickets during rush periods are meant for certain disadvantaged groups) but no proper enforcement machinery, and that bureaucrats are openly unethical. In that case, once again the licenses will come to have prices; it is just that these will now be called "bribes." (2) If there are rules and bureaucrats are meticulously ethical in their behavior, once again there will be no scope for the man of influence, because who gets the licenses is then decided in advance by the rules.[39] The scope for the influential person therefore exists in that intermediate situation where individuals are not so unethical as to openly sell what they are not supposed to and not so fastidiously ethical that they cannot convince themselves that they are doing a favor, and in its guise perform an indirect exchange.

Secondly, if the demand for licenses among the bureaucrats is pairwise compatible, that is, person i needs what j can give *and vice versa*, then one would expect that, over time, every pair would develop mutual trust and do each other favors, thereby doing away with the need for a go-between.[40]

---

[39] It follows from this discussion that the man of influence may or may not be socially desirable. In some situations he could be a desirable person activating a sluggish bureaucracy. But he could also in some cases be seen as a surrogate for bribery, diverting licenses, intended for certain socially disadvantageous groups, to the highest "bidders" instead.

[40] There may be rare cases where demands are not pairwise compatible and yet all exchanges take place without a man of influence in the middle. Thus, considering the act of giving gifts within the family, Malinowski (1957: 82) points out that at first sight it appears that here there is no exchange, even indirect, involved. But that, he argues, is an error stemming from "not taking a sufficiently long view of the chain of transactions;" and once we do so we would discover "that the system is based on a very complex give and take and that in the long run the mutual services balance." This kind of exchange is, however, distinct from the economist's model, because individual behavior cannot be explained in terms of utility maximization, even though the group ends up maximizing utility.

A final comment on exchange. What the above model tries to show is that in some situations where all individuals claim to be doing favors, the favors can be grouped into pairs that balance out and therefore do not constitute favors at all but are really exchanges. Yet it would be wrong to claim that these exchanges are conventional market exchanges. They are indeed more akin to what sociologists refer to as "social exchanges", namely "voluntary actions of individuals that are motivated by the returns they are expected to bring and typically do in fact bring" (Blau, 1964: 91). At first sight there appears to be no difference between this and economic exchange. If the action is "motivated by the returns," then that is exactly what economic exchange involves. That part of economic and social exchange is indeed common. The difference lies in the fact that in performing an economic exchange, if one party does not fulfil his obligation, we could consider it a breach of contract and the offended party could gather people or use the law to either get the other person to pay or recover what he has already paid or given. If, on the other hand, A gives B a gift and never gets a return gift, he can feel let down but he cannot ask for his gift back. He would simply have to decide not to give B a gift again. It is precisely for this reason that trust plays a much more important role in social exchange than in economic exchange. And it is for this same reason that the *reputation* of the man of influence as a man of influence is crucial in ensuring that the equilibrium in our model does not break down.

6.6. Concluding Remarks

Power and influence are complex concepts, and it is quite likely that these concepts have so many facets and nuances that it will never be possible to capture them all in a single definition. As Dahl (1957: 201) observed:

> If so many people at so many different times have felt the need to attach the label power, or something like it, to some Thing they believe they have observed, one is tempted to suppose that the Thing must exist. . . . and [a] more cynical suspicion is that a Thing to which people attach many labels with subtly or grossly different meanings in many different cultures and times is probably not a Thing at all but many Things.

Indeed, the difficulty could be even more profound and Lukes (1974: 4) has argued: "I maintain that power is one of those concepts identified by Gallie as 'essentially contested,' which 'inevitably involve endless disputes about their proper uses on the part of their users.' "[41]

Even if the concept is inherently contentious, at any point of time the actual contentions could be more than the inherent ones. Consequently, there is a case for trying to reduce the areas of actual contention. In a sense, this chapter is an attempt to do so. The scope of this exercise was limited to examining one kind of power. The focus was on power and influence, which work through triadic and, more generally, multiple relations. In each of the models discussed, there was some asymmetry between agents. In the models in Sections 6.2 and 6.5 there is an agent, who, despite having no endowment of his own lives well and perhaps better than the others because of certain mutually reinforcing conjectures in the minds of agents.

In Section 6.3 one agent extorts more from another agent than is witnessed in conventional theory because he threatens – explicitly or through a reputation for vindictiveness – to destroy the latter's relation with a third agent if she does not accept his offer. In this model, the exploited agent, in fact, gets a *negative* utility from her transaction with the powerful. To explain something like this, beginning with standard economic theory, at first sight it seems as if we need to give up the axiom of rationality. What this model tries to show is that that is not necessary. We could get the same result by exploiting the fact that human social relations are triadic.

---

[41] The subquotes are from Gallie (1955: 169). It may be worth noting that Gallie's essentially contested concepts are required to be "appraisive." Thus it may be questioned as to whether "power" is essentially contested *in the sense of Gallie*. It is easier to agree that it is essentially contested in a primitive sense.

7. On Advising Government

7.1. A Science of Advising?

Once we begin to take an endogenous view of government, as proposed in the previous chapters, it is no longer evident that there is scope for advising governments in the simple manner in which economists are supposed to. In the traditional models of economics, government is a receptacle of exogenous variables and an agency waiting to carry out the recommendations of the wise – in Bhagwati's (1990) words, "a puppet government." So it seemed natural that we should advise governments on how best to run the economy and, when something went wrong in the economy, take the government to task. Milton Friedman (1986) described this as the "public interest" conception of government and lamented that some of his own sage advice had no impact because he had made precisely this mistake of thinking of the government as a public-interest institution.

If prices are very high, few economists would say that producers should lower the price. If, seeing high unemployment in an economy, a person – for instance, a politician – advises entrepreneurs to employ more laborers, or consumers to demand more goods, this typically causes economists to share a laugh. Firms and consumers, they are quick to point out, have their own aims and objectives; so it is naive to treat them as exogenous agents who can be persuaded to behave in ways other than they do.

The same economists then go on to advise government, to take steps to lower prices or curtail unemployment or expand the fiscal deficit or curtail the fiscal deficit, forgetting that the individuals in government are also, like the consumers and producers, agents with their own agenda. So if it is laughable to advise firms and consumers, it is laughable to advise governments. One of the conclusions that we will reach in this chapter is that there *is* scope for advising governments but this may have to be done differently from the way we (at least claim to) do it currently, and, to the extent that there is scope for advising government, there is scope for advising all agents of an economy.

Viewed through Machiavellian lenses, the economist's faulty conception of government is not so much an act of folly as a ruse or an act of strategem. It is the existence of such puppet agents and organizations that justifies the existence of the traditional policy adviser. And economists like to give advice. As O'Flaherty and Bhagwati (1997) observe, "Many economists like to think of themselves as active participants in history, not as members of a contemplative order trying to understand a world they cannot influence".

Once we endogenize the state, so that the agents of government are also part of the economy, with their own motivations and strategies, the role of advising becomes ambiguous. And this happens in ways that have not always been appreciated, even by those advocating the more sophisticated view of government. To understand this, consider the Arrow–Debreu model of general equilibrium. In it, individuals choose points from their budget sets, and then buy and sell goods; and out of this emerges what are called equilibrium prices. All individuals in this economy are well-informed and have their own objectives. In this economy what person i *says* does not affect what person j *does*. In brief, it is an economy that works in silence. This is not to deny that in the Arrow–Debreu world people may be chatting, laughing and singing, but it is simply that that aspect of their lives does not impinge on what happens in the domain of economics and in the marketplace.[1] Having studied such a model in which i's speech has no effect on what j does, the policy economist has gone on to give advice. But what is advice but a set of spoken or written words? If the advice is based on a model in which words cannot have any significant effect, then it is surely inconsistent to believe that the *advice* can have an effect.

This is closely related to what Bhagwati, Brecher and Srinivasan (1984) described as "the determinacy paradox:" Once we treat all agents as part of the system we are studying, the system seems to become fully determined, leaving no scope for the policy adviser.[2] O'Flaherty and Bhagwati (1997) elaborate on this argument with several analogies. They argue, for instance, that in a fully deterministic world there is no freedom of choice; whether we have orange juice or milk is predetermined. This is a position that has been taken by a long line of philosophers. Levi (1997: 222), for instance, points out: "If Jones had sufficiently detailed information about the model and his environment, deliberating about his morning menu would be pointless. What he will eat has, as far as Jones is concerned, been settled." He then goes on to relate this to the problem of advice giving. Essentially

[1] This is an analogue of "epiphenomenalism" in philosophy, which maintains that, while the human mind is a reality, it has an existence entirely separate from that of the human body and, more generally, matter; and so events in the mental world cannot influence what happens in the material world.

[2] While the mainstream of economics has overlooked this paradox, there is a small body of writing that has tried to contend with this problem. *See* Magee and Brock (1983), Barro (1984), Friedman (1986), Austen-Smith (1990), and Robinson (1996).

the point is that, in a fully determined world, advice cannot change the advisee's choice. However, as I argue in the Appendix to this book, this widely held view turns out, on closer analysis, to be flawed. Determinism and freedom of choice are not mutually inconsistent. It is entirely possible that what action an agent chooses is (1) predetermined and, at the same time, (2) depends on the advice he gets. The full argument is spelled out in the Appendix, but it may be noted here that (1) and (2) turn out to be consistent once it is recognized that the advice that the adviser gives is also determined in a fully deterministic world.

So, while the view that determinism and free choice are mutually inconsistent is incorrect,[3] "the determinacy paradox" points to a valid and important inconsistency in conventional economic thinking. You cannot model the world as an Arrow–Debreu economy and then proceed to give meaningful advice.

Before we go on to grapple with the nature of and scope for policy advice in an economy with an endogenous government, it is useful to classify different kinds of faulty advice. There are two broad ways in which a piece of advice can be considered defective. First, advice can be "wrong advice" in the sense of it being based on an erroneous view of the world, so that *if* it were followed, it would not bring about the kind of world that it was intended to bring about. Second, advice can be "futile advice" in the sense that it either urges the advisee to do something that is beyond the advisee's control or is transparently against the advisee's interest (North, 1989).[4] "Wrong advice" is therefore like the doctor who prescribes aspirin to a patient concerned about hair loss.[5] It is ironical but should come as no surprise in the light of the above discussion that the pervasive error of the advising economist has been that of "futile" advising.

In the *Economic Times*, New Delhi edition, of July 12, 1991, Abhijit Sen presents, with his usual clarity, a set of detailed instructions about what the Indian government should do about India's foreign-exchange problem. But, having done so, and just as the reader begins to warm to the idea that here at last is the solution to a stubborn problem, Sen goes on to observe, "But for this [that is, for his advice to be followed] the existing culture in government must be turned upside down." But what is the value of advice the prerequisite for which is that the entire culture of the existing government be turned upside down? This is virtually tantamount to saying that

---

[3] Dixit (1997) also argues against this view, though for reasons different from mine.

[4] The analysis that follows is largely taken from Basu (1997).

[5] With the appearance of news items every few days about one more illness that aspirin can cure, I am aware that this example may become invalid by the time the book goes to print!

the advice cannot be followed. So whatever else might be the value of such an essay, as advice it belongs to the category of "futile."

In the *National Review* of September 30, 1996, we find Deal Hudson advising America on how to recover its "intellect and its freedom." "Our best bet," he argues, is the "church-related university, illumined by the light of faith, confident in its curriculum, rooted in history, concerned for the student as a whole person." In such a university, he goes on to urge, the primary concern should be "the development of character, the discernment of true values, and the preparation for heaven." The trouble with this advice is that it seems compellingly beyond the reach of anybody.

Without questioning the content of the advice, one can multiply the examples given above of advice that is futile – for which there is no hope of even the most diligent advisee being able to carry it out.

A very different set of problems arises once we move away from traditional models of the economy to ones where one person's utterances can influence another's action. Such a world raises not only issues of analytical interest to the economist or the game theorist but also moral dilemmas for the adviser. And if we are ever to have a science of advising, we will need to contend with these issues and dilemmas.

7.2. Advising Endogenous Government

To make room for advice that will not fall on deaf ears, a *necessary* step is to move away from the Walrasian world to one in which information is imperfect and asymmetric. In particular, we shall assume that government consists of individuals (the politicians) with their own aims and objectives but who have inadequate information about the implications of the projects and plans from which they have to choose one. On the other hand, there are the advisers (the economists) who, through training, research or, for that matter, clairvoyance, have information about the effects of each project and plan. But they are not allowed to choose; they can only advise the politicians about what to choose. In brief, we are taking a small step towards a more realistic model of government by recognizing that (1) government is not an exogenous agent but a collection of individuals with their own motivations, and that (2) information in society is incomplete and asymmetric. It is interesting to note that Green's (1993) model, while addressing very different issues, nevertheless uses an argument concerning asymmetric information and communication to explain the emergence of parliamentary democracy.

These assumptions make it possible for one agent to influence another through advice. But (1) and (2) above are by no means *sufficient* for this to be so. Moreover, the *manner* in which advice is given turns out to be quite different from what is generally presumed. The aim of this and the next section is to demonstrate these assertions by constructing some simple game-theoretic examples.

If the adviser and the advisee have the same objective function, then all is well. There is scope for "cheap talk" and advice takes place in the usual way – that is, by saying that x should be done when the adviser believes that x should be done (Farrell and Rabin, 1996).[6] Trouble arises when the adviser and the politician have different aims.[7]

Let me assume that the adviser (player 1) works entirely in the interest of the people,[8] while the politician (player 2) is self-interested; and the people's (and, therefore, the adviser's) interest is not the same as that of the politician.[9] The simplest illustrative example of this is where there are two projects: N (a nuclear power plant) and T (a thermal one), from which the politician has to choose one. Like all such projects, the impact of each project on society is very complicated, and the politician does not know what effect the projects will have on his and other people's welfare.

We can formalize this information structure by supposing that there are two states of the world, w_1 and w_2, which occur with probability $\frac{1}{2}$ each. In the language of game theory, "nature" makes an equiprobable choice between w_1 and w_2. In w_1, the payoffs from N̄ (that is, from having the nuclear power plant) to the adviser and the politician are, respectively, 1 and

---

[6] Even here one can have trouble if there is coordination of action needed between the adviser and the advisee and there is a non-zero probability of an item of advice failing to be common knowledge after it is announced. This was illustrated with the example of Rubinstein's (1989) E-mail Game in Chapter 2.

[7] An interesting, related problem is analyzed by Gilligan and Krehbiel (1987). A large group of people or the legislature often find it useful to appoint a subcommittee to acquire information on some specific matter and then propose suitable legislation to the legislature. The information acquired by the subcommittee gives it power to direct legislation to serve its own interest better. Complication arises from the fact that the legislature knows this. Gilligan and Krehbiel show that, as long as the preferences of the committee and the parent body are not too divergent and the costs of committee specialization not too large, it is in the interest of the parent body to adopt a "restrictive procedure" that prevents the parent body from amending the committee's proposal. It has to either accept it as it stands or stay with the status quo.

[8] Nothing formal hinges on this assumption but it prepares the ground for some moral dilemmas that are discussed later.

[9] It is important to understand that the fact that one may try to delude one's listeners does not in itself suggest a selfish motivation. As Goffman (1959: 18) points out: "It is not assumed, of course, that all cynical performers are interested in deluding their audiences for purposes of what is called 'self-interest' or private gain. A cynical individual may delude his audience for what he considers to be their own good, or for the good of the community."

0 and from T̄ the adviser gets 0 and the politician gets 1. In w_2 (that is, if the state of the world turns out to be w_2), the payoffs from N̄ and T̄ are reversed. The adviser knows which state of the world has occurred and makes the first move. He has to choose between saying "Do N" and "Do T." These two actions are denoted by N and T in state w_1, and by N' and T' in state w_2. The politician hears the advice but does not know whether w_1 or w_2 has occurred, and has to choose between the nuclear and thermal power plants. The politician's choice is implemented and the players reap payoffs as already explained.

This game is described using the standard device of a game tree in Fig. 7.1, and is called the "Orthogonal Game." Note that nodes x and y belong to the same information set, which captures the idea that the politician cannot tell whether he is at x or y when he is at one of them. In both these nodes he has just heard his rather taciturn adviser say "Do N." And, since he does not know whether w_1 or w_2 has occurred, for him x and y are indistinguishable. His choice of the nuclear and thermal plants at these nodes is denoted by n and t. What will be the outcome of this game? Will the adviser be able to influence the choice of the politician?

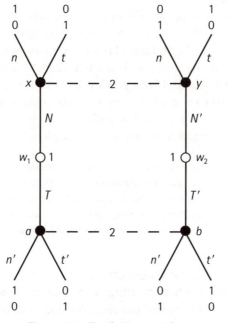

Figure 7.1. The Orthogonal Game

Let us first check intuitively how they will play this game. Suppose w_1 occurs. The adviser will want the politician to choose the nuclear project. Let us suppose that he is naive, and so says exactly that: "I advise you, Sir, to go for the nuclear project" (the "Sir" being a judicious addition to ensure upward career mobility), or, equivalently, "Do N." The politician, knowing about his adviser's "strange" political leanings, would, it seems, choose the thermal plant. This happens in the same way that a child, told by the mother not to watch channel 29 that evening because there will be "a boring film", *Last Tango in Paris*, knows that that is one evening when the child must not watch *Mr. Roger's Neighborhood*, and instead turn to channel 29.

If the adviser were rational and knew that the politician would do the opposite, then the above outcome would not occur. The adviser may then give the false advice "Go Thermal" and hope that the politician will go nuclear. (Indeed, there are not too many mothers who would instruct their children as in the above paragraph.) But, of course, if the politician knows that the adviser is rational and that the adviser knows that the politician is rational, then this simple trick of the adviser will not work.

It is actually easy to check that the only Nash equilibrium is one in which the adviser's advice is completely uncorrelated to which state of the world actually occurs and the politician's choice is completely uninfluenced by the adviser's advice.

What the above example points to is not just the difficulty of advising but to some deep problems of communication in general. Addressing this more general problem, Glenn Loury (1994: 432) points out in his engaging essay on self-censorship and political correctness: "There is always some uncertainty when ideas and information are exchanged between parties who may not have the same objectives. Each message bears interpretation." He goes on to point out how he himself (as a prominent commentator on racial issues in the United States) has to be cautious (p. 435):

> I must tread carefully as I try to express my particular "truth." If you will "read between the lines" for my true meaning [. . .], then I am determined to write between the lines – avoiding (or embracing) certain "code words", choosing carefully my illustrative examples, concealing some of my thinking while exaggerating other sentiments – so as to control the impression I make on my audience.

As Sunstein (1996) has so eloquently argued, a society confronts some of this same problem when drafting a law, because words can convey meanings beyond the literal and can therefore hurt sentiments, console and inspire people.

It may appear that the problem that the Orthogonal Game highlights is the difficulty of advising when preferences are *diametrically opposite* between the adviser and the advisee. As O'Flaherty and Bhagwati (1997) observe: "Saddam Hussein is unlikely to revise the Iraqi agricultural price system just because some American economists tell him that doing so would be nice."[10]

This naturally leads to the suggestion that for an adviser to play a positive role there must be a reasonable affinity of interest between the adviser and the politician and, more generally, the speaker and the listener. Thus O'Flaherty and Bhagwati speak about the importance of the "coincidence of interests," and, to stress that this need not be a non-generic special case, add that "coincidence does not have to be exact." In the same spirit, Loury (1994: 436) remarks, "If we know a speaker shares our values, we more readily accept observations from him . . . ;" and "when we believe the speaker has goals *similar* to our own, we are confident that any effort on his part to manipulate us is undertaken to advance ends similar to those we would pursue ourselves" (italics added).

What I want to illustrate, however, is that the prognosis is gloomier than these observations suggest. In the sort of setting that we are considering here, which is also the setting that most commentators in this field presume, similarity of objectives is not enough. Anything short of an exact coincidence of preference may result in a complete breakdown in communication. This paradoxical result is driven by a kind of "infection" argument where a small anomaly or some informational event far away becomes pervasive and has real effects (see Morris and Shin, 1995). This is proved in the next section by constructing a game that I call "Cheater's Roulette." While the game is created by me to illustrate the problem of information transmission, the problem, in the abstract, has been known for a while, especially since the seminal paper of Crawford and Sobel (1982).

7.3. Cheater's Roulette

To illustrate the result mentioned in the last paragraph, consider a continuum of projects $\Omega = [0, 1]$. As before, what effect each project has on the adviser and the politician is known by the adviser but not by the politician. The adviser gives a piece of advice to the politician that takes the form

---

[10] And, as the Orthogonal Game shows, neither should Saddam Hussein not revise it *because* he has been asked to revise. Such a response would also make him vulnerable to manipulation.

of saying "Do x," where $x \in \Omega$ and the politician then chooses some $y \in \Omega$. We shall describe a way of measuring the nearness of the preferences of the politician and her adviser, and show that, unless the preferences are identical, the politician will not pay any heed to the adviser's advice.

Some abstraction makes it easier to describe this game, which I call **Cheater's Roulette**. It consists of a roulette board, the circumference of which is a unit circle. Let us call the northernmost point 0 and the same point also 1 (in the same way that in a clock 0 and 12 refer to the same point). This is illustrated in Fig. 7.2. The circumference then is our set of projects $\Omega = [0, 1]$.

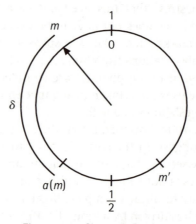

Figure 7.2. Cheater's Roulette

The board has a "hand" which is pivoted to the center of the roulette board. The hand can be made to spin. The line with the arrow in Fig. 7.2 represents the hand. The game is played as follows. The politician sits where she cannot see the board. The hand is given a spin (by "Nature" let us say) and after it comes to rest the politician is asked to choose a point from Ω. If the hand comes to rest at point m, as shown in the figure, then the politician is paid as follows. She gets 100 dollars if she chooses m (that is, guesses that m is the outcome); 0 dollars if she chooses the point diametrically opposite to m (i.e. point m' in the figure) and the payoff drops off linearly (though monotonically would do) as she chooses points further and further away from m.

This may be stated formally as follows. For any two points x, $y \in \Omega$, define the distance between them, denoted by $d(x, y)$, to be the shortest distance between x and y along the circumference. It follows that

$$d(x, y) = \min \{|x - y|, 1 - |x - y|\}.$$

If Nature selects $m \in \Omega$ and the politician $x \in \Omega$, then the politician's payoff is $[100 - d(x, m)200]$. Note that $d(x, m)$ can vary between 0 and $\frac{1}{2}$. Hence the payoff varies between 100 and 0.

The adviser in this game is actually an accomplice who *watches* Nature's selection (and so he knows more than the politician, as advisers are expected to in reality) and whispers a piece of advice to the politician about what she should choose.

The adviser also gets a payoff, which depends on what Nature and the politician choose. This may be described as follows. Note that whatever Nature chooses is the politician's ideal point. Let us suppose that the adviser is to the "left" of the politician and define the "adviser's ideal point," $a(m)$, to be a point which is at a distance of δ ($\leq \frac{1}{2}$) to the left of m. An illustration of $a(m)$, where δ is $\frac{1}{4}$ is shown in Fig. 7.2. To remind ourselves that $a(m)$ depends on δ, we could write it as $a_\delta(m)$ but I am not doing so for reasons of notational simplicity.

If Nature selects m and the politician chooses x, the adviser is paid 100 dollars if $x = a(m)$ (that is, if the politician chooses the adviser's ideal point), 0 dollars if x is diametrically opposite $a(m)$ and the payoff falls off linearly as x moves away from $a(m)$. Formally, the adviser's payoff is $[100 - d(x, a(m))200]$. If $\delta = 0$, then the adviser's preference is exactly the same as the politician's and his every advice will be taken by the latter. The paradoxical result is this: if $\delta > 0$, then no matter how small δ is, communication will break down totally between the adviser and the politician. The only Nash equilibrium is one in which the politician ignores her adviser's whisper in making her choice.[11] Attention is throughout restricted to pure strategies.

In order to sketch a proof of this, I need to introduce some new terminology. Let the adviser's strategy be denoted by ϕ where $\phi : \Omega \to \Omega$. For every selection $x \in \Omega$ by Nature, $\phi(x)$ is what the adviser asks the politician to choose. Similarly, the politician's strategy is c, where $c : \Omega \to \Omega$. For every advice $x \in \Omega$ given by the adviser, $c(x)$ is the element of Ω that the politician chooses.

Hence, if Nature selects $m \in \Omega$, the politician chooses $c(\phi(m))$ and her payoff is $[100 - d(c(\phi(m)), m)200]$. And the adviser's payoff is $[100 - d(c(\phi(m)), a(m))200]$. Since Nature selects by spinning the hand, it selects from a uniform density function on Ω. Hence, given ϕ and c, we can compute the expected payoff of each player. Let (ϕ^*, c^*) be a Nash equilibrium

---

[11] Some readers may wish to skip the proof of this claim, which stretches over the next few paragraphs, up to the point where it says, "*This completes the proof of the paradoxical result.*"

of this game. What we need to show is that $c^*(x)$ is independent of x (i.e. the politician's choice is independent of the advice she receives). That is, there exists $y \in \Omega$ such that $c^*(x) = y$ for all $x \in \Omega$.

First note that if $y \in c^*(\Omega)$, then there exist points z and x strictly to the "right" and "left" of y, respectively, such that $y \in [x, z]$ and no other point (i.e. other than y) in $[x, z]$ is in $c^*(\Omega)$.[12] If this were not true, we would find $x, z \in \Omega$ such that $c^*(\Omega)$ is dense in the interval $[x, z]$. Then c^* cannot be an optimum strategy for the politician. Let y be in the interior of $[x, z]$ such that for some $r \in \Omega$, $c^*(r) = y$. Then if Nature selects m such that $a(m) = r$, $\phi^*(m)$ must be such that $\phi^*(m) = r$. Clearly then, the politician would be better off deviating from her choice $c^*(r)$. This establishes the first sentence of this paragraph and thereby proves that $\# c^*(\Omega) < \infty$.

Denote $c^*(\Omega) \equiv \{x_1, \ldots, x_n\}$, where x_1 is the first point in $c^*(\Omega)$ at or to the right of 0; and $x_2, x_3, \ldots$ follow clockwise, as shown in Fig. 7.3. Suppose $n \geq 2$. It is now easy to check that c^* cannot be optimal for the politicians unless the length of x_i to x_{i-1} exceeds the length of x_{i+1} to x_i (lengths being measured along the counterclockwise arc). If this is not the case, it is possible to check that the politician can do better by choosing slightly clockwise away from x_i when the advice y is such that $c^*(y) = x_i$. Since the projects belong to a modular number system, it is not possible for the gaps between adjacent x_i's to increase throughout as we move in one direction. Hence, $n = 1$. *This completes the proof of the paradoxical result.*

What we have proved is this. There exists $x \in \Omega$ such that, for all $y \in \Omega$, $c^*(y) = x$. In equilibrium, the adviser's advice has no effect on the politician's

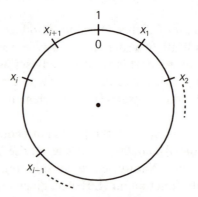

Figure 7.3. Cheater's Roulette (politician's strategy)

---

[12] For $x, y \in \Omega$, $[x, y]$ denotes the shorter arc between x and y, the tie being broken arbitrarily for x and y, which are diametrically opposite to each other.

choice. The politician just arbitrarily picks a point $x \in \Omega$. It follows that in equilibrium the adviser just babbles – he gives advice that conveys no information about the state that has occurred (that is, Nature's choice).

Before proceeding further, it may be useful to explain my use of a unit circle as opposed to the more-conventional unit interval. The immediate reason for doing this is the mathematical convenience of being able to describe one person as being at a distance δ to the "left" of another, irrespective of the latter's location. Second, this description can capture some very real problems. Some years ago, the Ministry of Finance in Delhi was considering changing the time of the annual budget of the Government of India (currently the budget year starts on April 1). There were many real issues involved. A budget in October, for instance, would mean that the government would know how the monsoons had affected the country and therefore be better placed to plan ahead. There were, in fact, so many variables involved that expert advice was sought about when the budget year should start. If we now think of the unit circle as representing the calendar year from January 1 to December 31, then this problem has the same algebra as our model.

Can advice then have *no* role unless there is a total coincidence of preference? Despite the above result, the answer to this question is in the negative. First, by allowing the use of mixed strategies we can open up the possibility of some communication. Second, there is now a small body of literature that shows that even when precise advising can be shown to have no role, ambiguity in speech or vagueness of expression can be used to convey *some* information from the speaker to the listener (see Crawford and Sobel, 1982 and Stein, 1989). This, in itself, is a very interesting result because it shows how moving away from precision to ambiguity may help us to actually convey more.

Third, we could appeal to the fact that the outcome of Cheater's Roulette is *paradoxical* and urge the reader to reject the game-theoretic solution. In this respect Cheater's Roulette is akin to the Traveler's Dilemma, discussed in Chapter 2, because in that game it is (in a sense) rational to reject playing the game rationally because it seems reasonable to expect that the other player will do the same. Now put yourself in the shoes of the adviser in the Cheater's Roulette game and suppose that δ is very small (that is, the adviser and the advisee have almost identical objectives). If the roulette hand stops at m, one reasonable way of thinking is this. "A Nash equilibrium play could make both of us lose a lot. So why don't I advise something in the vicinity of m. Surely the politician will also realize that the Nash equilibrium play does us no good and so choose something in the vicinity of what I advise."

This is not watertight reasoning, but nevertheless not one to be dismissed. Note also that "the vicinity of m" and "the vicinity of what I advise" are imprecise expressions. But, as argued in Chapter 2, meta-rational behavior depends on the use of imprecise (and hence realistic) categories of thinking.

No matter how we seek to resolve the problem, one thing is evident. Barring the nongeneric special case in which there is a complete coincidence of wants, *it does not pay to give the advice that one believes in.* That is, the same morality that leads you to think that "X should be done" prompts you not to *say* "X should be done." This creates a moral dilemma that may have no easy solution, and this is the subject matter of the next section. But before moving on to it, I want to dwell on three caveats to the present analysis and a related observation.

First, we have in this chapter, for reasons of tractability, taken "advice" to be simple normative statements or, more generally, any message that can influence behavior by *informing* the advisee. However, in reality, advice often takes the form of persuasion, which involves attempts to influence the advisee's *preference.* What complicates this is the fact that people often voluntarily go for this kind of advice. This is true not just of the alcoholic seeking counselling, but in politics and in government there is the continuous play of forces jockeying and buffeting to influence preferences and of individuals voluntarily leaving themselves vulnerable to preference shifts.

Second, there are social institutions that work to bring the interest of the adviser and the advisee into alignment. Note that an adviser typically belongs to a profession. If it is medical advice we are talking about, the adviser will belong to the medical profession; if it is legal advice, he will belong to the profession of law; and if it is economics advice, he will be a member of the economics profession. When a person works as a professional, he or she is supposed to work in the interest of his or her advisee. Hence, even if the adviser – say a doctor – has an innate preference that is divergent from the preference of the advisee – for instance, the latter happens to be a tenant occupying his rent-controlled apartment who is seeking advice on the right diet for prolonging his life – the doctor is supposed to have a moral commitment to give advice *as if* his preference is the same as his advisee's. Frequently the profession as a whole, formally or informally, tries to ensure that individual members of the profession adhere to this code of professional responsibility (*see* Larson, 1977; and DiMaggio and Powell, 1983, especially pp. 152–3). In addition, many professionals will, for reasons of their own morality or social norm, adhere to such a code. And, even if that were not the case, it is possible to think of a repeated game model, where, for reasons of reputation, it will be in the adviser's interest to behave as though he had the advisee's preference. I do not, at this stage, know if this is formally true, but it should be possible to check this claim through formal modeling.[13]

Third, once we move away from the assumption of preferences being mutually known, communication (and, for that matter, certain kinds of actions) may acquire a new strategic dimension whereby the communicator seeks to influence the belief of the listener about the communicator's preference. Preferences of political actors are often important to others because they indicate what the politician might do in contingencies that arise in the future (some of which may not even currently be conceivable). Thus it is arguable that President Clinton supported the Helms–Burton Act, discussed in the previous chapter, not because he believes in it (there is actually some evidence suggesting that he does not) but because he wanted to *appear* more conservative before the 1997 presidential election and thereby create the expectation that in future decision-making he will pick the more conservative alternative.

By assuming that preferences are exogenously given and common knowledge among the agents, the present essay stays clear of these complications. But they are important in reality and deserve to be on the agenda for future research.

Finally, the related observation. I have posed the problem of communication in the asymmetric context involving an adviser and an advisee. The same problem can, however, also arise when the agents involved are symmetrically placed – for example, the members of a parliament taking a vote or the members of a jury deciding by majority. An interesting paper by Austen-Smith and Banks (1996) illustrates how the dilemma of not revealing one's information sincerely can arise in the context of problems such as the celebrated Condorcet jury theorem. In their model, this can happen even when all members have the same preference.

7.4. A Moral Conundrum

An act of speaking or writing usually has consequences for the world. The Communist Manifesto was nothing but some words on paper. So were the Bible, the Koran and even *The Satanic Verses*. But these "words" have had consequences for the world of action, creating or destroying wealth,

---

[13] Related ideas have been explored in the literature on trustworthiness in repeated interactions (Dasgupta, 1988; Greif, 1993; Greif, Milgrom and Weigast, 1994), and may provide cues on modeling why giving good advice may be individually rational.

stirring human beings into acts of bravery or cowardice. Hence, anyone who writes or speaks has to take into account the consequences of the writing and the speech. This is especially so for those who write for and speak to large audiences. The scientist writing *positive* science can at least claim no *inconsistency* if he chooses to write whatever is the truth, with no thought to the consequence of his writing. On the other hand, a scientist, or, for that matter, anybody, making a normative statement may face a deeper moral conundrum, and a problem that is virtually one of consistency. The politician beseeching the public to act, the economist advising the politician, and the journalist urging the economist to say something all face this problem. Unlike the positive scientist, these people cannot disclaim having a normative purpose because their very act of speaking reveals such a purpose.

As we have already seen, when an expert or an informed person utters something, people try (or should try) to elicit information from that utterance, in the same way that the politician in Cheater's Roulette tries to deduce the outcome on the roulette board from his adviser's whisper. Similarly, if you read or hear Mr. Stephen R. Covey, the author of popular improve-yourself books such as *The Seven Habits of Highly Effective People*, telling you to be goal-oriented or to keep "the end in mind," you have reason to believe that *he* believes in being goal-oriented. Given that it seems unlikely that Mr. Covey's goal is to make *you* goal-oriented; and his much more likely goal is to maximize the sales of his books, you have reason to suspect that some of the things he advises people are the advice people *like* to hear. And you could decide, not totally unreasonably, that, given the great success of his books, following not his advice but him himself is the more profitable strategy. Of course, you may be wrong in attributing the best-seller motive to Mr. Covey; he perhaps has a missionary purpose. But the fact remains that people look for meanings other than the one explicitly stated.[14]

Now suppose you want to tell the government: "Government should do *x*." This will make people try to guess what you know and they do not, make them act in certain ways and, let us suppose, bring about the kind of world that you do not morally approve of. And suppose your giving the opposite advice will bring about a desirable world, in terms of your own morals. Then you face a moral conundrum, because what is in conflict is not your self-interest with your moral judgment but your morals with your morals. Should you say what you believe in or should you say the reverse and bring

---

[14] This is the subject matter of Kuran's (1995) engaging book.

about the kind of world that you believe in? Note that a person making a normative statement cannot even use the alibi of being normatively disinterested. He has to face the dilemma.

Hence, this is a conundrum that one has to confront if one wishes to advise and pronounce publicly on policy. It may be possible to construct models of repeated advice, which bring the two moral options discussed in the above paragraph into alignment. That is, it may be morally best to say what you actually believe in because otherwise your "strategic" behavior will get revealed in the long run and people will not take you seriously anyway. But till such a formal result is established and also when we are working outside such a repeated-game framework, we have no option but to leave this problem as an open-ended issue. And, moreover, till this is resolved we will be right in trying to read between the lines of not only what politicians and other government officials say, but also what the economic adviser and the economist say in public life.

8. The Concept of "State"

8.1. Preamble

A central purpose of this monograph is to advocate a more inclusive conception of government in the social sciences, especially economics. Various aspects of this view have been developed and discussed in the previous three chapters. The aim of the present chapter is simply to wrap up this analysis by articulating this point of view as clearly as possible and also to caution the reader against possible misinterpretations of this viewpoint.

It is natural for us to take government for granted. Government is a necessary concomitant of the state and, for certain discourses, it is the state.[1] Yet in the history of human beings, state and government are relatively modern institutions. People belonged to tribes and had chiefs rather than governments and heads of states. This is true even in some contemporary situations. Many tribespeople – for instance, those living on the Andaman and Nicobar Islands in the Bay of Bengal are not aware that they are Indian nationals. To them, the agents of the state – the police, the civil servants – are not representatives of the "law" but, on the contrary, illegal trespassers on whom the use of poison arrows is considered well worth the poison. Barring some such small exceptions, however, all people in today's world treat government and its agencies as part of life.

As Strayer's (1970) elegant little book reminds us, this was not always so.[2] This is of course partly a matter of definition, but it is safe to assert that up to as late as the eleventh century AD there were no national states as we know them now. There were some small city-states and there were empires. According to Strayer, state as a moral authority, with a monopoly of the legitimate use of physical force and as an institution for providing public goods, is a phenomenon of the last millennium.[3] And several activities of the

---

[1] In this book itself, there has been no need to draw a sharp line between government and state.

[2] The origin of the state is a subject of immense controversy and diversity of opinion, the difficulty being created not just by the lack of facts, but the lack of definitions agreed upon.

[3] The emergence of primitive states in Mesopotamia, China, the Indus Valley and elsewhere is equally important, though its causation and character are very different. The emergence of the primitive state nearly 5000 years ago has been described as "the most far-reaching political development" in history (Carneiro, 1970) and is a subject of immense interest. I shall, however, confine my remarks here to the emergence and nature of the modern state.

In speaking of the moral legitimacy of the modern state, one must guard against the risk of going too far. Even when one talks of the very modern institution of representative democracy, one

government that we today take for granted were not a part of governmental activity till even more recently. A general system of tax, especially direct tax, is a surprisingly modern institution. Great Britain adopted an income tax in 1798, rescinded it for a while in the nineteenth century, then broadened its coverage, and finally reached the modern system of universal taxation only around the turn of the twentieth century. Piecemeal attempts at taxing income had started earlier.[4] By the thirteenth and fourteenth century there were taxes imposed by the public authority in some cities of Europe, especially Italy. But these were quite arbitrary, both in terms of how much had to be paid and who was to be exempted. A little later, France attempted something more universal with the *taille*, which was a tax based on the estimated incomes of the farmers. Something similar was also being attempted around the same time by the Mughal rulers of India. What did predate direct personal taxation was the practice of taxing international trade and even internal trade by stopping freight *en route* and charging a toll.

What was lacking in all these early practices was legitimacy. Taxation was imposed through the power of the state or the local authority without the recognition of this being a legitimate charge. Often, no single authority had the monopoly for imposing tolls, with the consequence that it was the stronger authority rather than the one recognized to be legitimate that collected the tolls, in a manner somewhat reminiscent of the *rangdari* tax described in Chapter 1.[5]

The lack of legitimacy in the public eye was a hangover of the early concept of the state, where tax was a symbol of oppression rather than of belonging. Slaves and conquered people were routinely plundered to finance the ruling classes and the kings. Taxes were naturally viewed as a transfer from the oppressed by the rich and the powerful. They were used to keep away foreign aggression and to maintain peace in the local community; but these were the concomitant of taxes, not their central purpose. The view of taxes being a collection in the interest of the taxpayer, one that promotes equity and economic growth among the community of those who

should be aware that the moral legitimacy of many of its laws may be questionable. As Macey (1997: 1) reminds us, laws are often created not because they are "legitimately needed, but because the outcomes spontaneously generated by private ordering often do not serve the interests of the politicians, legislatures, and special interest groups that are uniquely able to supply law." In commenting on Macey, Rutten (1997) has drawn our attention to the fact that norms do not have to be morally sound in order to survive – a point that is borne out by some of my examples in Chapter 6.

[4] The widespread practice in tribal societies of giving gifts in kind to the chief – a practice that has remained unchanged over long stretches of history – is also a kind of tax.

[5] For a philosophical discussion of what constitutes a "legitimate state," see Copp (1999).

pay, is a relatively recent idea. This closely mirrors the concept of the state itself. As Douglas North (1989: 107) wrote:

> Throughout most of history the State has not provided a framework conducive to economic growth. Indeed the Mafia would be a more accurate characterization of the State in the past [. . .]. There were of course exceptions. [. . .] But they were exceptions; and a State that is self-consciously concerned with the performance of the economy is a relatively modern phenomenon.

These are facts that will be worth keeping in mind when we eventually turn to examining how the social scientist's concept of the state has itself evolved.

Why did the state – or rather the state as we now know it – emerge in the twelfth and thirteenth centuries? This is a subject matter for history and one that may well require the longevity of a historian's professional life for successful investigation, but one suggestion in Strayer's essay is particularly interesting. The twelfth and thirteenth centuries saw a steep rise in learning and literacy. It therefore allowed the codification of law and the signing of contracts in a way that may not have been possible earlier.[6] This gave rise to the need for an enforcer of contracts, and government soon became that ubiquitous "third party" that enforced contracts, or at least tried to. Modern society, it is arguable, would be unsustainable without an institution for supporting contracts and covenants, that is, without a widely shared set of beliefs that a subset of the population will take action to enforce contracts (because if they did not, they would, in turn, be punished). The prosperity of contemporary economies owes as much to the slow evolution of this institution as it does to the many sudden scientific breakthroughs.

As the institution of government has evolved, so has the social scientist's conception of government. The early attitude within the economics profession was inspired by two conflicting facts: the discipline's preference for precision and its failure to precisely characterize government. This led to an abandonment of effort to seriously model government; it was left aside as somehow exogenous to the domain of economics and markets. With the

---

[6] I write this with some unease, since institutions in history seldom have clear points of origin. Though modern law, enforced by the state, is distinct in character, legal systems have existed far back in history and exist now in tribal societies where the hand of the state is weak (*see* Basu, 1998b, for a discussion). Ancient laws such as the Code of Hammurabi in Mesopotamia, which dates back to over 2000 years BC, and the laws outlined by Kautilya in his famous book on statecraft, *Arthashastra*, for the Maurya dynasty in India around 300 BC, were undoubtedly legal systems, as are the rules and regulations in contemporary primitive societies such as the Lozi people of Barotseland, as described by Gluckman (1955). Hence, in thinking of the law as a modern construct enforced by the state, one has no choice but to draw an arbitrary line.

rise in the recognition of the role of governance in the efficient functioning of markets (Stiglitz, 1989), there have also occurred some fine attempts to model government (*see, for instance*, Olson, 1993; Tirole, 1994; Dixit, 1996). But let us step back a little. Much of the initial provocation for research in this area came from arguably the most influential writer on the state, namely Thomas Hobbes, and in particular his *Leviathan* (1651). Some of the most engaging contemporary writings on the origins of the state, such as Taylor (1976), are rooted in the Hobbesian tradition, whether or not these agree with Hobbes's view.

Those who know nothing else about Hobbes know his observation that, in the absence of the state, the life of man is "solitary, poor, nasty, brutish and short" (Hobbes, 1651, ch. xiii, para. 9). According to Hobbes, in the "state of nature," that is, before the emergence of the state, self-seeking human beings lead a life of anarchy and chaos and are at war with one another.[7] In such a state there is no sense of justice and no sense of right and wrong. To assure that such a state is not just a figment of his imagination, Hobbes, never too fussy about the sources of his empirical evidence, added, "There are many places where they live so now. For the savage people in many places of America . . . have no government at all and live at this day in that brutish manner. . . ." (ch. xiii, para. 11).

The way to break out of this is for individuals to give up their own rights in favor of an individual (or an assembly of individuals), who is empowered to punish and enforce the common good. It is this realization on the part of individuals that results in the creation of the state. In Hobbes' own words (ch. xvii, para. 13), "The only way to create such a common power as may be able to defend them from the invasion of foreigners and the injuries of one another and . . . live contentedly, is to confer all their power and strength upon one man, or upon one assembly of men. . . . This is the generation of that great Leviathan. . . ."

Michael Taylor (1976) formalized Hobbes's theory as a Prisoner's Dilemma in which the state of nature is the equilibrium that arises when individuals pursue their self-interest with no outside force.[8] The Sovereign

---

[7] Even when the war is not literally so, life is bad enough, since the war that occurs in the state of nature "consisteth not in battle only, or the act of fighting, but in a tract of time wherein the will to contend by battle is sufficiently known. [. . .] For as the nature of foul weather lieth not in a shower or two of rain, but in an inclination thereto of many days together, so the nature of war consisteth not in actual fighting, but in the known disposition thereto during all the time there is no assurance to the contrary." (Hobbes, 1651, ch. xiii, para. 9).

[8] From Hobbes's own description, it is not always clear (and Taylor is aware of this) whether he is talking of the Prisoner's Dilemma or a game with two equilibria (one Pareto-superior to the other), so that what the players face is a coordination problem.

in this model can be that outside force which can lead people to cooperate and thereby achieve Pareto optimality. Taylor goes on to discuss voluntary cooperation and cooperation through governmental enforcement, but that is not my concern here (though I will argue in the next section that the distinction between voluntary and government-enforced may not always be meaningful). What his discussion of Hobbes' nicely demonstrates is the source of the 'third party' view of government. This, as has been argued in Chapter 5, is the basis of the standard view of government and many of our contemporary misunderstandings of the concept of state.

8.2. The Standard View and Its Brood of Fallacies

As discussed in an earlier chapter, in traditional economics textbooks, "government" is treated as *exogenous* to the economy. It controls certain variables – for instance, the amount of money supply in the economy, or the size of the fiscal deficit – and provides certain public goods, without having any compelling reason for doing what it does. It is this character-ization that made us direct all our advice at the government. Consumers were busy maximizing utility and entrepreneurs their profits, and so it was only the agents of the state that were considered pliable enough for advice giving to make sense. This view of the government has become so pervasive that it has entered our everyday discourse.

Consider the following observation about how the Brazilian economy can realize its great potential, taken from *The Economist*, March 27–April 2, 1999 (Brazil Survey, p. 5): "But to seize that opportunity, this survey will argue, Brazil needs a radical rethink of the workings of all levels of gov-ernment. Only then will it be able to realise its tantalizingly rich potential and overcome its huge problems." One hears or sees statements like this all the time, in newspapers and in talks given by policy economists. One is told how Nigeria has done poorly because successive governments have squandered money, or how India could have done well if it were not for the politicians. The responsibility is always laid at the doorstep of the govern-ment. These observations may be right in themselves, but one can think of other observations involving other agents of an economy, which are also right but sound wrong to the economist's "trained" ear. If, for instance, all entrepreneurs began producing more, despite the fact that this resulted in losses for themselves, that may help an economy take off. If ordinary citizens ate less and worked more hours, that may give the economy a boost. But social scientists and responsible journalists seldom advise entrepreneurs to produce beyond their profit-maximizing point and consumers to eat less than they do.

The journalist's penchant to single out government as the cause of the economy's predicament is a reflection of the widespread belief that, if things are to change, the process has to start with the government, and this, in turn, shows how pervasive and influential the economist's view of government as exogenous to the economy has been.

Our poor understanding of government has showed up in other places too. Some economists recommend that individuals should be entirely free to pursue their own interest, free from government intervention. Similarly, some economists have argued that institutions that have emerged out of individual actions are optimal; they are there because their benefits outweigh the costs (*see, for instance*, Anderson and Hill, 1975; and Posner, 1981). Government, according to this view, is an organization that distorts these natural civic institutions. Such a view is made possible only by not asking ourselves where government itself has come from. Government did not create government; so we cannot castigate it as one more manifestation of the evils of government. As discussed in the previous section, government, as we now know, is a fairly modern institution. It has evolved through the ages, through a multitude of individual actions. Hence, if we maintain that individuals, left to themselves, bring about desirable institutions, then we cannot say that such institutions need to be protected from government. This is because government is itself such an institution.

Moreover, to take the view that it is all right for individuals to bring about institutions that help them cooperate, but without creating a government that intervenes, amounts to placing an exogenous constraint on *individual* effort. It is the fallacy that some politicians commit when they say that government should get out of charitable and welfare work and leave these to community efforts. What this misses out on is that government itself is one such community effort. This is not to deny that a distinction can be drawn between community and government (*see, for instance*, Taylor, 1982) but voluntariness is not the key to that distinction.

To see the intricacy of this argument and the ease with which we can err in our conception of government, let me draw on the other work of Taylor, which I have already discussed in the previous section: Taylor (1976). As he observes in his Preface, in the West the most popular justification of the state is that "without the state, people would not act so as to realize their common interests; more specifically, they would not voluntarily cooperate to provide themselves with certain public goods." The roots of this view, he argues, go back principally to Hobbes, and also to Hume. Taylor's book is meant to be a critique of this view. He is right in challenging it, for it is based on the "third party" (or exogenous, or "puppet") view of government that we have already taken to task. However, one does not have to be a careful reader to see that his criticism is very different from the one being made in this book. Taylor shows (*see, also,* Rutten 1997) how individuals can voluntarily cooperate, for instance, through repeated play of the Prisoner's Dilemma (for the technical derivation of this result see Chapter 2). This then becomes the basis of his rejection of the Hobbesian recommendation whereby individuals create the Sovereign, who then ensures order and cooperation among the citizens by "creating appropriate laws and punishing transgressors" (Taylor, 1976: 104).

The error in this viewpoint is to characterize the government-led path to order as a "coercive one" and the repeated Prisoner's Dilemma path as the "voluntary one." Hence, Taylor's (1976) critique also commits the fallacy of the exogenous conception of government. Since in reality government is itself a creation of the individuals and is run by the individuals, the government-led path to social order is nothing but a self-enforcing equilibrium among the individuals – a point that is implied in a thought-provoking paper by David Friedman (1994). After all, even in the repeated Prisoner's Dilemma, cooperation arises from the threat of punishment to deviators from the cooperative path. Just because in the Hobbesian route the "punishers" are *called* members of government, this does not make the Hobbesian path any more coercive than the one sustained by a trigger strategy in a repeated game.

In brief, we cannot maintain that (a) institutions that emerge from the actions and choices of free individuals are desirable and (b) big governments are undesirable. (Social norms, as we have seen in Chapters 4–6, can lead to as much oppression as the state.) Much of the popular debate concerning "big" and "small" governments is of such poor intellectual quality precisely because it is rooted in this fallacy. We can argue that governments are often too big and too oppressive, but we have to construct such an argument on the negation of (a).

The endogenization of government is a large research project. The works of Buchanan (1968), Taylor (1976), Dixit (1996) and many other contemporary writers have contributed building blocks to this project.[9] Yet as the several examples in this and the earlier chapters show, it is easy, in the course of research, to stray into the same fallacies that one had set out to

---

[9] *See, for instance,* Brock and Magee (1978), Findlay and Wellisz (1982), Bhagwati, Brecher and Srinivasan (1984), de Jasay (1985), Grindle (1991), Meier (1991), and Acemoglu and Robinson (1998).

avoid. The almost universal view of law as an instrument for altering the strategy sets or payoff functions betrays our inadvertent commitment to a concept of government as an exogenous agent. The model of law, proposed in Chapter 5 as a set of dicta that do nothing to the payoff functions or the sets of strategies open to the players but merely influence the players' beliefs and create new focal points, is a consequence of the inclusive approach to the state taken seriously and "all the way." If the concept of law discussed in Chapter 5 seems new, it is only a reflection of the endogenous theory of the state not being taken seriously, even when we claim to abide by it.

8.3. State as Beliefs

What our analysis points towards is a much more elusive concept of "state." Like the approach taken to law in this book, the view of the state that naturally emerges from the inclusive approach is that of nothing but a bundle of beliefs and expectations in the minds of the people. The state, in the end, is nothing more tangible than the ordinary citizen's belief, that, if he behaves in a certain way, the agents of the state, who are simply other citizens, will punish him or reward him, along with the beliefs of the agents of the state that if a person behaves in a certain way then they ought to punish or reward that person and, if they do not do so, others will punish or reward them, and so on. In other words, these beliefs must be self-fulfilling because they result in an outcome that is a subgame perfect equilibrium.

Once again, as in the case of law, there being a state or not, and there being one kind of state or another, are not properties of the rules of the game being played by the citizens, nor of the strategy sets or payoff functions, but of the beliefs in the players' mind and, through that, the outcome of the game.

While this concept of the state contradicts what most textbooks of economics teach, it builds on an ancient legacy – that of David Hume. It is impossible not to marvel at the depth of Hume's understanding of collective action. He had none of the modern tools of analysis, such as game theory and decision analysis; yet the conclusions he reaches, using pure intuition and reason, are quite breathtaking. The section, "Of the Origin of Government," in Hume's (1739) classic, *A Treatise of Human Nature*, is a remarkable statement on the *raison d'être* of the state. He begins by giving an account of the frailty of human decision making, including a remarkable statement of dynamic inconsistency and salience – almost as if he had read Akerlof (1991). He argues, like Hobbes, that, without a government, human beings are doomed to the "state of nature," which can be "wretched and savage." So one needs governance and government. Where Hume makes no mistake is in recognizing that this government has to emerge from the same group of people who suffer in its absence. Given that human beings are selfish and myopic, how can they be expected to dispense justice that brings about the common good? Hume does not manage to give a full answer to this, but he recognizes the importance of the question. He says that human beings can emerge from the state of nature by giving extra powers into the hands of some individuals in such a way that it is not against the interest of these persons to dispense justice. So the act of governance must be compatible with the interests of the agents of the state, since they are also human beings. And once this is done, society can have order and progress (Hume, 1739, Bk. III, Sec. VII):

> Thus bridges are built; harbours open'd; ramparts rais'd; canals form'd; fleets equipp'd; and armies disciplin'd every where, by the care of government, *which tho' composed of men subject to all infirmities, becomes, by one of the finest and most subtle inventions imaginable, a composition, which is, in some measure, exempted from all these infirmities.* [italics added].

In a later essay, "Of the First Principles of Government," Hume (1758) had puzzled about the sources of state influence on social and economic outcomes. He wrote (p. 32 of the 1987 edition), "Nothing appears more surprising to those who consider human affairs with a philosophical eye, than the easiness with which the many are governed by the few . . ."; and he reaches the remarkable conclusion that those who rule do so by the force of opinion: "It is therefore *on opinion only that government is founded*; and this maxim extends to the most despotic [. . .] governments, as well as to the most free and most popular" (italics added). Hume's view of government clearly sits well with Havel's theory of despotism. And the same idea is echoed in David Friedman's (1994: 10) observation, "I will accept one [the tax collector] and fight the other [the robber] because of my beliefs about other people's behavior – what they will or will not fight for [. . .]. We are bound together by a set of mutually reinforcing strategic expectations."

One seeming counter-argument to this intangible conception of government is to observe, at the minimum, that all governments have some manifestation in concrete and mortar, not just figuratively but literally. There are the buildings, such as the White House in Washington, 10 Downing Street in London and the Casa Rosada in Buenos Aires. So, if nothing else, the citizens cannot walk across these areas because the buildings block the way. They cannot walk across the open lawns that *would* have been there if the US government, and therefore the White House, did not exist. So, it seems, the set of strategies open to individuals in the economy game are changed by virtue of the existence of government.

All the observations in the above paragraph are correct, excepting the final sentence. The fact that the actions available to the US citizens now are different from what would have been available to them if the US government did not exist (or existed in some other form) does not mean that having a state (or a different form of state) amounts to the people of the United States playing a different game. It instead means that having a state has meant that *today* US citizens have reached a different node of the same game. And at this node the actions available to individual players are (and, therefore, the subgame is) different. If one goes back in time and thinks of Americans as embarking on a long game with a state or without a state, the game would be the same. But, of course, having a state influences (or, more correctly, *is a set of*) beliefs and "opinions" – to use Hume's term – and may therefore influence the outcome or the path of play. Hence, if, in 1999, after a few hundred years of the game having started, we look at the strategies available to individual players, we may well find a difference.

To see this more concretely, go to the game shown in Fig. 2.8 of Chapter 2, replacing the payoff 0 with −1.[10] Suppose that this is the economy game being played by two players; then the view that I am asserting (and claiming a Humean heritage for) is that having a state or not cannot influence the game. But it can influence beliefs (in fact, to have a state *is* to have a certain set of beliefs) and therefore the *play* of the game. So having a state may result in player 1 playing L in period 1, though she would have played R if there were no state. Now suppose that there is a state and we are in the second period; player 2 will find that he has no choices. On the other hand, if there were no state then in the second period he could have chosen between l and r. But this alteration in the actions available to a player because of the state is not a change in the game but a mere reflection of the fact that the players have reached a different node in the same game.

The subgame stretching in front of us *today* is itself a game, so can we not say that the game that we have open to us today would have been different if there were no state or a different form of state? We have to be careful in answering this question. If having the state or not was a matter of the

---

[10] I do this for the purely technical reason that it renders all strategies subgame perfect. Hence, in working with this example we do not have to worry about treading outside the equilibria.

past, then the answer is "yes," for the reasons given above. Having a state may have resulted in differences in our landscape, for instance, in having new buildings, bridges, submarines and areas protected by barbed wire, and also in different behavior on the part of other nations, and so brought us to a different node. And so, the game stretching in front of us today onwards may well be different. If, on the other hand, we are considering the state vanishing today or the form of government getting altered today, then the game open to us today cannot be changed. How we *play* the game may well change because of the change in the form of government or the disappearance of the state, but not the strategy sets and the payoff functions, that is, the game itself.

This means that, as in the case of law discussed in Chapter 5, when we write down a model of the full economy, having a state or not having a state cannot be thought of as something that alters the payoff functions of the players. It can only influence beliefs and, through that, the outcome. Nevertheless, there is a sense in which we can say that the subgame in front of us today is different by virtue of there *having been* a state. Hence, in an extensive-form model of the economy, there is a sense in which our standard language of the state is more likely to be right than for a normal-form construction, but we have to be careful nevertheless, since this treads very close to the fallacy of exogeneity.

Moving on now to a related matter, note that, while a state is, at a fundamental level, nothing but beliefs, the *kind* of beliefs that the state induces in a game has some distinguishing features. In a state, not *everybody* is expected to be involved in upholding the law. The expectations are invariably asymmetric. There are some individual players – by definition, the agents of the state, such as the police, the judges and the bureaucrats – from whom the actions to uphold the law are expected. Given a state and its laws, when I, an ordinary citizen, do something to violate the law, I expect punitive action from one of these upholders of the law and when these upholders of law violate the law, they expect punishment from other upholders of the law. Of course, I am an ordinary citizen and they are the upholders of law not exogenously but as a concomitant of the beliefs.

There are therefore several reasons why, despite the state, at a fundamental level, being merely a bundle of beliefs, we can point to the state, or at least to different manifestations of the state, in the street. When we walk down a nation's capital, we point to government buildings and the functionaries of the state; when we see corruption, we point to the politicians; when we think of Brazil not realizing its potential, we lament that the government in Brasilia does not behave differently; and, when NATO bombs

Serbia, it drops pamphlets assuring the civilians that NATO wishes them no harm and that it is only their government that it dislikes. First, in most of these cases the state (that is, a particular set of beliefs) having being there for a while, there are manifestations of the state in the form of past actions (putting up a building, fencing off a ground, and so on). Secondly, the state being there means that the players have beliefs about what a *subset* of players would do if a player violated the law.[11] This subset consists of the agents or the functionaries of the state and is at times treated *as* the state. This is what ensures that, though our modeling of the state is frequently faulty, the language of government and state that we use in our everyday discourse is not necessarily flawed. It may hide behind it a defective view of government, as an agency exogenous to society, but not all our reference to government can be taken as evidence of that. With this caveat in mind the remainder of this chapter turns to a discussion of practical matters concerning the role of government and governance. It does this, keeping in mind that it is an inclusive government that we are talking about and so many of the liberties that an economist can take with an exogenous government are no longer permitted.

8.4. The Dane County Farmers' Market

The Dane County Farmers' Market is a weekly market that is open every Saturday morning during the summer and autumn months in Madison's Capital Square. It is meant to be an outlet for local producers to sell fresh, usually organic, farm products. For buyers, it provides old-world charm and the opportunity to do some leisurely shopping and taste local non-commercially produced foods. To a visitor, the Dane County Market is like the ideal of a free market: several small producers set up their small temporary stalls and compete for customers. But there is no jostling and chaos, the competition seems to run entirely on the basis of price and the quality of the food being sold. The prices are low and the fruits, vegetables, eggs and flowers are visibly fresh and of good quality. If the visitor happens to be an economist steeped in conventional neoclassical wisdom, this will be

---

[11] It is interesting to note that in drawing a distinction between an order that is a "convention" and an order that is a "law", Weber (1922: 34) relies precisely on whether the enforcement is a general responsibility of the people (convention) or a special responsibility of *some* people: "An order will be called . . . *law* if it is externally guaranteed by the probability that physical or psychological coercion will be applied by a *staff* of people in order to bring about compliance . . ." (his italics).

of no surprise since competition, which is not hindered by centralized controls and rules, is, according to mainstream doctrine, supposed to achieve
precisely this.

But in this case the lay person's bewilderment will be more to the point
than the economist's composure, because a little bit of research reveals that
behind the harmony of the Farmers' Market is a small-print green booklet
of 18 pages that specifies a remarkably detailed set of rules and the penal-
ties for violating these rules. The rules do not simply talk about cleanliness
and how stalls are to be set up and how, prior to setting up shop, the vendor
must seek permission by completing an "Application For Permission to
Sell," but also about a variety of other matters: "Raw fruits and vegetables
must be grown from cuttings grown by the vendor or from seeds and
transplants. . . . Purchased plant materials must be grown on the vendor's
premises for at least 60 days before they can be offered for sale at the
market. . . . Eggs must be produced by hens which have been raised by the
vendor for 75 percent of their production weight. . . . Sellers must not bring
pets into the Market for health and safety reasons. The sale or giving away
of animals on the Capitol grounds is prohibited. . . . Vendors must discour-
age sales to people in vehicles or lengthy double parking by customers. . . .
Vendors selling wild-gathered items must have an application to sell filed
with the market prior to arrival at the market and either have proof of land-
ownership or show written permission from the landowner to gather the
product. . . . Vendors must have photocopies of all necessary licenses. . . ."

The Farmers' Market is a nice example of the role of a Humean government in microcosm. The same people that buy and sell have set up for themselves a set of rules that they are then supposed to abide by. They have also
put aside some people to carry out the administration and enforcement.
The analogy is not exact, since this is a state within a state, and so the
vendors and the buyers have to abide by the laws of the United States and
the state of Wisconsin.[12] Moreover, for a variety of rule violations the Board
of Directors of the Farmers' Market no doubt take the help of the actual
police force and judiciary of the nation. Nevertheless, it is an illustration
of the importance of governance for the economy and market to function
efficiently.

---

[12] The interaction between different layers of government is the subject of ample literature. The
central government can at times reinforce and strengthen local governments, but it can also create
disincentives. In India, the village-level *panchayat* often resembles a local community-level
administration, such as the Farmer's Market bureaucracy. The literature on local government and
its interaction with the state is large: *see, for instance,* Wade (1988), Seabright (1996), Singh (1997),
and Bardhan and Mookherjee (1998).

Is the harmony that prevails in the Dane County Farmers' Market an outcome of voluntary cooperation or the coercion of government? Posing the question in this manner makes it evident that voluntariness and coercion are not mutually exclusive categories. The rules place restrictions on individual vendors (and also some on buyers) and so, at one level, there is coercion. But at the same time the rules are, by and large, the outcome of the combined wishes of the people who participate in the Market to enable the Market to function more effectively. So they are voluntary. In talking of government, the important distinction is not between voluntariness and coercion because, in the final analysis, the outcome that comes to prevail must be the equilibrium of the game that takes account of all agents, including the enforcers of the law. The important distinction is that in a government-based equilibrium, the players play asymmetric roles. Some perform the economic activities (such as the vendors), while others take on the role of enforcing the law by punishing the violators. If we look at only a part of the game – in particular, only the players involved in economic activity – the government-based equilibrium appears to be coercive (since these players seem to face restrictions from outside), while an equilibrium in which players participate symmetrically or, more importantly, no one specializes as an enforcer, appears to be voluntary. But this is no more than a matter of appearance. The illusion is created by comparing a part of one system with another system in full.

The above discussion draws our attention to the fact that in some games there may be two ways of reaching an efficient outcome, via having some players specialize in enforcement and alternately without such players (where each player combines the role of an economic agent and enforcer). But in other games we may not have such a choice. To take Hume's famous example, two neighbors may agree and succeed in draining the meadow they possess in common, but it becomes difficult and may be impossible when a thousand persons have to agree to such action. In the latter case they may have to think of official enforcers. However, unlike in some of the older work, we cannot simply wish into existence exogenous enforcers but should instead think of setting aside some of the thousand to do this task, and design this in a way that it is in the interest of the enforcers to enforce.

It is easy to try to elicit some message from the discussion above about whether government is good or bad and about whether government should be small or big. But that would be wrong. In fact, the search for such general propositions is a remnant of precisely the kind of thinking that this monograph is criticizing.

Much harm has been done in the past by trying to base policy on broad-brush beliefs, such as government intervention being good or bad, or markets being left free or regulated. In several countries there have been attempts to introduce a free market economy, without noticing that in the economies where the free market works the market is embedded in a certain structure of governance and social norms. Consequently, such reforms have often backfired, resulting in chaos and the breakdown of the very market that they were supposed to nurture (Platteau, 1994; Stiglitz, 1999). If a visitor to the Dane County Farmers' Market went home without having seen the green book, and tried to replicate the market by simply clearing some area and inviting farmers to come and set up stall, it is likely that this would end up in inefficiency and bucolic disorder.

Part IV. ETHICS AND JUDGMENT

9. Welfare and Interpersonal Comparisons

9.1. Preliminaries

It is time now to move on, from the central story of this book to some of its by-products in other fields. This part of the book is a foray into the related discipline of welfare economics and ethics. These are large subjects on which volumes have been written; and it would be foolhardy to enter this domain in the closing chapters of a book if the aim were to present an even-handed discussion. But evenhandedness is not the strength of this book, as must be evident to the reader by now, and no attempt will be made to make amends for that here. Instead, the aim of these two chapters (9 and 10) is to build up to some special topics within welfare economics on which it is possible to bring a new perspective using the results and propositions of the earlier chapters. We are, for instance, now able to shed new light on rule and act utilitarianism and deontological ethics, and mount an unusual criticism on utlitarianism and the conventional modeling of rights. These are the subject matter of Chapter 10. The present chapter is concerned with some "preliminaries" of welfare economics: in particular, a discussion of the meaning of welfare and interpersonal comparisons. These are concepts taken for granted in the next chapter. The caveats are discussed here.

"Proponents of the economic approach to law find in welfare economics a framework for understanding large bodies of common law and develop-ing new law," wrote Jules Coleman (1982) in setting out to investigate the relation between law and welfare economics. The view of "law and eco-nomics" as normative theory and its relation to utilitarianism and liberty has recently been emphasized and written about by Nussbaum (1997). It is arguable that, just as human beings have preferences and selfish interests, they also have a sense of morality and moral judgment. This is true whether or not they live by their morals. For most people, morals, like social norms, influence behavior. But whether or not they do so, people almost invariably *possess* a sense of morals. A kleptomaniac, or even an ordinary thief, may well believe that it is wrong to steal. Moreover, when we try to concep-tualize an ideal state or the drafting of laws for the running of a nation, we usually do so in terms of this innate moral sense of ours. It is for this reason that the study of law and government is closely connected to welfare eco-nomics and, more generally, to ethics.

While in much of social science writing our preferences are treated as primitives, it is recognized that our moral judgments are open to suasion, reason and cogitation. One must be careful, however, not to draw *too* sharp a contrast between preferences and morals in this respect. Our preferences also respond to reason, suasion and societal concerns at large. Simple folks, gradually making their way into sophisticated society, learn not to like the wines they once did. (This usually happens after a period of *pretending* not to like these.) But it is probably true that a person's preference is more of a primitive than a person's morals. Morals, like the social norms discussed in Chapter 4, are more susceptible to change in response to society-wide changes than preferences.

Given the importance of moral judgment in conceptualizing the state and its laws and the openness of these judgments to reason and persuasion, it is not surprising that the literature on what are the *correct* morals is very large.

In the present chapter my focus is on the informational feasibility of some ethical systems, and so it is best viewed as providing the informational foundation for the discussion in the next chapter. There is a substantial literature that recognizes the close relation between information and value judgments (See Sen, 1974; D'Aspremont and Gevers, 1977; and Hammond, 1976). Indeed, our inability to make interpersonal comparisons of certain kinds may sharply reduce the possibility of using certain kinds of welfare judgments and so may prevent us from taking some particular moral stance. If, for instance, we cannot compare one person's change in utility with another person's change in utility, then we will not be able to use utilitarianism in most situations. Hence, before joining in the debate on whether one system of welfare judgment is better than another, it is worth being clear about what we mean by and the scope for interpersonal comparisons. That is the subject matter of this chapter. In the process, I want to demonstrate that one influential method of interpersonal comparison, namely that propounded by what may be called the Chicago school, and widely used in labor economics and in evaluating institutions, suffers from a serious problem of inconsistency.

Before proceeding to examine the Chicago view, I shall dwell on a philosophically deep, though less operational, approach: the method of "extended sympathy." This has been widely used in social-choice theory (Sen, 1970; Hammond, 1976; Strasnick, 1976; D'Aspremont and Gevers, 1977; Arrow, 1977) as an approach to interpersonal comparisons. While extended sympathy cannot be faulted on grounds of inconsistency, I shall argue in the next section that its philosophical foundations are open to doubts and its use *as an instrument of interpersonal comparison* needs rethinking.

Broadly speaking, there are two grounds for attacking any judgment on interpersonal welfare. First, we can adduce reasons why a particular comparison is unappealing. For example, it could be pointed out to one who believes that equal income implies equal welfare that, though John and Tom have equal incomes, John knows how to "use" money, and is, consequently, better off. Such arguments are not compelling but merely *persuasive*. Second, we could point out some logical inconsistency in the method of interpersonal comparison. For example, the view that if two individuals receive the same basket of goods then their welfare levels are the same is inconsistent in a world where people's preferences are not identical and individual preferences reflect individual welfare. This is easily demonstrated. Let individual i prefer basket b_1 to b_2 and j prefer b_2 to b_1. Then obviously we cannot hold that i's utilities from b_1 and b_2 respectively are the same as j's. Such an argument is *compelling*.

In setting out to search for an acceptable method of interpersonal comparison, we should first weed out the logically inconsistent ones. Then we can use arguments of the first type from the preceding paragraph to decide on a particular comparison method from among all consistent ones. My concern here is mainly with the problem of logical consistency, for it is shown that the requirement of logical consistency is extremely demanding. Several methods of interpersonal comparisons, including the one implicit in the Chicago approach, falls foul of logical consistency. The argument used against the method of extended sympathy is, however, of the first type.

9.2. If I Were You . . .

There was a time when the whole discussion of interpersonal comparison would be viewed with skepticism. Robbins (1938) argued that interpersonal comparisons were ascientific. The problem stems from the fact that the overt state of an individual does not always reflect the state of her mind: it is *possible* that when Mona Lisa smiled she was happy, or that the "untouchable" in India with no income is happier than the wealthy Brahmin. This phase of skepticism appears to be over. It seems to be agreed that we can make some welfare comparisons, though we should specify clearly what our basis of comparison is. Many ways of making interpersonal comparisons have been suggested over the years (Harsanyi, 1955; Pattanaik, 1968; Simon, 1974; Becker, 1975; *see also* Kaneko, 1984, for a discussion). One example discussed by Becker (1975) is interesting because it typifies a common error. He suggests that "evidence as to which of two people has the greater desire for something can be obtained by seeing which of them is willing to work harder" (p. 483). But this presupposes that people's disutilities of work are of identical intensity. For if I had a greater distaste for work than you, then I could be working less hard than you to obtain "something" but at the same time desire this "something" more intensely than you. Hence, in outlining a method of how to make interpersonal comparisons, Becker starts off by making certain interpersonal comparisons, namely between different people's disutilities of work. This kind of erroneous argument has frequently been used to justify unequal incomes. It has been claimed, for instance, that if i works harder than j and earns a greater income, then this reflects i's greater desire for income.

In social choice and welfare economics, arguably the most widely used method of interpersonal comparison is that of "extended sympathy." **Extended sympathy** entails each person being asked questions of the following kind. Would you rather be person i in social state x or person j in social state y? Since I shall keep coming back to this question, it is useful to give the question a name. I shall call it Q. Let me also introduce the standard notation of writing (i, x) to denote "person i in social state x." Hence

Q: Would you rather be (i, x) or (j, y)?

The advantage of this approach is that it converts the problem of interpersonal comparison into a problem of *individual* choice. Hence, if deductions based on individual choice were scientific, as Robbins had suggested, then here was a basis for making interpersonal comparisons scientifically.

Of course it is possible that different individuals will give different answers to question Q so that, instead of having one standard for making interpersonal comparisons, we shall have several. Indeed, social-choice theory, based on extended ordering, begins by presuming that every person has a preference ordering defined on $N \times X$ where N is the set of individuals and X is the set of social states. *Given* these "extended orderings," some very powerful theorems have been established (see, e.g., Hammond, 1976; Strasnick, 1976; D'Aspremont and Gevers, 1977; Maskin, 1978; Roberts, 1980). My aim here, however, is to raise a more basic question. In particular, I shall argue that question Q is ambiguous in a fundamental way. Hence, if different people answer it differently, it is entirely possible that they are interpreting the question differently, in which case their answers are not comparable. The only way in which the ambiguity can be resolved,

but is to make the question trivial and everybody's answer would be the same. Either way we seem to run into an impasse.[1]

Let me illustrate the problem with an empirical case study. A few weeks after my arrival in London as a student, a street urchin threw a water balloon in my direction. No great damage was done and after a moment's vacillation I decided that the most judicious course of action was to ignore the incident and walk on. Just then, a large gentleman strode up to me and said in a tone not meant to hide his disapproval of my choice of strategy: "If I were you, young man, I would have thrashed that boy." My response was: "No, you would not because I did not." Given his declared proclivity for using physical force, it is needless to add that my response was kept at the level of an inaudible mutter and I never got to know his views on this philosophical issue.

One charitable way of interpreting the gentleman's remark is to claim that when people say "if I were you" what they mean is "if I were in your position." But this is highly ambiguous because it is not clear what "being in my position" means. If he was walking down a road and a boy threw a water balloon, would that mean he was in my position? Not quite, because just having arrived in a new country was an important part of the picture. If he had just arrived in a new country, was walking down a road and a boy threw a water balloon, would that mean he was in my position? Not quite. One can go on adding details from my past – my body weight, childhood education, and so on – in an effort to create a situation that describes "my position." If one goes the whole way, then the exercise becomes dull – and he would have done what I did. If one stops short of the whole way, the answer will depend on where one stops and is, therefore, inherently ambiguous.

Similarly with question Q. The answer depends on what being i in state x involves. Economists have tended to shy away from this question. In the literature on envy, this involves putting i's consumption vector into your utility function. While that is fine in the context of discussing justice

---

[1] An interesting example of how some questions have the chimerical quality of appearing deep occurs in Bertrand Russell's autobiography. Russell wrote that Wittgenstein used to believe that it is better to be good than clever. I have asked several people, including myself, the question: "Is it better to be good than clever?" Most people find this an interesting question, almost all answer it in the affirmative and then feel duly noble (I did) for taking such a noble position and being in the company of Wittgenstein. I am, however, now convinced that the question is a trivial one with only one right answer. It seems interesting only because of a quirk of the English language. Suppose that instead of "better" the word used in English was "gooder", in the same way that we say "taller" for "more tall". But now the question becomes trivial: Is it gooder to be good than clever? The answer is: yes, just as it is cleverer to be clever than good! If people gave different answers to the question, it would not reflect their different attitudes to life, but merely their different under-standing of the question. Something similar is true of our question Q.

and envy-freedom, this is not quite acceptable in doing interpersonal comparisons. Sen (1973), who considers the matter, points out that "putting oneself in the position of another includes the exercise of having his tastes and mental make-up as well" (*see also* Pattanaik, 1968). But, if to remove ambiguity one becomes *completely* like another person, then a society in which you are *i* is completely indistinguishable from a society in which you are *j*. In that case, it is not clear that your attitude should be anything other than one of indifference. And in that case, extended orderings will cease to give any information about preferences and attitudes.

As mentioned earlier, my arguments here are not meant to be compelling but merely persuasive. And it is enough if the reader is persuaded that question Q is either trivial or fundamentally ambiguous.[2] Much greater thought has to go into it to give it a clear and operational meaning, and till that happens people's answer to question Q may not be a good basis for making welfare judgments about different social states.

9.3. Income and Welfare

Let me now turn to a more practical approach to interpersonal comparison and see how well this stands up to scrutiny. Most studies of inequality are based on the distribution of wealth or income. The planner's concern for a better distribution is usually a concern for making *income* more equal. But for "equality" to mean an equal distribution of *income* is to rob some of the ethical appeal of egalitarianism. What we really seek is equality of *welfare or utility*. However, the preoccupation with income distribution may be justified if one assumes that income represents welfare and equal income between individuals means equal welfare. This assumption, which I shall refer to as the IRW (income represents welfare) view, has been attacked by several economists, including Milton Friedman and George Stigler. They have argued that equality of income does not imply equality of welfare. I shall refer to this viewpoint as the "Chicago" view.

---

[2] Gallie (1955: 169) had argued that certain concepts are "essentially contested," that is, ambiguity is an *inherent* feature of some concepts. It is arguable, in a similar vein, that certain *questions* are essentially contested. Clearly the information content of answers to such questions is likely to be slender.

Moore (1902) in his classic work *Principia Ethica*, took the issue of "*question* ambiguity" to be a more general problem of ethics. The first sentence of the Preface to his book declares: "It appears to me that in ethics, as in all other philosophical studies, the difficulties and disagreements, of which its history is full, are mainly due to a very simple cause: namely, to the attempt to answer questions, without first discovering precisely *what* question it is which you desire to answer."

Both these viewpoints represent different ways of making interpersonal comparison[3] and, in particular, they are attempts to answer the question: When can we say that two individuals are equally well-off? It will be argued that the answers provided by both the IRW and Chicago schools have serious logical problems. I shall, in particular, closely examine the Chicago view and the concept of "equalizing differences" because these have been extremely influential. "Equalizing differences" are today a part of common parlance in mainstream economics.

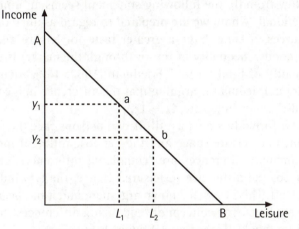

Figure 9.1. The leisure–income space

The Chicago school's argument against the IRW view is easily summarized. If two individuals face the same feasibility set in the income–leisure space, then there seems very little reason for saying that the person with the lower income is worse-off. And yet we would be forced to say this if we held the IRW view. As a prelude to some further analysis, let us explain this diagrammatically. Let two individuals face the same budget constraint, shown as line AB in Fig. 9.1. Individual 1 chooses point a and individual 2 chooses point b. According to the IRW view, 1 is better-off than 2 since 1 earns y_1 and 2 earns y_2. Clearly the Chicago school is justified in pointing out that this is unreasonable since individual 2 may be earning more but he also gets less leisure.

[3] Actually what these represent are different ways of making weak level comparability (Basu, 1980). For definitions of different comparability types and the algebra of interpersonal comparisons, which is now quite well developed, *see, for instance*, Sen (1970), Basu (1983a), and Blackorby, Donaldson and Weymark (1984).

This argument is now formally stated as an axiom: (I) If two persons choose from the same budget set in the income–leisure space, then it cannot be said that one individual is better-off than the other.

This is an appealing assumption and it quite rightly cautions those who are preoccupied with *income* distribution alone. The Chicago school goes on further to assert that a large amount of inequality in a capitalist economy is of the above kind, that is, illusory. Casual observation casts doubts on such an assertion, but now is not the occasion to go into that debate.

Arguments of type (I) have had considerable influence on economic thinking. Now from (I), the following statement seems an innocuous step: "Given individuals whom we are prepared to regard as alike in ability and initial resources, if some have a greater taste for leisure and others for marketable goods, inequality of return through the market is necessary to achieve equality of total return." Friedman (1962: 162).[4] Hence, in terms of our diagram, Friedman is arguing that the difference in income, $y_1 - y_2$ offsets the difference in leisure, $L_1 - L_2$.

This is now formally stated as: (II) If two persons face the same budget set in the income–leisure space and they choose different income levels, then these income differences are "equalizing differences," that is, they compensate for the difference in leisure.[5] Hence, the two individuals are equally well-off. This is a well-known argument and it has been frequently repeated to students. The concept of "equalizing differences" has appeared in standard textbooks (for instance Stigler, 1966).

It will be argued here that the logical foundations of (II) are dubious. It may also be argued that (II) is unappealing, that is, arguments of the first type from Section 9.1 may be used against it, but that is not my concern here. It can be demonstrated that, on purely logical grounds, (II) is unacceptable.

Since this logical problem arises even with the IRW view, I shall keep the proof general by assuming that utility is a function of just two variables, x and y, which are represented on the two axes in Fig. 9.2. So x and y could be two goods, or leisure and income. We assume individual utilities are ordinal and indifference curves are the usual smooth contours in two-dimensional space. We demonstrate that (II) implies a type of level

---

[4] Similarly, Friedman (1962: 162) says that if the amounts of leisure are different, then "if both were paid equally in money, their incomes in a more fundamental sense would be unequal."

[5] The Chicago school has argued that income differences could also reflect differences in the pleasantness of the job and the work environment. In order to keep our argument simple, we assume that there are no differences in pleasantness of jobs and work environment; only the hours of work vary. The main results hold even without this assumption.

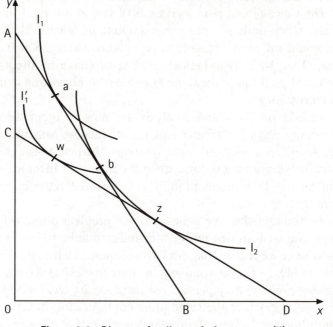

Figure 9.2. Diagram for disproof of statement (II)

comparison that is internally inconsistent. Let $u(d, i)$ denote the utility of individual i at point d. I_1 and I_1' are individual 1's indifference curves and I_2 is 2's indifference curve. Let both individuals face the same budget set, AOB. Then individuals 1 and 2 will choose a and b, respectively. By (II), $u(a, 1) = u(b, 2)$. Now let prices change and both individuals face the budget set COD (CD being tangential to I_2). Then individuals 1 and 2 will choose w and z, respectively. By (II), $u(w, 1) = u(z, 2)$. But $u(b, 2) = u(z, 2)$, since b and z are both on I_2. Hence $u(a, 1) = u(w, 1)$. This is a contradiction since I is a higher indifference curve than I_1'. Hence, (II) is unacceptable.[6]

It is obvious that the IRW approach runs into this same logical difficulty. Assume that two individuals have the same amounts of leisure and same

---

[6] One objection to my argument may be that if x is leisure, then the budget constraint can only pivot around a point on the horizontal axis (representing 24 hours) and feasibility sets like AOB and COD cannot both occur. This is not a serious objection. It is possible to conceive of realistic labor-market situations that allow for budget constraints to intersect. Consider a labor market of the following sort. A fixed amount, h, is paid for eight hours work a day, employers refusing to employ people for less than eight hours a day. For every further hour, there is an overtime rate of w per hour. Then it is quite possible to construct, by varying h and w, budget constraints that intersect.

income. This means that, by the IRW view, the two individuals are equally well-off. The Chicago criticism against IRW would not hold in this particular case, since both get the same amount of leisure. However, our objection would still hold. Let there be two goods, x and y, which these two people buy. Then by a hypothetical exercise of changing the prices of x and y, we could go through the same arguments as above and demonstrate logical inconsistency.

Some remarks on the above analysis are now in order. Lerner, who argued in many ways for greater equality of income, was aware of this logical problem, as is obvious from his book (Lerner, 1944: ch. 3). And so he constructed arguments for a greater equality of income, which are not based on the IRW assumption. These are unaffected by the above discussion.

It may be thought that the genesis of the problem discussed above is the same as the well-known problem of index numbers. This is not true. This is clear once we realize that, for two individuals with identical preferences, the problem of level comparison need not exist, even though the index number problem may persist. For instance, let two individuals with identical preferences face the same price configuration in time t_1 but let i have more money income than j (and assume that they consume the same amount of leisure). Then, by most criteria, i is better-off than j. In time t_2, the prices change so that the consumption bundles chosen in t_1 are infeasible for both i and j. Now, clearly, we cannot unequivocally (that is, independent of the nature of the indifference curves) say whether i is better-off in t_1 or t_2 and the same goes for j. This is the index number problem. But j may be judged better-off than i in both t_1 and t_2, that is, there is no problem of level comparison in each time period.

Till now in this section, different methods of level comparisons (e.g., the IRW approach and the Chicago approach) were criticized purely on logical grounds, that is, only arguments of the second type from Section 9.1 were used. However, there can be important noncompelling arguments (i.e., of the first type) against assuming that if two individuals choose from identical feasibility sets, then their welfare levels are identical. Consider, for instance, the case of John, the vegetarian, and Tom, the meat-eater. Suppose that they have the same income and they face the same price vector. But if the price of meat is "exorbitant" and vegetables are "cheap," then there may be good reason to believe that John is better-off than Tom. A similar implication can be drawn from some remarks of Kenneth Arrow (1995: 8): "As Anatole France remarked somewhere, 'The law in its majestic equality forbids the rich as well as the poor from sleeping on park benches.' (The updated version would be that the law, or at least custom, permits the poor as well as the rich to sleep on park benches or street corners.)" On the one hand this law seems to expand or curb *everybody's* feasible options in the same way, yet we know that it relates to different kinds of people (in this case the rich and the poor) differently.

Having demonstrated that, in a world where preferences differ, the assumption that if two individuals choose from identical feasibility sets they are equally well-off is logically inconsistent, the question arises as to what alternative method of level comparisons can we suggest? I have discussed some of this in Basu (1994c). There is, however, no escape from the fact that there is no known fully satisfactory way of making interpersonal comparisons. This does not make it ascientific, as was once suggested; and, even more importantly, that is no reason for not making interpersonal comparisons. The latter would lead us to declare lots of pairs of social state as noncomparable, and if we are to make policy choices then the judgment of noncomparability is also a judgment.

The chapter that follows begins with an evaluation of utilitarianism. One criticism against utilitarianism is that it involves interpersonal comparison and that, too, of a fairly strong variety. It is true that this creates some concern about the basis of utilitarian judgments, but that is not the criticism that I will be concerned with here. My concern is about the *domain* of application of utilitarian principles and, for that matter, all consequentialist ethics. This is a criticism not generally made in the literature. In addition, it is rooted in the kinds of problems of rationality and social norms that I have been concerned with in the earlier chapters.

10. Utilitarianism and Rights

10.1. Basic Concepts

The aim of this chapter, as already explained in Section 9.1, is to critically evaluate utilitarianism and consequentialism as moral principles of decision-making; and also to study the scope of rights and individual liberty. In doing so, I draw on some of the methods of analysis developed in the earlier chapters of the book. Moving away from equilibrium-selection norms, back to rationality-limiting and preference-changing norms, observe that what limits relentless, selfish optimization on the part of individuals is a commitment to morals. But what is morally correct behavior? The answer to this can influence how we choose and behave. Moreover, no matter how we ourselves behave and no matter how the agents of government actually behave, we have come to expect moral behavior on the part of such agents. But the conventional view of what constitutes morally correct behavior runs into difficulty once we take seriously the methods of analysis introduced in Chapters 4–8. Hence, the aim of this chapter is not to build further on the central thesis of an inclusive view of government and society, but to derive some lessons from that for welfare economics.

This section provides a quick review of some dominant schools of thought in modern welfare economics and also defines some of the terms of the debate.[1] Some of these definitions will become clearer through their use in the next sections, but the process of initiation is important for those unfamiliar with the field. In addition, some of these terms have been used in several senses in the literature, and so it is important for me to clarify my use of terminology, which draws on welfare economics rather more than on moral philosophy.

Arguably, the most widely used system of moral judgment is utilitarianism. According to **utilitarianism**, a person should choose the action, from among those available to him, that maximizes total utility or happiness of all human beings. There are contexts where "utility" and "happiness" need to be distinguished from each other; but for my present purpose the distinction is unnecessary; so in this chapter I shall be unfussy about these terms. Welfare economists have tended to treat the term "total" in the above

[1] For a more thorough review, the reader is referred to Sen (1987).

definition of utilitarianism to mean a sum, that is, the addition or sum of every person's utility. This introduces some bias towards inequality in choices based on utilitarianism, a fact that can be corrected if, instead of summing everybody's utility, we were to use some other method of aggregation. But this is again not my concern here; so I will use the term "total" somewhat ambiguously, allowing it to represent different kinds of aggregation, as moral philosophers usually do.

Utilitarianism is part of a more general system of ethical evaluation, often referred to as consequentialism. **Consequentialism** requires that the goodness of an action be evaluated in terms of its consequences. No action is, in itself, good or bad. Thus a consequentialist would not, typically, be able to use a moral principle such as "one must never tell lies," because he has to evaluate each lie in terms of the consequences that the lie has. A system of ethics where one obeys certain rules irrespective of their consequences is called "deontological ethics." Thus people who adhere to principles like "you must always keep a promise" or "you must never use violence" are typically thought to be believers in deontic principles.

It is now easy to see why utilitarianism is a form of consequentialism. This is because it requires us to evaluate actions in terms of their impact on people's utilities or, in other words, on utility consequences.

The above classification is not without its ambiguities. One may, for instance, rightly wonder what exactly "consequence" means. What if I describe an action, such as telling a lie or breaking a promise, as part of its consequence? After all, one consequence of breaking a promise is a broken promise. While admitting that this ambiguity might arise in some contexts, it suffices here to note that there are contexts where we intuitively distinguish between actions and their consequences. Basically, what we need to allow for is that two different actions can lead to the same consequence. Between two such actions, a consequentialist cannot express moral preference for one over the other, whereas a believer in deontological ethics can.

Another problem arises from the fact that some rules of behavior may be derived from purely consequentialist or, more specifically, utilitarian premises. Consider for instance a person who, through cogitation, reaches the conclusion that the rule not to tell a lie is one that maximizes total utility and therefore follows the rule not to tell a lie. This is not really a problem. Such a person is a utilitarian and a consequentialist, because she does not value the rule *in itself* but because it maximizes utility. At times, this kind of an ethic is referred to as "rule-utilitarianism" or "rule-consequentialism" (see Brandt, 1959; and Smart and Williams, 1973). **Rule-utilitarianism** requires a person to act according to rules of behavior that, if followed by all, results in the maximization of aggregate utility. **Rule-consequentialism** is defined similarly. **Rule-utilitarianism** is traditionally distinguished from **act-utilitarianism**, which requires us to evaluate each action on its own. From the definition of utilitarianism, given in the third paragraph of this chapter, it is plain that what I am calling "utilitarianism" here is act-utilitarianism.

Further, it is not always clear – and this is a matter of debate in philosophy – whether we can really distinguish between rule-utilitarianism and act-utilitarianism (see Gibbard, 1965). If we are free to make a rule as complex as we like, clearly a rule can single out each action separately, in which case rule-utilitarianism would never prescribe an action different from act-utilitarianism. Suppose I begin with the belief that I should always tell the truth. Then one day I encounter a situation where I can save someone's life only by telling a lie; and, upon some thought, I reach the conclusion that it is morally incumbent on me, *in this case*, to tell a lie because that will enhance aggregate utility. Does this moral judgment of mine *have* to be described as act-utilitarianism? The answer is "no," because I can specify a rule that accommodates this "exception." The rule could be something like: You should never tell a lie except when that saves a life. This strategy seems always possible. That is, it appears that we can endlessly refine a rule so as to make the prescription of rule-utilitarianism identical to that of act-utilitarianism.

I will show below that (for reasons that are similar to the ones used for modeling self-control in Chapter 3) this is not always so – that one can construct examples where act-consequentialism differs from rule-consequentialism – and I shall try to persuade the reader that in such situations it is rule-consequentialism that we should try to follow.[2] Given that rule-consequentialism differs from consequentialism in the direction of deontological ethics, my argument may be viewed as a move *towards* deontology.

Before getting into the main argument, it is useful to remind ourselves of the meaning of act-utilitarianism, which is the target of attack of the next section. For that I can do no better than quote you Gibbard's (1965: 212) whimsical but compelling definition: "Act-utilitarianism tells us that if we have hired a boy to mow our lawn and he has done so, we should pay him only if we can find no better use for the money."

---

[2] Though my argument applies to consequentialism in general, I shall pose the problem in the context of utilitarianism.

10.2. Escher's Waterfall and a Critique of Utilitarianism

Consider the following moral dilemmas.

1. A dying man confides in you that buried in his back yard is a large collection of gold and he asks you to promise him that you will not dig it out and give it away to people. If you wanted to be moral, what should you do? In particular, should you make the promise (which will allow the old man to die in peace), and then, after he dies, should you dig the gold out and distribute it, say, to the poor?[3]

2. You have just returned from a trip to the Amazon and your grandmother, who is confined to her house, loves to hear about distant lands and, having no idea of what the Amazon is like, asks you to describe what you saw. Should you describe what you saw (which you know will make her happy) or should you quickly think through several imaginary experiences and describe to her the one that will make her the happiest?

3. You are running in the 100-meter race in the Olympics and you are about to cross the finish line ahead of everyone else. Should you do so or should you quickly calculate[4] the happiness that will be generated if you win and the happiness that will be generated if Carl, who is just behind you, wins; and then, if the latter turns out to be greater, slow down and let Carl pass?

Unless one conjures up unnecessary complications, the utilitarian prescription in each of these cases is as follows. In case 1 you should promise the dying man that the gold will remain under the ground and then, after he dies, you should take it out and distribute it among the poor. In case 2 you should pay no heed to what you saw and describe the most-happiness-giving scenario to your grandmother. In case 3 you should make the calculations and let Carl pass if that gives greater total happiness.

I have tried these questions on a variety of people, including many of my students. To question 1, a large number say that their morality would have them behave as utilitarianism prescribes.[5] In the case of question 2, fewer go along with the utilitarian prescription. They feel that the utilitarian prescription amounts to giving in too wantonly to lying for too small a gain in welfare. On question 3, everybody seems to feel that the right action is to violate the utilitarian norm.

---

[3] Needless to say, you should assume that distributing the gold increases the sum total of happiness in the world. In other words, I am urging you not to display your knowledge of general equilibrium theory and take the easy way out of the moral dilemma by arguing how the increased supply of gold may cause a sufficient drop in price so as to leave the recipients worse off.

[4] Assume that the calculation can be done instantaneously and costlessly.

[5] I hope they do not make this too public, because it may cause a sharp decline in the happiness of dying old men.

There is, it seems to me, something right about these reactions. We want to be concerned about consequences but we also must draw a line somewhere. To me a major problem of a philosophy such as utilitarianism is that it does not specify a domain over which it is to be applied. This criticism occurs at two levels. Let me call these the philosophical and pragmatic criticisms.

The philosophical problem, which I can state at best somewhat inarticulately, is this. Is it at all meaningful to prescribe a certain principle of choice without specifying the set or domain of alternatives over which one is to apply this? Would not this be wrong in the same way as writing down a function without making it clear what its domain of application is? Note that in the definition of utilitarianism early in this chapter, there is no mention of "sets" or "domains of decision" where one should use the utilitarian principle. The presumption, of course, is that the principle should be used everywhere.[6] But is "everywhere" a well-defined set? The answer is "no." To treat these arbitrary collectivities – for instance, "the set of everything" – as sets is to run into a minefield of philosophical conundrums.[7] This means that, to apply utilitarianism, or for that matter any consequentialist principle, meaningfully, one must specify the *set* of alternatives over which one should choose following this principle. And since all the conceivable actions open to a person probably do not comprise a set, there must exist domains over which one is exempt from applying this principle of choice. In brief, for a consequentialist principle to be meaningful, its domain of application *has* to be restricted. The philosophical problem of utilitarianism is that a true utilitarian is supposed to always and everywhere adhere to this principle.

The pragmatic problem of utilitarianism is easier to explain. (In stating it, I will ignore the philosophical problem.) It arises from the recognition that too relentless an application of a principle such as utilitarianism may be *self-defeating*. Consider moral problem 3 described above. Suppose all Olympic runners were card-carrying utilitarians. Then, soon, no one would want to watch Olympic races, because the word would get around that the runners are moralists who do not try to win but maximize social welfare,

---

[6] This is precisely what allows Gibbard (1965) to apply the utilitarian principle at the point where the boy who was supposed to mow the lawn has mowed it and the only decision remaining is whether to pay him or not.

[7] It is arguable that the celebrated "Russell paradox" is a consequence of this. One way to avert the paradox is to reject that the "set of everything" is a set. A proof of this occurs in Chapter 11, p. 233.

and the winner is not really the fastest runner but the one whose victory maximizes social welfare. We may respect the runners for their saintliness but would not want to waste time watching them run. The joy that one gets from following the Olympics would be lost, and – here is the dilemma – the end result of each runner trying to maximize total utility may be a net lowering of total utility.

The same possibility arises in the context of speech. Can the practice of telling lies in order to enhance aggregate utility be self-defeating? This has been a matter of biding concern for moral philosophers. To see this, return to the first two moral dilemmas described above. Suppose everybody decides to be a true utilitarian. So they lie to the dying man that they will guard the gold and they tell their grandmothers not what they saw but what they expect will make their grandmothers happy. In such a society, speech will soon lose most of its power to convey information. And if such an instrument as speech loses power, society may well be worse off in terms of the same criterion that led to the telling of lies in the first place. In other words, utilitarianism may be pitted against utilitarianism. Is this really possible? Harrod (1936) certainly believed so,[8] as did Hodgson (1967). The matter has also been discussed by Brandt (1959), Gibbard (1965) and Parfit (1984). I believe the answer to the above question is "yes," but for reasons more complicated than suggested by these authors.

Let me proceed to set up the problem formally, answer it, and then we can discuss its implications. I shall construct my argument in terms of truthfulness and lying, though the same story can be told for keeping promises and winning races.

Note first that language has at least two uses. First, there is the "normal" or "serious" use, which allows us to communicate and exchange information. For its normal use, what matters is "the meaning of what is said." Habermas (1989: 159) describes this as the "original mode of language." Second, there is what has been described as the "etiolated" or "parasitical" use (Austin, 1962), whereby language is used by the speaker to bring about some state of the world. I shall here use the terms "honest" and "strategic" to represent, respectively, normal speech and parasitic speech. If a potential murderer asks me about the whereabouts of a potential victim and I say, "He has gone left," knowing full well that he has gone right, I am using

---

[8] Here is Allan Gibbard (1965: 212) paraphrasing Roy Harrod's argument: "If people always broke promises when breaking them would produce more good than keeping them, however, then nobody could trust a promise. The whole social value of being able to make promises on which people can rely would be destroyed."

language strategically to bring about a certain state of world. Note that if language was never used honestly, there would be very little scope for its strategic use.

Let us consider a game in which each person has to choose between using language honestly and using it strategically. I shall call these strategies 1 and 0. If a person chooses 0, it means that she will tell a lie if that enhances whatever it is that the person is trying to maximize. The choice of 1 means a commitment to total honesty in speech.

Assume that all these individuals are committed utilitarians, so if they decide to tell a lie it will only be to enhance *social* welfare (or, equivalently, aggregate utility). This means that if one person switches her strategy from 1 to 0, then social welfare must rise.[9] The question that the above-mentioned philosophers and economists have been concerned with is whether this is compatible with the possibility that, if everybody switches over from 1 to 0, then social welfare falls (because speech now loses its power). I will show that the answer is "yes" but for more complex reasons than the ones considered by the earlier commentators.

To make all this more precise, suppose that N is the set of individuals or players, and the number of players in N is given by n, where n may or may not be finite. Though I will often work with the case where n is infinite, this is only for mathematical convenience; my results would be unchanged if there were a finite number of individuals, as long as they had an infinite number of decisions to take among them. It is now clear that a set of strategies chosen by the n players (one for each player) is a vector, $x = (x_1, x_2, \ldots)$, where, for each player i, x_i is either 1 or 0. I shall call x a **strategy vector**. The strategy vector consisting of all zeros will be denoted by 0 and the strategy vector consisting of all ones will be denoted by 1. A player's pay-off function, f_i, is a real-valued function such that, for every x, $f_i(x)$ specifies i's payoff.

It is interesting to note that the above game is a Prisoner's Dilemma if, given other players' choice of strategy, each player prefers 0 to 1, but if everybody chooses 0 then they are all worse off than they would be in the case where everybody chooses 1. Clearly, the game *can* be a Prisoner's Dilemma because we can set $n = 2$ and choose numbers exactly as in the standard Prisoner's Dilemma (see Chapter 2) to represent payoff.

Now let us suppose we place a restriction on the above game such that, for all i, $f_i = f$ for some payoff function f. In other words, this is a game in

---

[9] This is assuming that occasions do indeed arise when a lie enhances social welfare. If not, the word "rise" would have to be replaced with "not fall."

which everybody is trying to maximize the same thing. Such a game is called a **unanimity game** in game theory.

Assume now that all individuals are utilitarians. This means that all players will have the same payoff function or objective function. In other words, what I am considering here is a unanimity game in which everybody is interested in maximizing social welfare.

Now we can ask formally the question that the economists and philosophers were asking. Is it possible to think of a payoff function f that has the following two properties: (i) If strategy vectors, x and y, are such that, for some player k, $x_k = 0$ and $y_k = 1$, and, for every other player i, $x_i = y_i$, then $f(x) > f(y)$; and (ii) $f(0) < f(1)$.

Note that (i) asserts that a single person switching over to using speech strategically (that is, telling lies whenever that enhances social welfare) does indeed enhance social welfare, while (ii) says that if everybody chooses to use speech strategically, then social welfare actually falls.

Now, to the question whether there exists a function f that satisfies both (i) and (ii), the answer is: yes if and only if n is infinite. As I mentioned above and will explain below, n being infinite means that society has an infinite number of *decisions* to make (which is plausible). It does not necessarily mean that there exists an infinite number of *players*. For those interested in relating this to the Prisoner's Dilemma, note that my answer can be paraphrased into asserting that a unanimity game can be a Prisoner's Dilemma if and only if the number of decisions to be taken in this society is infinite.

To prove my answer, consider first the case in which n is finite. Start from the strategy vector $1 = (1, \ldots, 1)$. Now, one at a time, in this vector switch a one over to a zero. If (i) is true, then each such act must register an increase in payoff. Since we can go from 1 to 0 in a finite number of such switches and each such switch increases payoff, the payoff must be higher at 0 than at 1. Hence, (ii) is false. Thus telling lies or breaking promises to enhance social welfare can never be self-defeating in a finite-decision society.

However, the claim is valid for infinite-decision societies. To see this, suppose n is infinite. I shall give a constructive proof of how both (i) and (ii) may be valid. Let the payoff function, f, be as follows. Consider a strategy vector, x. It must be true that either $\Sigma_t x_t$ is a finite number or it is infinite. If it is finite, let

$$f(x) = -\Sigma_t x_t \qquad (10.1)$$

And if it is infinite, let

$$f(x) = 1 + \Sigma_t (0.5)^t (1 - x_t) \qquad (10.2)$$

Now, it is easy to check that $f(0) = 0$ and $f(1) = 1$. Hence, (ii) is satisfied. Next note that as a single element of a strategy vector, x, switches from 1 to 0, $f(x)$ increases, no matter whether $f(x)$ is given by (10.1) or (10.2). Hence, such changes always increase payoff, thereby ensuring that function f satisfies (i). That ends the proof. Following Basu (1994b) I shall call this the "Waterfall Game."

Equations (10.1) and (10.2) are strange functions to use, but they serve our purpose by providing one of the easiest proofs one can think of. If we want a more reasonable payoff function, the mathematical problem becomes harder, of course, depending on what we mean by "reasonable." One additional quality that one may seek in the payoff function is that it be symmetric in the strategies of different individuals. Note that, currently, different players have different impacts on f. This is obvious from examining (10.2). Clearly, player 1 switching from 1 to 0 has a much bigger effect on the payoff than player 9. What if we want everybody's effect to be the same? In other words, can we find a function f that satisfies properties (i), (ii) and, in addition, that of symmetry?

As I have tried to show elsewhere (Basu, 1994b), the answer to this question is a *qualified* "yes." I have been unable to give a constructive proof for this. What I did show (in Basu, 1994b) is that if the axiom of choice is true, then the answer is "yes." The proof of this is rather detailed. I shall not go into it here because it does not bear on my main argument in any serious way. But some of the intuition of the result may be conveyed as follows.

Note first that the result that I proved above is similar, *technically*, to the result proved in Section 3.3, though there my concern was with individual decision making and not strategic interaction between the players. This paradoxical result, as I noted there, is reminiscent of Escher's painting of a waterfall (*see* Fig. 3.1). The water keeps flowing downwards but it ends up on top. Interestingly, the waterfall is not symmetrical everywhere, because at one point the water drops sharply. For a pictorial representation of the paradox in the symmetrical case, one can once again turn to M. C. Escher. His painting *Ascending and Descending* illustrates the same paradox, with no exceptional behavior anywhere. Each step takes you higher (by an identical amount), but in the end you find yourself lower down. The analogy is obvious. Each lie may raise social welfare, but when everybody begins to tell lies, social welfare falls.

With the background knowledge that we *could* have restricted the payoff function further, such as by requiring that it satisfy symmetry, I shall, in the discussion that follows, confine myself to the simple payoff function of the Waterfall Game, that is, one that satisfies (i) and (ii).

First, a technical comment. How should we interpret the case of $n = \infty$? In economics it is standard to model large societies as ones with infinite population. So we could assume that the result we get in the case of n being infinite tells us what we can expect in large societies. I find this interpretation unpersuasive both in economics and here. Fortunately, there is another way of interpreting n being infinite. Suppose we have a society with a finite number of individuals – and let me assume, without loss of generality, that there are only two individuals – but each of them has to make an infinite number of decisions, where each decision problem involves choosing between 0 and 1. Let me, in particular, assume that, for every positive and *odd* integer, person A has to choose between taking 1 and 0; and that, for every positive and *even* integer, person B has to choose between taking it 1 and 0. Now, when both persons have made all their choices, we will have an infinitely long vector of zeros and ones, just like a strategy vector in the Waterfall Game. Now, if we use the same payoff function as in the Waterfall Game, we have the same paradox, but with a finite number of individuals – though the number of decisions that the individuals have to take is infinite, which seems quite conceivable to me. If n is infinite in any of these two senses (infinite population or infinite decisions), we shall say that we have a society with an infinite decision problem.

So what we have showed is that Harrod's (1936) and Hodgson's (1967) conjectures are right only for societies with infinite decision problems. Harrod (1936: 147–8), while remarkably clear about the possibility of utilitarianism conflicting with utilitarianism and also that this arises when there is a large number of decisions to be made, seems to have missed the importance of infiniteness. He talks of "a million lies" having an effect that exceeds the sum of the effect of each lie. As my formalization of this argument shows, this cannot happen with a million or even a trillion lies; we have to cross over to the domain of infinite decisions.

Let us see what else we learn from the construction of this paradoxical game, that is, a game in which (i) and (ii) can both be satisfied.

Its most important implication is that there may be reason for us to abandon an adherence to a philosophy of consequentialism, and the reason lies in consequentialism itself. Take, for instance, utilitarianism. As I pointed out earlier, the philosophy of utilitarianism as traditionally propounded urges people to apply the utilitarian principle to *all* choices. What I have just demonstrated is that there may be circumstances such that, *if* people followed this advice,[10] they would end up bringing about a world where there is less aggregate utility than one in which people violated utilitarianism on some occasions.

The Waterfall Game also helps us draw a line between act- and rule-utilitarianism. As explained earlier, the distinction between these two has always been considered somewhat ambiguous and I have shared this feeling. This game shows, however, that in *infinite*-decision societies these two moral principles may be legitimately distinguished from each other. Clearly, in the Waterfall Game act-utilitarianism would recommend that individuals should use speech strategically, that is, choose 0. Rule-utilitarianism, on the other hand, does not prescribe this behavior. What it prescribes depends on what we mean by a rule. Let us begin by considering the simplest of rules.[11] Here are two of them: "Be honest" and "Be strategic." Rule-utilitarianism would prescribe the former (recall (ii)). If we allow for more complicated rules – for instance, prescribing different kinds of behavior for different people – or if we interpret the Waterfall Game in two-person terms and ask each person to choose 1 in some situations and 0 in others, then rule-utilitarianism may make more complicated prescriptions.[12] But the upshot is the same: there is reason to adhere to some rule-based behavior in life.

This brings us close to the idea of *karma*. For certain activities there are predefined reasons, almost obligations, for undertaking them. One runs in the Olympics in order to win. One speaks in order to convey something. One makes promises to keep. When one tells a boy that he will be paid if he mows the lawn, it is expected that one will pay the boy if he mows the lawn. These are all one's *karma*, which is not quite duty but something that one does because one is supposed to do so (Barrett, 1999). The supposition is a moral primitive. There may nevertheless be reason to deviate from these. If one learns, after the boy has mowed the lawn, that he will use the money to buy a gun and shoot people, one may decide not to pay him. But such considerations must be exceptional.

These preordained rules of behavior in different domains – you run in a race to win it, you take an examination to pass in it – not only makes life possible and gives meaning to a variety of activities, which would lose all

---

[10] Ignore here the philosophical problem mentioned above and assume that the advice *can* be followed.

[11] In fact, it is possible to argue that a rule ceases to be a rule if it becomes too complicated. See Schlicht (1998) for a discussion of the idea of "rules."

[12] If by a rule we mean *any* strategy vector, then in the Waterfall Game there is no best rule. For every strategy vector, one can think of another that does better.

purpose if we were perennially prompted by moral, consequential considerations, but they limit the domain over which one uses act-consequentialism or act-utilitarianism. In some philosophical systems, such as those of deontological ethics, the obligation to live by some rules instead of consequential considerations are moral primitives. What I have argued here is that some of the reasons for these exceptions to utilitarianism may be founded in utilitarianism itself.

10.3. Rights and Liberty

We have thus far discussed morality without any mention of rights; and the mention of obligations occurred only in the last few paragraphs. Yet in the literature on moral philosophy, rights and obligations have been frequently discussed in the context of utilitarianism. One question that has been debated is whether having rights is compatible with utilitarianism. The boy who mowed the lawn, it seems to us, has the right to be paid. But utilitarianism suggests that he should be paid if and only if that increases aggregate welfare. To quote David Lyons (1982: 111): "Bentham held that institutions are to be evaluated *solely* in terms of human welfare. Unless we assume that arguments based on moral rights converge perfectly with those based on welfare, it should seem that a utilitarian like Bentham would be obliged to reject moral rights."

The analysis in the previous section suggests a way out of this dilemma. Since it was shown that an adherence to utilitarianism must not (and it was conjectured that it can not) be taken to mean using the utilitarian principle for *every* decision in *all* walks of life, my argument makes room for the use of other moral criteria, such as rights and obligations. Moreover, if one distinguishes between moral rights and legal rights (as does Lyons, 1982), where "moral rights" denote primitive or natural rights and "legal rights" are those that may be derived from other principles and that are predicated on their being socially recognized, it is arguable that rule-utilitarianism is compatible with legal rights.[13]

The conflict between utilitarianism and rights has been discussed in modern times from a different perspective provoked by Amartya Sen's work on rights and liberty (Sen, 1970). I believe that the approach to law proposed in Chapter 5 has an important bearing on this debate; and the remainder of this section is devoted to the subject.

---

[13] Though Lyons himself contests this.

What Sen demonstrated was a conflict between the principle of libertarianism and the Pareto principle. In particular, he showed that a commitment to a minimal libertarianism (which gives individuals some minimum rights) may amount to a violation of the Pareto principle. The violation of the Pareto principle basically means that society may end up choosing a social state x when everybody prefers social state y. Now note that if everybody is better off in social state y, then no matter how we compare interpersonal utilities, aggregate utility at y must be greater than aggregate utility at x. Hence, a violation of the Pareto criterion implies a violation of utilitarianism, no matter how we make interpersonal comparisons. So Sen's liberty paradox implies as a corollary[14] that the principle of liberty is incompatible with utilitarianism.

What has been debated extensively, since the appearance of Sen's work, is the *meaning* of liberty and individual rights; and that is where I want to join in. Sen's approach was rooted in the tradition of John Stuart Mill (1848, Book 5, chapter 11, p. 306), who had argued that "there is a circle around every individual human being which no government, be that of one, of a few, or of the many, ought to be permitted to overstep." I shall refer to this here as the **liberty primitive**. More specifically, the argument was that each person has a "recognized personal sphere" such that decisions within this sphere are for him or her to take, no matter what view others take of this decision. A typical example of this may be as follows: Whether person i reads D. H. Lawrence's *Lady Chatterly's Lover* (option x) or not (option y) should be thought of as a decision in person i's personal sphere. In other words, i has the right to decide between x and y, regardless of whether others get more utility from x or y.

This much is widely agreed upon; the controversy occurs in trying to formalize this intuitive idea. I must, however, register my hesitation about even this informal notion of individual right. Despite the declaration that the recognized personal sphere is a moral primitive and one has a right to choose within this irrespective of what others feel, my hunch is that what alternatives we regard as being within a person's personal sphere is influenced by the *presumption* that these are matters that do not strongly affect other people's utility. The examples typically found in the literature

---

[14] The corollary is obvious if an individual's right is deemed to be valid irrespective of the strength of other people's feelings, because the conflict between liberty and utilitarianism can now occur over the choice between a single pair of alternatives. The conflict with Pareto is, however, not as obvious since it cannot occur over the same pair of alternatives. I would have to qualify this last remark if we considered a framework where an individual could himself have a preference that overruled his own right: see the next footnote.

lend support to this view – whether i reads Lawrence's novel or not is person i's right, whether i wears a red shirt or a blue shirt is i's right.

Do we consider these to be within i's right (or i's personal sphere) for reasons that are unconnected to utility? I do not think so. On the contrary, one of the reasons why we consider these choices to be i's right is precisely because of our *presumption* that these choices do not affect other people's utility strongly enough one way or the other. I should clarify that I am not saying that other people's utility not being strongly affected is a sufficient condition for a choice to belong to a person's personal sphere, but merely that that is a factor.[15] So even if we consider the choice between x and y to be in i's personal sphere to start with, we may legitimately want to reconsider this if evidence is brought to us that i's choice of x will cause j acute suffering.[16]

In a richer framework in which it is recognized that the same level of utility can hide different kinds of emotions or mental states, I would be tempted to argue that a person's right may be limited by another person's utility, depending on the kind and intensity of emotion that underlies that utility. Suppose a girl wants to wear a fur miniskirt and a man objects. Most of my readers will agree that her decision to wear a fur miniskirt is her right, but I think we should at the same time agree that, depending on the basis and nature of the man's objection, we may be willing to overrule her right. Consider two alternative motivations for his objection. First, he is a prude and an authoritarian who likes to impose his morals on others. Second, he is allergic to fur, which causes serotonin imbalance in his head and makes him acutely sad. It seems to me reasonable to argue that it is her right that must be upheld in the first case but in the second case there is reason to overrule it.

I shall return to this later. Let us for now accept the liberty primitive. Sen formalized it in the framework of social choice and precipitated the celebrated contradiction with the Pareto principle. Some philosophers and economists have objected to such a social-choice-theoretic formulation and have argued that rights are best formalized as game forms.[17] Broadly

[15] There may be conditions where an individual herself may be willing to forego a certain choice because of one's regard for the well-being of other human beings. In that case, "rights" (interpreted as one's preference being realized) can clash with "rights" (interpreted as one having the ability to exercise choice): *see* Subramanian (1994).

[16] Some may be tempted to argue that this new evidence means that x is no longer x, but a new social state x'. In that case the belief that if x and y are in i's personal sphere then i has full right to choose between x and y, irrespective of what others feel, becomes *trivially* valid because any change in other people's feeling will now be used to relabel x and y.

[17] See Gaertner, Pattanaik and Suzumura (1992) and Deb (1994) for a general statement of this approach. Some have argued that Nozick's (1974) informal argument was an argument in favor of the game-form approach. One of the first attempts to model rights in the context of games – strictly speaking, in terms of "effectivity functions" – was by Gardenfors (1981).

speaking, a game form is a game in which the payoff functions of the players are left unspecified. According to this approach, to say that a person has the right to a certain set of actions means that only those actions are available to her. So the strategy set of a player in a game form captures the rights of a player. Suppose player 1 has the right to invite player 2 to a party and player 2 has the right to go or not go, if invited (but he does not have the right to go to the party if he is not invited). Then, according to Gaertner, Pattanaik and Suzumura (1992), the game form shown in Fig. 10.1 captures this rights assignment. And no matter what the outcome of this game is, individual rights are upheld. In other words, according to them, rights being upheld is a matter of what choices players have and not what the outcome happens to be.

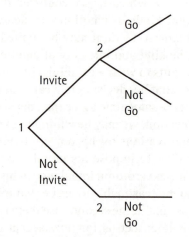

Figure 10.1. Game form showing a rights assignment

The approach to the modeling of law that I have espoused in this book suggests that this game-form model of rights is inadequate. The use of games to model rights is probably a move in the correct direction, but we need to go further. Let me explain.

According to the game-form view of rights, a change in people's rights would result in a change in the game that the people are playing. Consider a society in which person i does not have the right to steal j's wallet. By this approach, i's stealing j's wallet is not an available action for i. If we now think of an altered system of rights in which a person does have a right to steal wallets, then the game is taken to have changed.

It is, however, eminently arguable that i's not having a right to do something does not mean that i *cannot* do that thing. I would therefore take the view that a change in rights should not be construed as a change in the feasible set of actions.[18] Stepping back from these academic debates, let us ask ourselves what it really means to say "Person i does not have the right to steal j's wallet." It means that if i *does* steal j's wallet, then someone else (j or a policeman, for instance) has the right to take some punitive action (call it y) against i that, otherwise, that person would not have the right to. Thus i having a right to action z means that if i chooses z, then someone else j will not have the right to some action y that punishes i. This idea of the innate interdependence of rights has been stressed by several writers. Hart (1979: 19) writes: ". . . to have a right entails having a moral justification for limiting the freedom of another person and for determining how he [or she] should act." More pertinently, Lyons (1979: 5) argues: "When others are under an obligation to me and threaten to default, there are actions that I might appropriately take which I would not otherwise be justified in taking."

This interdependent character of rights is very similar to the concept of law described in Chapter 5. And, by the same argument as there, it follows that rights cannot influence the game – although they may influence the *outcomes* of games by creating expectations, beliefs and focal points.

There is a second criticism of the game-form formulation of rights. Note that this approach treats a right as inviolable, no matter what others feel. Once we deviate from this and take the view that a person's right need not be upheld in some contexts, depending on the extent and nature of others' suffering caused by this person's exercising of his or her right, whether a person has a certain right or not depends on the payoffs that players earn from different outcomes. This means that a change in the payoff function can cause a change in the rights. Hence, the rights depend on the entire game and not just the game form. This is, however, a criticism that I shall not bother about here.

A bit more formally, a structure of rights, then, is a specification of a subset of (admissible) actions from among all the actions available at each information set of a game (or game form). Given a certain structure of rights, whether the rights are violated or respected is a property not of the game but of how the game is played. If i does not have the right to hit j and in playing the game he hits j, we can say that rights have been violated. Interestingly, whether a right has been violated or not is not just a property of the outcome of a game but of the strategies used. This, of

---

[18] The distinction between feasibility and admissibility in the context of rights has been drawn and used by Fleurbaey and Gaertner (1996).

course, complicates the story because you cannot tell by looking at how a game is actually played whether rights have been violated or not. The violation of rights (and therefore the satisfaction of rights) cannot be reduced to behaviorism.

To see this, consider a game in which player 1 moves first. She may or may not invite player 2 to a party. After that it is player 2's move, and he has to choose between hitting and not hitting player 1. Let us take the structure of rights to be as follows. Player 1 has the right to invite or not invite player 2 and player 2 does not have the right to hit player 1. The game tree is shown in Fig. 10.2, and the strategies that are admissible under the rights structure are marked "(R)."

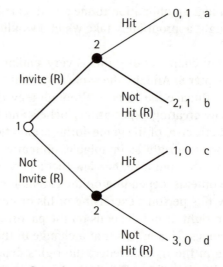

Figure 10.2. Game form showing potential violation of rights

Clearly, if the outcome of the game is such that the players reach terminal node a or c, then there has occurred a violation of rights. What I am arguing is that that is not the only way in which rights may be violated. Suppose players choose the strategies that are marked in Fig. 10.3 by bold lines. The game will terminate at b, but it is arguable that rights have been violated. This is because the strategies may be interpreted as follows. Player 2, it is expected, will hit player 1 if he is not invited, and so player 1 does what is rational under the circumstances: she invites player 2. This is the case of invitation at gunpoint that Gaertner, Pattanaik and Suzumura (1992) talked about, and it is easy to agree that this involves a violation of rights.

In sum, games may be the appropriate instrument for describing rights; but rights do not specify the game, they merely denote some actions as admissible; and rights are violated not only if a nonadmissible action is actually used but if it is intended to be used at some unreached node of the game. There is no compelling reason why an arbitrary specification of rights will be satisfied in society. If, in fact, the rights assignment is such that no equilibrium play of the game satisfies the rights, then some rights are bound to be violated. If there are equilibrium strategies that satisfy the rights, then the rights *may* be satisfied. I use the word "may" because there is nothing in rights themselves to ensure enforcement. If rights are to influence behavior, this can only happen through its influence on players' beliefs, expectations of other people's behavior, and focal points.

10.4. Morals and Solipsism

The analysis of moral behavior is important because human beings have innate moral instincts. Unlike the self-centered "rational man" encountered in economics textbooks and also in the new political science literature, human beings, in reality, are often guided by altruism and have an instinctive urge to be moral. It is true that self-interest usually dominates our decisions. But for most human beings it is tempered by morals. Interestingly, human beings want to be moral without quite knowing what that entails. This is the reason why moral philosophy is important. It can help us sort out whether we should be concerned, for instance, about aggregate utility or some deontic principles – justice, equity, and so on – given that we *want* to be moral.

I am taking here a rather solipsistic view of moral philosophy. And that is what it should be. It is not clear that there is ever a reason for morally labeling *other* people's actions, and even less, other people. Since the social sciences function on a presumption of determinism (as discussed in the Appendix to this book), human behavior is assumed to be prompted by causes; and we can track these causes back to heredity and environment. This is an ancient topic in philosophy; what I have tried to show in the Appendix is that this philosophical point of view is compatible with the belief that individuals can have freedom of choice and free will.

So a person who steals money does indeed *choose* to steal money. And this is not inconsistent with the fact that, given his heredity and environment, he would choose in no other way. In other words, at one level, human beings are like billiard balls. They are moved and jostled by forces beyond their control. So to apply moral categories to them is almost as absurd as calling a billiard ball immoral. There are actions of human beings, and even human beings, that are harmful for the world. But at a certain significant level they are harmful in the same way that tornados are harmful. We do not condemn tornados. In the case of human beings it may be reasonable to publicly condemn them, but only because such criticism may deter people in the future from indulging in harmful behavior. But the true purpose of ethics and moral philosophy must be to guide one's *own* action.

Part V. CONCLUSION

11. Some Concluding Remarks

11.1. Introduction

The central propositions of this book, such as the need to take an inclusive approach to the state and to think of markets as embedded in social norms and institutions, have been stated clearly (as clearly as I could). So I will not dwell further on these. There is, however, another important part-message-part-criticism of standard economics, which has permeated through several chapters and has been stated more by implication than directly. This concerns the domain of a person's preference and payoff functions. I will refer to this in brief as the "pdomain problem." The "p," meant to be silent, is a reminder that the problem pertains to Preferences and Payoff functions.[1]

The reason why I did not want to bring this up in the main chapters of the book is that this criticism is still rather ill-formulated, and also because it is a methodological criticism and so it affects our view of norms and the state by implication rather than directly. Yet it is an important criticism. It questions the very description of an economy as a game. To work out its full ramifications is a separate project. It therefore seems apt that I use this last chapter to spell out the pdomain problem by drawing on discussions that have occurred throughout the book, though often between the lines. The problem has important implications for mechanism design and our conception of the free-rider problem. These implications are discussed in Sections 11.3 and 11.4.

11.2. The Pdomain Problem

In most models of economics, in general equilibrium theory and in game theory, it is assumed that agents have well-defined domains or feasible sets

---

[1] "... The name is Psmith. P-smith."

"Peasmith, sir?"

"No, no. P-s-m-i-t-h. I should explain to you that I started life without the initial letter, and my father always clung ruggedly to the plain Smith. But it seemed to me that there were so many Smiths in the world that a little variety might well be introduced. ... So I decided to adopt Psmith. The p, I should add for your guidance, is silent, as in pthisis, psychic, and ptarmigan." From P. G. Wodehouse's *Leave it to Psmith*, Harmondsworth: Penguin, 1983, p. 35 (original publication 1923).

of options or strategies from which they choose. In consumer theory, we usually start from the non-negative orthant of the n-dimensional Euclidean space, with each of the n dimensions representing each of the n goods available in society. Then, given a consumer's income and the prices faced by her, we take the subset of all vectors of goods that can be purchased within her income. The set thus specified is the consumer's **feasible set**. Freedom on the part of the consumer is then equated with the ability to choose freely from this set. But, as noted in Chapter 4, in reality a consumer can do many things other than simply picking vectors of goods. She can loot, plunder and abuse; she can cajole, shout and intimidate. Likewise, in game theory, we specify the set of options open to each player as part of the description of the game. Usually this set is quite limited and in ways that are at variance with what reality allows. This makes it difficult to jump from our models to reality. And the problem is more complex than the literature on bounded rationality suggests.

As was discussed in Chapter 4, the policy implications of the First Fundamental Theorem of welfare economics become clouded as soon as we explicitly recognize that in economics we (that is, the researchers) restrict human choice to a smaller set than what reality allows. If, with this assumption in the background, we establish that giving individuals the freedom to choose as they wish leads to social optimality, at first sight this looks like a case for free-market policies. However, a little thought reveals that this freedom is nothing but the freedom to choose from a set, which is severely restricted to start with, by assumption. Thus, from another perspective, the same theorem seems to be making a case for restricting individual freedom. Hence, one reason why our models fail to capture reality is this initial assumption, which is so germane to our models that it is not even stated as an axiom or an assumption. It is, in the language of the Appendix to this book, an embedded assumption.

What about getting out of this problem by assuming that the feasible set consists of "all possible actions" or "everything"? This creates two problems. First, we know that, ever since Bertrand Russell discovered the "Russell paradox," such magic words as "the set of all actions" or "everything" may not define a set at all, and treating these as sets runs us into deep paradoxes. We got glimpses of this problem in Chapters 4 and 10.

Most people find it difficult to understand how a certain collectivity or assemblage can ever be *not* a set. This is undoubtedly a philosophically troublesome matter, since a set, in most discourses, is a primitive and so not easy to define.

One method that logicians have used to check whether a certain collectivity constitutes a set is to begin by assuming that it *is* a set and then try to establish a contradiction. If they succeed, then the initial assumption must be false; what was taken to be a set could not have been so. This is exactly how it is determined that the "set of everything" is not a set. Here is a proof. Suppose there exists a set of everything. Call it U. Now consider the set of all those elements in U that are not elements of themselves. Call this set X. Now, since any proposition is either true or false, one of the following must be true: (i) X is an element of itself; and (ii) X is not an element of itself. It is worth pausing to understand what it means for a set to be an element of itself. The best I can do is to explain with an example, which Bertrand Russell gave in his *Autobiography*. Consider the set of all spoons. Clearly this is not an element of itself, since the set of spoons is not a spoon. So this is an example of (ii) above. Now consider the set of everything that is not a spoon. Since the set of everything that is not a spoon is not a spoon, it is an element of itself. Hence, this illustrates (i) above.

Continuing with the proof, suppose (i) is true. Then, by the definition of X, X is not an element of itself, which is a negation of (i). Hence, (i) cannot be true. So (ii) must be true. But if (ii) is true, then, by the definition of X, X is an element of X, which is a negation of (ii). Hence, what we have is a contradiction, which suggests that our initial assumption – that there is a set of everything – is false.[2]

The second problem is more mundane. Our culture, our social and moral norms and, simply, the limitations of the human mind imply that in trying to maximize payoff or utility we do not search through all the options available to us. It is almost as if these factors – culture and the mind's limitations – are like a torch beam that lights up certain subsets of the feasible actions, which we then consider and optimize over. Hence, even if we *could* identify the enormous feasible set available to a person in a certain situation, to assume that the person will maximize over this domain, and from that to predict his behavior, would frequently lead to errors, since a person's choice behavior in reality depends on which options this torch of culture lights up. This is troublesome for two reasons. First, this set from

---

[2] There is no novelty in this proof. I have just proved in words what can be found formally established in books of logic and set theory: see, for instance, Halmos (1974). The proof is not, however, foolproof. The contradiction is established by using certain rules of logic, which we take for granted, such as: if we start with a set and isolate those elements of the set that satisfy a certain property, then what we have is another set. It is possible to argue that what the contradiction in the end establishes is a negation of one of these rules or axioms that we take for granted.

which individuals actually choose is unlikely to coincide with the textbook assumption of individuals choosing from a set defined by what is financially feasible (that is, the budget set in consumer theory) or technologically feasible (that is, the production possibility set in the theory of the firm). Second, this set may evolve and grow during the process of decision making. We saw this in the case of the Cuban Missile Crisis, discussed in Chapters 2–4. A large part of the deliberation among Kennedy and his advisers was to discover what strategies were open to them, and the strategy that they actually chose was not among the ones that they were initially considering.

The pdomain problem also crops up in moral systems, such as utilitarianism or Rawlsianism. Usually these are prescribed for *all* our choices. Utilitarianism, for instance, is defined as a moral system that prescribes that, faced with a choice between several alternatives, we should choose the one that maximizes total human happiness or utility. Implicit in this statement is the fact that this rule ought to be applied to all choices. Bentham (1789: 11–12) was quite clear on this: "By the principle of utility is meant that principle which approves or disapproves of every action whatsoever, according to the tendency which it appears to have to augment or diminish the happiness of the party whose interest is in question: or, what is the same thing in other words, to promote or oppose that happiness." And he went on to add that this should hold for "every action whatsoever."[3]

While virtually all the terms in the utilitarian prescription have been subjected to debate and scrutiny, what has escaped notice (as discussed in Chapter 10) is the implicit clause that the rule be applied to *all* choices. The same is true of Rawlsianism.

But, as we have just seen, "all" is not a meaningful domain. Therefore these moral rules, as they are conventionally prescribed, are difficult to interpret properly and, arguably, impossible to follow. A more correct approach would be to formally define the domain or set over which the rule applies. And since such a set cannot include "everything," there must be choices where the rules do not apply. So just as no one can optimize over all possible available actions, one cannot apply moral rules of behavior over all possible actions. There will always be actions that we undertake for no *reasons*, let alone to maximize payoffs or utility. Likewise, there will always be actions we do not even consider; so our not choosing such

---

[3] It is not evident here that Bentham is talking of the well-being of the community as a whole (as distinct from the well-being of some specific individual). But that becomes clear later. My concern here is anyway not with the domain of human beings but the domain of possible actions, and on this Bentham is unambiguous: the principle must apply to all.

an action is not out of any consideration of utility, morality or altruism. We exclude these actions by instinct. Let me refer to such alternatives as "instinctively excluded."[4] My conjecture is that the **instinctively excluded actions** are much more numerous than the elements in the domain over which we use our rationality and reason to choose. In addition, the assemblage of all instinctively excluded alternatives may not even constitute a set.

The belief of the traditional economist (and that of the new political scientist), that individuals choose the best from among all available alternatives, has led to important errors in our conception of the world. This has, for instance, led to the view that, whenever human beings can free-ride, they will do so. What this fails to recognize is that there are areas where we do not free-ride simply because we do not even *consider* the actions that would amount to free-riding. Such actions are instinctively excluded. In most homes, all family members have access to the refrigerator, yet the refrigerator, unlike the local common, does not suffer from "over-grazing." There are institutes where hundreds of people are given keys to the library, where they can borrow books by writing it down in a register. Economic theory predicts that such libraries will be empty in no time. That does not happen. At the end of a taxi ride, often we can run away without paying. Most people do not do so.

Some of these choices researchers *can* explain by convoluted constructions of rationality. But in reality we do not take many of these actions simply because we do not even consider them. This can be for force of habit, deep-seated cultural norms, our moral training or, simply, limitations of the mind. The instinctively excluded elements may be very hard to predict and model; and so it may not be unreasonable for researchers to ignore them on occasions, and get on with their task. The mistake occurs when, having assumed these excluded options away, we forget that we did so, and craft policy as if such options do not exist in the world. This has interesting implications for our understanding of games and free-riding, the subject matters of, respectively, the next two sections.

---

[4] The "normative loopholes" discussed in Chapter 4 are elements of a person's instinctively excluded set. This is, in turn, closely connected to what in the law and economics literature is called a person's "internalized obligational norms" (Eisenberg, 1999). By this terminology, an agent's normative loophole consists of actions that lie beyond his or her internalized obligational norms.

Note that, in this discourse, the actions that are defined to be "instinctively excluded" are actually a motley group, consisting of actions that we reject outright because we are morally programmed to do so, or because our social norms and culture rule out such actions, or simply because we are not even aware of the availability of such actions.

11.3. Games and Reality

The idea of a "game" that is used to model social, economic and political interactions comes originally from parlor games, such as Bridge, Chess and Hex. This analogy was used to introduce the idea of games in Chapter 2, and it draws our attention to the fact that the heart of any game is a set of rules. These rules specify a set of permitted actions open to each player at each stage of the game. What the discussion in the above section alerted us to was that these "rules" apply rather differently to parlor games and to real-life games.[5] In parlor games it is not in a person's interest to violate the rules. In Chess, a player does not kick the opponent's king off the board in an effort to win. However, in the game of life, people often steal another's initial endowment even though that may not be considered a legitimate move. The reason for this is that, in Chess, if one does such a thing like kick the opponent's king out of the board, one by definition loses the game. Hence, actions chosen outside the set specified by the rules of the game cannot, *by definition*, lead a player to victory. The payoff function (in Chess this can be thought of as taking values of 1 (win), 0 (draw) and −1 (lose)) is either not defined for moves that constitute a violation of the rules of the game or defined as constituting a loss for the player making such a move. Hence, in parlor games we do not have to, typically, worry about players violating the rules, or at least doing so openly, because it is not in the players' interest to do so. This can, however, not be said for games in reality. When we think of two firms as being locked in a duopoly game, the rules certainly do not allow a player to hit the other player on the head if he lowers the price or to throw the other player's output into the sea. But obeying this rule is not necessarily in the players' interest. In a duopoly the players' aim is to maximize profit, and profit is not necessarily lower for actions that lie beyond the rules of the game. It may be that the player *can* earn a higher payoff by throwing the opponent's output into the sea. In real-life games, the payoff function that the player seeks to maximize happens to be defined not only for actions that are inside the player's strategy set (that is, the set of actions permitted by the rules of the game) but also for those outside, and there is no guarantee that the outside options will not give a greater payoff than the ones within.

Some may object to my distinction between parlor games and reality by pointing to the fact that there are parlor games where one can cheat and

---

[5] This classification is reminiscent of Bernard's (1954: 415–16) distinction between "parlor games" and "sociological games".

still win. Any skillful Bridge player can give you a lesson or two about how to cheat at Bridge and increase the chances of a win. But this criticism is not pertinent to the point that I am trying to make. What it shows is that the distinction that I am drawing between parlor games and real-life games is not a sharp one. But what is central to my argument is to recognize that there *are* two different kinds of games: ones in which to violate the rule is, by definition, to get a lower payoff; and ones where that is not necessarily true. All I am asserting is that these two kinds of games may have to be analyzed very differently. I am also suggesting that the games that economists and political scientists are concerned with are typically, but not necessarily, of the latter kind. But even if that were not the case, the point of needing different kinds of analysis would remain.

Another response to this argument is to assert that we all know that a game is an inexact representation of reality; so there is no value in having this pointed out. What the above discussion shows is that a game as a depiction of reality is inexact in a rather significant way and one that has not always been recognized.

The problem being discussed here is distinct from the vexing question of where the rules of a game come from and how they evolve (Kreps, 1990: ch. 5) but it has a bearing on it. It suggests that in analyzing the origin and evolution of games we must distinguish between the two kinds of games talked about above. The evolution of Chess is a fundamentally different process from the evolution of landlord–tenant relations. And this has much to do with the fact that in the former game, violating the rules (while the game is on) is not in the interest of any player, by the very definition of the payoff function. In the landlord–tenant game, first of all the rules are fuzzy (Kreps, 1990), and, second, the rules can change through small violations and cheating over time. These are matters hard to formalize because games are usually identified with their rules, and so it is not clear what it means for a player to violate the rules.

An interesting direction to proceed from here is to distinguish in a game between the set U of *all* actions available to a player and a subset X of it, from which the player actually (by consciously using his or her rationality calculus) chooses. I shall call U the **available set** or the **universal set** and X the **feasible set**. The payoff function is defined for all strategies in the available set. I am here ignoring the deeper criticism made above, that U may not be a set at all, and simply suggesting a way of recognizing that, in reality, players can do more things than what they typically maximize over, namely what the rules of the game permit. What I argued above is that in parlor games it is harmless to assume $U = X$, but not so in most real-life contexts.

The feasible set can be given different interpretations. It could, for instance, be thought of as the set of strategies that the player is aware of (perhaps initially). From examples such as that of the Cuban Missile Crisis, we know that, in reality, players are not always aware of all their available actions. Once the game begins, players may exercise their mind and discover "new" courses of action that they were not aware of earlier. The standard format of a game does not allow us to speak of this phenomenon, which is important in reality.

The feasible set could also be thought of as the set of strategies outside which a player's norm does not allow him to consider. This would be close to the approach taken in Chapter 4 when discussing rationality-limiting norms. This would open up the possibility of studying the implications of changing social norms.

In general, we could think of the feasible set as consisting of actions permitted by the "rules" of the game. This characterization makes explicit what it means for a player to violate the rules. This is useful, since in most social applications of games, games are intrinsically identified with rules.[6] It is not evident, though, what "rules" mean in many of these cases, because it is not clear what their violation implies for a player. But this is precisely the reason why we need to set out from some such generalized characterization of a game. It will force us to confront what "rules" mean and imply, instead of taking them as given. Especially when we step beyond analyzing some narrowly-defined classroom exercise, to addressing larger questions about the economy and polity, the standard game can easily become a constraint. Directing research to break out of this straitjacket will be one game well worth our time.

11.4. The Free Rider

It is evident that knowing which economic arrangement or mechanism is incentive-compatible and which is not is not simply a matter of the economic arrangement or mechanism but also of the norms of the individuals involved and more generally what is instinctively excluded, since that determines the true feasible sets of individuals or, in other words, the sets of options that individuals may actually exercise. Frequently one hears economists saying, "Naturally, bureaucrats will not work. They have no incentive to do so, since their pay or job security does not depend on how hard they work." Or, "Firms must be given the right to fire workers if they

---

[6] An insightful discussion of this occurs in Field (1984).

shirk work. Otherwise, shirking will be a foregone conclusion." But while these may be true in some societies, there is nothing natural or foregone about these. Just as family members do not clear out the refrigerator just because it is not kept locked and just because there is no punishment for cleaning up its contents, it is *conceivable* that workers will not shirk even when there is no punishment for shirking and that bureaucrats will work hard – here I am asking for the reader's indulgence – even though that does not influence their pay. This could be because shirking and not working hard are instinctively excluded in the society under consideration. If we look around us with an open mind, it is indeed staggering the amount of free-riding that we do *not* do.

It follows from what is argued above that a completely *incentive-compatible system* (that is, one in which there does not exist any action that is instinctively excluded but that is otherwise feasible and that enables the agent to do better by violating his prescribed code of behavior) is almost (and perhaps fully) impossible to design. We have, in the end, to rely on the fact that in every society there are actions that individuals do not even consider. A poorly designed system of incentives – and we see a lot of that in society – is one where there is scope for cheating *in areas where people do not have normative restrictions on taking the action that amounts to cheating.* Because what is normatively permitted can change over time and across societies, a system of incentives that may be optimal in one society, at a certain time, may fail to be so in another society at another time.[7] A good system of incentives may, over time, turn out to be defective as the individuals in society discover actions that were earlier instinctively excluded. A good system of incentives cannot therefore be reduced to theorems and formulas. The old-fashioned belief, namely that in designing good economic policy and even in predicting the behavior of economic agents the context matters, may be right after all. The intuition of the designer about what people's feasible sets are is an essential ingredient in designing incentive-compatible mechanisms, which work in practice. This is one reason why entrepreneurship is inevitably in part a matter of knack. The entrepreneur (who has to design mechanisms of rewards and punishment within the firm) has to guess at what the feasible sets of his employees are and then design incentives accordingly.

---

[7] The spectacular success of the Grameen Bank in Bangladesh naturally led to attempts to replicate it in other countries. But somehow it did not work as well. Most analysts attribute this to a failure to replicate it exactly. What these analysts miss out on is that the success of an institution such as the Grameen Bank relies not just on its explicit structure and organization but also on the social setting in which it is being tried, the relationship between the members who form the groups that monitor one another, their social norms, and their culture. The study by Ghatak and Guinnane (1998) is an exception that lays considerable emphasis on precisely such factors.

Just as good tennis cannot be reduced entirely to a set of instructions that one can read up from a book, but must rely on the intuition and judgment of the player, good economic policy cannot be entirely codified into a set of formulas to be used. There will always be things that a good policy-maker can do but that the policy-maker – or an economist – cannot write down in a form that can be transmitted to another person.

This is not to deny that in designing good economic policy there is much that can be scientifically analyzed and codified for use by policy-makers; but an important step in designing effective policy is to recognize that there is also a lot that is not amenable to such treatment.

11.5. Conclusion

This book has been concerned with the shortcomings of mainstream economics that show up as the methods of economic analysis cross boundaries and spill over into other disciplines such as politics, law and sociology. It is a testimony of the distance that economics has come from its founding in the eighteenth century that we can even dare to ask the kinds of questions that the modern economist does. But success can breed the closing of minds. Spurred by the elegance of our mathematical tools of analysis and the theorems and lemmas, economics has, ironically, grown insular as it has reached out to larger domains of applications. Economic theory has become synonymous with enquiry into the mathematical and technical foundations of the discipline. What we often forget is that economics is founded in society and politics as well; and economic theory ought to include in its ambit the understanding of the social and political foundations of economics. This is important not only to take economics beyond its boundaries but even to understand it more fully in its own territory.

An inquiry into the social and political foundations of economics has to be, by its very nature, a slow and lengthy process. The book was intended to spur interest in such research. I believe that such an inquiry will allow economists to go beyond the narrow concerns of economics and enable them to understand and speak meaningfully on larger issues, such as what causes an economy to succeed and what causes stagnation, the interconnection between democracy and economic progress, and the causes of the rise and fall of totalitarianism. I hope the book will play at least a small role in enabling us to address these issues. But even if that were not to happen, and it merely restrained us from pronouncing on these matters as if we had the answers, that too would be no small achievement.

Appendix. Notes on Methodology: Various and Sundry

"Yes, you fall when your life is over." Bahadur, a member of a tribe of nomadic hunters of Nepal, who climb high trees to gather honey, when asked by the National Geographic photographer, Eric Valli, if anyone ever falls from the trees.[1]

A1. Introduction

On the methodology of science, the best strategy is to say little of one's own but find faults in others intrepid enough to disregard this rule. Natural and social scientists are usually quite incoherent when they try to say *how* they do what they do. Some of the greatest scientists have failed when they have ventured to explain to us what the correct methodology of their science is. More tragically, lesser scientists who have tried consciously to follow the method outlined by the *éminence grise* in their fields have produced lesser science.

Hence, this Appendix offers very little by way of advice on what methodology the social scientist should follow. Instead, it devotes itself to the altogether more pleasurable task of picking holes in the methodologies advocated by others. More generally, in this essay I try to inject some skepticism into what social scientists do, and argue that we can never really know anything with certainty. So when we construct models of human behavior, society and economic functioning at a very basic level, these are acts of faith; indeed, there is no escape from that.

The discussion that follows is a miscellany of comments and observations on methodology. It criticizes Friedman's methodology, defends Hume's law, dispenses with Hare's rule, interprets methodological individualism, and comments on the link between determinism and choice. Some of these are referred to or underlie some of the arguments in the book, but, more importantly, this Appendix is intended to underline the skeptical and cautious approach to knowledge that this monograph adopts.

---

[1] *National Geographic*, vol. 193, no. 6, June 1998, p. 92.

A2. Knowledge and Skepticism

How do we know what we do? We may fail to predict inflations, business cycles and the rise and fall of nations but to me what is more remarkable is how in so many domains we *are* so good at making predictions. When I keep a book on the table, I "know" that it will not fly away and it does not. When I leave the apple in mid-air, I "know" that it will fall downwards and it does. How do we know these things? It is difficult to avoid the feeling that perhaps we do *not* know these things; we are just lucky or, more precisely, we have just been lucky thus far. Our minds *happen* to predict things in a way that, over a wide domain, matches reasonably well what actually happens. Our *reasoning* (for example, that the book will not fly because books have not flown off in the past) is, as a little introspection will show, fallacious or vacuous. The wonder is that this kind of fallacious reasoning leads us to a conclusion that is so often right.

How does it come about that our minds are so programmed as to predict tolerably well what nature does? I am unable to answer this, but I can explain why we do not see a world that is otherwise. This is for reasons of natural selection and evolution. A human race endowed with a mind that is *not* programmed so as to be able to predict nature's moves at all would make so many wrong predictions that such a race would not survive. Hence, the fact of our survival ensures that our minds are programmed so as to have predicted nature's moves reasonably well. But it is important to be clear that, as with all natural-selection arguments, this has little power of prediction. It offers no guarantees that we will continue to make reasonably good predictions. Since this book, on some occasions, uses evolutionary arguments,[2] it is worth stressing that such arguments provide only a limited explanation.

An even more amazing manner in which our minds are synchronized with nature is evident when we consider how we relate to time. In order to go into this, it is important to appreciate that what we consider to be two equal intervals of time is a matter of definition. That is, the fact that we consider the time gap between 10 a.m. and 11 a.m. to be the same as the gap between 11 a.m. and 12 noon is simply because we have *chosen* to keep time by the turning of the Earth.[3] We could instead have chosen to keep time by the falling of the leaves onto the White House lawns. That is, we could

---

[2] Typically, an *evolutionary* explanation of why agents have a certain characteristic x takes the form of demonstrating how an agent without x will fail or is less likely to survive.

[3] This is not strictly true, but virtually so. For my discussion this is a good enough approximation.

define the time gap between every consecutive falling of leaves to be equal. Most people's first reaction to this will be that this is absurd. For one, this will mean that in October time would pass much faster than in April. But such a reaction is explained entirely by our conditioning. Because we are used to keeping time by the turning of the Earth, we react in this way. If we were used to this new definition of time gaps, we would simply say that the Earth turns faster in April than in October.

With this in the background, now consider the following experiment. Strike a gong and ask a person, without a watch and sitting in a room where the sun casts no shadow, to let you know when she thinks that ten minutes have passed since the gong was struck. What is surprising is not that most people get it wrong but that no one gets it *too* wrong, that no one tells you in less than one minute or after two hours that she thinks that it is ten minutes. Moreover, many people can beat on a drum thrice so that the time gap between the first two beats is the same as the gap between the last two. But what does it mean to say that the time gap is the same? As we just saw, this is a matter of convention. It simply means that the number of degrees that the Earth turns during one gap is the same as the amount it turns during the other gap. What is surprising is the synchronization of our *intuitive sense* of time gaps with the turning of the Earth and, by virtue of that, with one another. How does our mind count time without a watch, without watching shadows or without some *external* device, given that what we call equal time gaps is after all a matter of convention?

It is now accepted that human beings, like computers, have internal clocks. But what does that mean? It can mean, for instance, that our mind calculates time by keeping tabs on our pulse. This may not be the internal clock that biologists talk about, but it is a nice and plausible example; so let us go along with it, treating it as our internal clock. So it is our pulse that gives us our sense of rhythm, our ability to enjoy percussion instruments. This, in itself, is interesting, but what makes it especially so is that our pulse rates are synchronized with the turning of the Earth on its axis[4] and with one another's pulse rates. That is, for every 360-degree turn of the Earth there is a reasonably fixed number of beats that a person's pulse takes. If during one minute (i.e., during a $[360/(24 \times 60)]$-degree turn) my pulse beats 80 times and during another minute it beats 8 times or 800 times, I would not be able to play the drum or appreciate percussion instruments,

---

[4] This is one reason why it is more convenient to measure time, as we do, by the turning of the Earth. It enables us to have an intuitive sense of how much time has passed, which would not be the case if we measured time by the falling of leaves. Nevertheless, the point remains that what we consider equal lengths of time is a matter of definition.

and I would be dependent on the (external) watch in a way that is difficult to imagine. Of course, even if my pulse did not beat a fixed number of times each day, if all watches were set to the beating of *my* pulse instead of the turning of the Earth or whatever it is that watches are synchronized to, then it would be others who would be out of synchrony, some days would take much longer to pass than other days, and I would never know that I have fever from the reading of my pulse. And if all our pulse rates were matched with one another's but not with the turning of the Earth, then you would be able to enjoy my playing the drum but some days would take longer to pass than others.

It is hopeless to expect some science to explain this synchronization between our internal clock and chosen external clock (that is, in my example, the pulse and the turning of the Earth);[5] this is fundamentally a philosophical problem. All we can say is that if this were not so, the human race might not have survived; we would have mistimed ourselves out of existence. So what we see once again is simply the case that has survived the sieve of natural selection.

This is related to the view taken in "evolutionary epistemology," that what we know is the result of evolutionary processes. This is illustrated nicely by Lorenz (1977: 6) when he observes: "Even the slipper animalcule (paramecium), which, when it meets an obstacle, first recoils slightly and then swims on again in a random direction, 'knows' something literally quite 'objective' about its environment. [. . .] The paramecium 'knows' only that the object is blocking its progress in the original direction, but as 'knowledge' this will meet any criteria which, from our own infinitely more sophisticated standpoint, we are able to apply."

As this discussion must suggest, there is reason to be skeptical about whether we know anything. Infinitely more sophisticated we may be, but in a certain fundamental sense our "knowledge" is no different from that of the paramecium. This is not to deny that most of us think that we do know many things and we act *as if* we do. So this must raise the question: How do we get to think we know what we think we know? In answering this question it is difficult to do better than Hume did nearly a quarter of a millennium ago. Our knowledge is, in an essential way, based on our experience. Causal links between different events can never, according to Hume, be discovered through pure introspection and deduction. They have to be

---

[5] It may reasonably be argued that we have chosen to keep time by the turning of the Earth precisely *because* it matches our pulse. But the question still remains: How come our millions of pulses match one another and there exists external clocks that match our pulses?

based on the repeated observation of the events and their order; logic cannot reveal causality. One can go further and question the very existence of causality. Causality is much more likely a construct of the human mind than an inherent feature of nature. If we find that event E is closely conjoined with event F, in particular that every time E happens F follows, we begin to *believe* that E causes F. Cause is a construction of our mind. In brief, what is being argued here is that causality is learned through experience; but, at the same time, causality is not discovered by our mind but created by it. Given that our mind is programmed to match nature, as we have just seen, it is a very useful construct and so it may be all right, in most circumstances, to use the language of causation *as if* it were an objective feature of nature.

The answer to the question near the start of the previous paragraph is that the *basis* of our knowledge of the world is repeated observation. It is, however, worth remembering that what we acquire is not knowledge but the presumption of knowledge. This is because, though human beings rely on induction, it is never clear why that is a reasonable thing to do. Induction relies on the claim that if we observe that something has happened invariably on n occasions and n is very large, then we have reason to expect that it will happen on the $(n + 1)$th similar occasion. We expect the sun to rise tomorrow because it has risen on all previous days. As Bertrand Russell pointed out, we can make the prediction stronger by basing it on the even more widely observed phenomenon that spinning bodies tend to continue to spin, since this would include not just our experience with the turning of the Earth but also tops and cricket balls.

Induction, however, often goes wrong. As Russell (1967: 35) himself observed: "The man who has fed the chicken every day throughout its life at last wrings its neck instead, showing that more refined views as to the uniformity of nature would have been useful to the chicken."

One reason why induction is unreliable is that the same experiment seldom (if ever) gets repeated twice. The sun has never risen on the kind of day that tomorrow will be. Hence, strictly interpreted, we never have any previous evidence, which is so necessary for the inductive step. One can try to get out of this by saying that one should not be too strict in interpreting "previous experiments;" what we need is not evidence on identical previous experiments but similar ones. This argument does not work because what we describe as a "similar experiment" has an essential circularity about it. Suppose a person who has never seen a kiwi fruit before is given one and asked if it will fall downwards when left in mid-air. Surely the person will predict that it will. Now if we ask her how she knew this, given that she has never seen a kiwi fruit before, she will say, for instance, that she has evidence from seeing what happens to similar objects suspended in mid-air – for instance, other fruits with which she has experience. But then why should the dropping of an apple be considered an experiment *similar* to the dropping of a kiwi fruit? Given that we cannot predict the *taste* of kiwi fruits from the taste of apples, how can we predict the *falling* of one from the falling of the other. No one will be foolish enough to say that a kiwi fruit must taste like an apple because, though one has never had a kiwi fruit before one can deduce this from *similar* experiments, namely that of eating apples. Surely, we will protest that that is not a similar experiment. In matters of taste kiwi fruits and apples are not similar, but in terms of falling downwards they are similar.

This use of the term "similar" is circular. We never did really predict the fall of the kiwi fruit *because* we have seen similar experiments with apples. Instead, we define the two as similar experiments because we somehow know that both fall downwards.

We are inevitably led back to the position that I took earlier. We cannot really know *how* the human mind makes predictions; all we know is that it does so fairly well; and the fact that we are around to see ourselves is the only part-answer that we can give as to why we are good at making so many predictions.

We cannot know anything but logical truths. All else we merely *think* we know. But given that our minds are so well programmed with nature, it will be harmless to use the language of knowledge, to say that we know *E* when what is really true is that we think we know *E*. So, in this monograph I have spoken of what we know without always reminding the reader of the caveat just mentioned.

A3. Assumptions

Still persisting with the subject of prediction but turning to a more mundane domain, let us consider a question that economists have to contend with: What is a good theory? One of the most influential answers to this question was given by Milton Friedman (1953), who argued that the goal of a good theory or hypothesis is to make "valid and meaningful (i.e. not truistic) predictions about phenomena not yet observed." From this, Friedman went on to analyze what constitutes a good assumption. Given that economists have been reviled for the strong and often untenable assumptions that they use, this is a subject that deserves consideration.

Friedman's (1953: 15) answer has the advantage of clarity: "The relevant question to ask about the 'assumptions' of a theory is not whether they are descriptively 'realistic,' for they never are, but whether they are sufficiently good approximations for the purpose in hand, [that is,] whether the theory works, which means whether it yields sufficiently accurate predictions." Thus if an economist assumes that businessmen consciously equate marginal cost to marginal revenue, this assumption will be taken as a good one if the predictions emanating from it are good, even if the assumption is false. In brief, according to Friedman, for assumptions to be judged acceptable, the predictions that follow from the assumption must be accurate. Though this has been a very influential idea, it is, I shall argue, flawed.

Clearly, when we say that for an assumption to be acceptable the predictions that follow from it need to be correct, even though the assumption itself may be false, we do not mean *all* predictions that follow from it must be correct. This is because one of the predictions of any assumption A is A itself. Thus it is not possible for all predictions to be true and the assumption to be not true. Friedman's methodology interpreted in this way would be uninteresting.

Hence, Friedman's position may be interpreted as saying that all *testable* propositions implied by A must be true. Then it is possible to have an assumption so that all its testable predictions are true but the assumption is not (testably) true because it cannot be tested. Indeed, Friedman does not talk of all the predictions of an assumption. What he seems to say is this. Let P be a prediction (for example, P can be "Firms maximize profit."). Let A be an assumption (or a set of assumptions) that implies P. Friedman says that if P is empirically true, then A is a good enough assumption even if A were false, or not *demonstrably* true. But note that if such an assumption A exists, then there must exist another assumption A^* such that A^* is demonstrably true and A^* implies P. This is because we can take A^* to be P itself. Likewise, consider Friedman's own example. Let P be "Firms maximize profits" and let A be "Entrepreneurs consciously equate MC to MR." Clearly A implies P.[6] But so does A^*: "Entrepreneurs equate MC to MR." Moreover, A^* must be testably true if P is testably true. Hence, unless we love false assumptions because they are false, there is no need to use them. We can always replace them with a true assumption. This was the gist of Samuelson's (1963) rebuttal of Friedman's argument.

---

[6] Of course, I am assuming that the total cost (revenue) function is differentiable and convex (concave).

One possible defence of Friedman's method can be that one may be able to find an assumption A such that P is not its only prediction. Suppose A also predicts Q. Now if we test P and find it to be true, then, by Friedman's argument, we accept A. Hence, we get to suppose Q is true, since Q is an implication of A. Hence, we seem to get something by using an assumption that is not in itself tested to be valid. To see this method in action, suppose that P is "As price rises, demand will fall." Let A be the standard assumptions of consumer theory – people prefer more to less, they have continuous and convex preferences, and so on – plus the assumption that the good is not a Giffen good. Then A does imply P, but it also implies Q: the effect of a change in p_1 on x_2 (utility held unchanged) is the same as the effect of a change in p_2 on x_1 (utility held unchanged), where p_i is the price of good i and x_i is the quantity of good i being demanded. So by this method we learn Q without actually having to test it.

I shall argue that this is an absurd procedure for acquiring faith in a proposition (for instance, Q). To see the absurdity of the procedure, consider another example. P is the same as before. Let A^+ be the conjunction of the above A and the assumption "All men wear hats." Clearly, since A implies P, then A^+ also implies P. Now suppose P is tested to be valid. Then by the above argument we should have faith in the other implications of A^+. But one implication of A^+ is that men do not get their hair wet even when it rains. Surely it would be absurd to believe that men do not have wet hair even when it rains *because* the demand curve is demonstrated to be down-ward sloping!

It follows that, given an assumption A that cannot be directly shown to be valid, we should have faith only in those predictions implied by A that are tested to be true. But in that case, why do we need the assumption at all, since we will have faith only in those propositions that are tested to be true?

Hence, contrary to Friedman's argument, assumptions are useful if we have reason to believe that they are true, either because they have been tested, or by introspection, or even by a hunch. Patently unrealistic assumptions cannot typically yield practically useful results; and when they do, they can be replaced, without loss, by realistic assumptions.

This is a principle that we should try to follow. At times, we may make an assumption that is patently unrealistic – for example, that an economy has only two goods, or that a society has two persons (or an infinity of persons). This can be for two reasons. At times we may do so, just to gain logical clarity on some point without expecting it to illuminate us about anything practical or real. At other times we may do so for brevity. For instance, suppose that I believe that "whatever is true for a two-person society is true for an *n*-person society." Then I could take the remark within quotes in the previous sentence as my assumption, do a two-person analysis and, citing this assumption, claim validity for an *n*-person world. Since these steps are exactly the same as the ones that I would take if I had assumed: "There are two persons in society," I may make the latter assumption, which is briefer and easier to understand, when what I actually believe in is the assumption quoted earlier. Indeed, when we analyze a two-person society or an infinitely populated society and *expect it to shed light on real societies*, we must be implicitly making the longer assumption.

Before going off the topic of assumptions or axioms, I want to introduce a taxonomy that is useful and that has been used in this book. Typically, when we want to criticize the assumptions behind a model, our tendency is to pick on the assumptions that are explicitly stated. Let us call these the **explicit assumptions**. Thus, in consumer theory, the assumptions that have been most frequently questioned are the ones written down explicitly as axioms – for instance, that human preference is transitive or complete or continuous or convex. However, it is arguable that some of the strongest assumptions are the ones that are never stated explicitly but are built into the framework of the model. I call the latter the **embedded assumptions** or **axioms**. In consumer theory, that a person has a preference relation is one such assumption. That the preference relation is crisp (that is, not fuzzy) is another such assumption. These are typically not written down as axioms but are implicitly treated as valid as soon as a book or a paper starts off by saying that "Suppose that a consumer has a preference relation that satisfies the following axioms."

What is an embedded assumption and what is an explicit assumption depends on the model in question. Thus, in old-fashioned consumer theory the existence of the utility function used to be an embedded assumption. The explicit assumptions were the properties of the utility function. This changed with the coming of modern theory (e.g., Debreu, 1959), which began with a preference relation and explicitly stated the axioms that allow us to deduce the existence of the utility function. There are other works (e.g., Arrow, 1959) that start even further back, from the embedded assumption of a consumer having a choice function, and on that they impose explicit assumptions to deduce the existence of a preference relation. However, each theory or model must have embedded assumptions. By their very nature they tend to escape notice and critical evaluation. The present book has been especially concerned with bringing to light the embedded assumptions of some of the economist's standard models, and evaluating them and suggesting alternative approaches and interpretations.

A4. Hume's Law

Hume's Law asserts that a should-statement can never be deduced from is-statements alone. In other words, if we deduce a normative statement or a prescription from some prior statements, then these prior statements must already contain some normative statements. This would not have been such an important law if it were not for the fact that it is so often overlooked. Overlooking this law has frequently resulted in economists and political scientists being unnecessarily worried about the policy implications of their positive research. A proper appreciation of Hume's Law is therefore an important aid in doing good and scrupulous research in positive social science.

Consider the sensitive topic of the relation between race and intelligence. To criticize empirical findings on this subject on the ground that it logically implies some unpalatable policy prescription, such as the curtailment of scholarship to a particular race, amounts to misunderstanding Hume's Law. From the finding that (1) x is less intelligent than y, we cannot deduce that (2) x should get less financial support from government for studies than y. If we do manage to deduce such a policy conclusion, we do so by unwittingly making use of some other prior normative statement (this follows from Hume's Law) – for instance, one that says that (3) if one race is established to be less intelligent than another race then this race should receive less financial support. Since (1) and (3) together imply (2), we do not have to suppress (1) just because we find (2) unacceptable. We have the option of rejecting (3).

Hume's Law assures us therefore that at least *this* worry need not thwart our effort at honest positive research. The prescription to implement or reject a policy can never be deduced from the positive statements that constitute one's empirical findings. We may criticize the empirical findings on the ground that they are flawed; we may criticize the *publication* of the empirical findings on the ground that it can hurt the well-being of certain minorities by providing ammunition to some fascist party or group. But we cannot reject the findings simply on the ground that they imply some unacceptable policy.

Before we accept Hume's Law as truth (as I am inclined to do), it is worth considering one possible exception to this law that has been discussed in the literature. Let us begin by clarifying what we mean by positive and normative statements.

Consider the following three statements:

  (a) If price rises, demand falls.
  (b) The US government should provide more welfare support to the poor.
  (c) India is today better off than it was in 1947.

Statement (a) is quite obviously a positive statement; it is a description of the world or an hypothesis. It may well be wrong, but that does not alter its status as positive. Likewise, (b) is transparently normative. It is a prescription, a statement of recommendation. What has on occasion been considered controversial are statements such as (c). At first sight, (c) looks like a positive statement because there is no explicit commendation in it. But nevertheless one can argue that there is an implicit recommendation – if you could through some choice of policy make India the way it was in 1947, then (c) suggests that you should *not* do so. Moreover, two people can fully agree on descriptions of India today and in 1947 and yet disagree on whether India was better off in 1947 or now. This can be because of their value judgments. One person may strongly mind the inequalities of current India and so prefer the relative poverty of 1947. These are very close to the grounds used by Hare (1952) to argue that a statement such as (c) should be treated as a normative statement. Likewise, the observation "This is a good apple" is a normative statement, though on the face of it it may appear to be positive. Hare's position seems entirely reasonable, and in this work we treat statements like (c) or "This is a good apple" as normative.

There is, however, need for a word of caution. Suppose a person fully describes an economy E and then says that

(d) E is optimal.

Is (d) normative? Here the context matters. If this were a discourse among noneconomists, statement (d) would have to be considered normative for exactly the reasons given above. However, among economists, especially economic theorists, (d) will typically be positive. This happens because the word "optimal" is used differently by economists and others. Economists have a definition for "optimal." By that they usually mean "Pareto-optimal." If the "optimal" in (d) refers to Pareto optimality, then two persons who agree on the description of E cannot disagree about whether it is optimal or not. That becomes a matter of definition. Under such an interpretation, (d) is positive. Indeed there would be nothing inconsistent for an economist to say that "E is optimal but awful." If, on the other hand, we use "optimal" in its usual, everyday sense, then (d) is normative.

Similarly, when game theorists describe the equilibrium of a game as "perfect" or even "divine," you may complain about their limited vocabulary, which makes them use such terms as "technical," but the fact remains that they are making positive observations. A divine equilibrium can be hellish.

Although normative statements reflect our values and, to that extent, are subjective, their use is nevertheless governed by some laws. One of them, propounded by Hare (1952) is now called Hare's Rule (Sen, 1966). It refers to a "universal principle": If in a certain context C you make a normative statement or pass a value judgment, then if the same context C arises again it may be presumed that your normative statement applies there as well. Let us take Hare's own example. In a compartment full of children, you tell a person "You ought not to smoke here." Suppose the person responds: "That is all right. I shall go to the next compartment and smoke. The compartment is identical to this one, including the fact that it has children." Then you will have to conclude that either he does not know what "ought" means, or he has decided to violate your moral injunction.

To take another example consider these two statements:

(A) Apple x is identical to apple y.
(B) Apple x is as good as apple y.

Hare's Rule asserts that (A) *implies* (B). Now, note that (B) is a normative statement, as discussed above; and (A) is a positive statement. Hence, Hare's rule suggests that in some situations we may have to violate Hume's Law. This was the argument of Sen (1966): One has to *choose* between Hare's Rule and Hume's Law; one cannot have both.

In what follows, I want to uphold Hume's Law. To me it seems questionable whether two separate situations or objects can ever be identical. If in the description of an apple we include its location in time and space, then of course two apples being identical will mean that they are the same apple. In other words, two apples cannot be distinct or separate and at the same time identical.[7] If the above assertion were correct, then Hare's Rule would be vacuous. There would be no context where it would apply. So, even if it were considered valid, it would not imply the negation of Hume's Law because of its vacuity.

Against this criticism, Hare's response would be that I am using the word "identical" wrongly, or too stringently. Surely, for two objects to be identical does not mean that they are the same. For one, including the location of the object in time and space as part of the description of the object may be going too far. This is certainly a plausible criticism. So let us assume that distinct objects can be (essentially) identical. It follows then that when we

---

[7] To quote Wittgenstein (1922, stanza 5.5303) on this: "Roughly speaking, to say of *two* things that they are identical is nonsense and to say of one thing that it is identical to itself is to say nothing."

declare two apples as equally good, this can be for two different reasons: because the two apples are identical, or because the two are not identical but whatever traits are better in one are offset by the traits that are better in the other. But now it seems perfectly reasonable to say that if statement (B) is made *because x and y are identical*, then (B) is not a normative statement. Otherwise (B) is normative.

This suggests an interesting twist to the distinction between normative and positive statements. Even if we know the meanings of the words, we cannot always judge whether a statement is positive or normative unless we know what reasoning prompted the statement. In accepting Hare's Rule, now there is no violation of Hume's Law, because if a statement of type (B) is made *because (A) is known to be true*, then (B) is positive and so there is no violation of Hume's Law.

A5. Methodological Individualism

A social science that explains social regularities and phenomena, such as reciprocity and inflation, wholly from the decisions and behavior of *individual* human beings is described as adhering to **methodological individualism** (henceforth, MI). Whether this is the right methodology for social science or not was once a matter of considerable dispute, which engaged the minds of leading economists and sociologists. Gradually interest in the subject died down, individuals continued to do social science research without, mercifully, trying to explicitly articulate the method that they were in fact using. But with this developed the feeling, especially among economists, that the problem of MI was either trivial or resolved in their favor.

Recently there has been a revival of interest in the rights and wrongs of MI, as evidenced in the works of Bhargava (1993) and Arrow (1994). The aim of this section is to evaluate this increase in interest and to present the reader with an open-ended and somewhat paradoxical problem concerning methodological individualism and normative judgments.

Bhargava's (1993) book summarizes the various points of view on the subject that have occurred in the social sciences; it is also meant to be a challenge to orthodoxy, especially orthodoxy within economics. He argues that MI is not trivial, and that there are versions of it that are intellectually sophisticated and deserve our attention; however, MI can be challenged and he goes on to construct nonindividualistic methodologies that, according to him, are at least as satisfactory as MI. What is remarkable and so rare in contemporary writing is Bhargava's flair for expressing the philosopher's anguish and elation. A variety of philosophers and scientists have suffered the anxiety of self-doubt, of not knowing whether what they are grappling with or have actually established is something profound or trivial. One has no difficulty in seeing that Bhargava means it when he writes (p. 5):

> On reading the literature one is swung between exuberance and despair, from feeling that all problems have been resolved to one that none has [. . .]. Gradually an intense frustration overwhelms the reader: perhaps there was nothing worth discussing in the first place. What on earth was all the fuss about?

What he settles for as the best face of MI is what in his book is christened "intentionalism." The **intentional man** is somewhere between the well-known but elusive *Homo economicus* and equally rare *Homo sociologicus*. He can choose and decide individually but he is not a relentless, maximizing agent. He has psychology and a sense of social norms, which get in the way of maximization and distinguishes him from the computer-like *Homo economicus*. Then, after going through some discussions of the limitations of MI, Bhargava develops the idea of "contextualism" as a challenge to MI, including intentionalism. The challenge consists of arguing that a variety of beliefs and practices in everyday life make sense only in the context of the society where they occur. Hence, in describing society or an economy, we are compelled to use concepts that are irreducibly social.

The problem with this thesis is not that it is unacceptable but that it is *too* acceptable, and it is not clear that the critique of social science on which it is based is a fair critique. To be on safer grounds while making this argument, I shall confine my attention mostly to economics.

Joseph Schumpeter is the person who coined the term "methodological individualism" and is at times treated as the original defender of this method. This is wrong, because there were others using the method and espousing its cause even before the term had been coined. The Austrian economist Carl Menger, for instance, published a book in 1883 in which he made a vigorous case for this method. This in itself is enough to deprive Schumpeter (despite his famous precocity) of any claims to paternity for this idea, 1883 being the year of Schumpeter's birth.

The reason why the sociologist's assertion that certain beliefs and concepts are inextricably social is unlikely to stir a hornet's nest is that, though many economists claim to be rigid adherents of MI, they do use and have always used social concepts and categories. This has been very convincingly argued recently by Kenneth Arrow (1994). Arrow points out how a variable such as price in a competitive model is an irreducibly social concept.

Each individual takes price to be given, but the price that comes to prevail is an outcome of the choices of the *collectivity*. So economists constructing equilibrium models, who claim to be hardened methodological individualists, are actually not so. They unwittingly follow a method that uses social categories and, therefore, is not too far away from what Bhargava is recommending, thereby making the recommendation partly futile.

I would argue that the more contentious and substantial methodological debate concerning individualism relates to the *permissibility* of a certain class of propositions in social science. Consider the following proposition:

> The landlord will undertake action *A because* it is in the landlord's class interest to do so. (Action *A* could, for instance, be: "refuse to hire a servant who has fled another landlord's employment and offers to work for this landlord for a very low wage.")

I shall call this proposition *P*. There are many economists and some political scientists (especially those belonging to the positive political-economy school) who believe that *P* is not permissible. I have sympathy with this. I do not deny that people do occasionally behave in certain ways simply because those are in their group or class interest; but as an axiom to be *generally* applied, I find *P* unacceptable. If I am to use an axiom like proposition *P*, I would usually want to first satisfy myself as to why it may be in the landlord's *self*-interest to behave in a way that is in his *class* interest. Or, at the very least, I would go along with *P* only in so far as there is no direct evidence or reason to believe that in this case the landlord's class interest does actually conflict with his self-interest. Hence, in explaining behavior, I consider the reduction (or at least the potential for reduction) to individual interest to be a worthwhile target. However, this does not negate the use of beliefs, concepts and variables that are irreducibly social. It is not clear that a researcher who does both (that is, resists explaining individual behavior solely in terms of its ability to serve group or class interests but uses concepts and beliefs that are inherently social) is an MI person or an anti-MI person – but neither is this a very important question. The important and contestable question is whether assumptions like proposition *P* should or should not be used. And as I just explained, I prefer to avoid such assumptions as far as possible, without making that course of action into dogma.

One reason why this must not be dogma relates to the discussion in Chapter 11 concerning how human beings, even when they optimize, do not do so over the domain of all actions open to them. Hence, there may well be actions that give greater utility than the chosen action but get rejected simply because those were actions that were not even considered. This implies that human beings may not seize every free-riding opportunity that comes their way.

In closing, I want to discuss one even more contentious matter. This concerns the use of nonindividualism in our normative statements. To those who insist on MI, and perhaps even to others, the problem that is outlined below constitutes almost a paradox – and certainly a challenge. I present it here as an open-ended problem for the reader without offering any "solution."

We often pass moral judgments on groups of people which cannot be reduced to the individuals in the group. Observations of the following kind are clearly not uncommon.

1. "It is a shame that no one in university U does research on poverty." Or,
2. "It speaks very poorly of the economics profession that so few economists in the 1930s were writing on the unemployment problem, despite that being one of the most important problems of that time."

Let us here concentrate on observation 1. If a person making this observation were asked: "Do you therefore feel that it is wrong that Professor X in university U does not do research on poverty?", the answer would typically be: "Of course not. I am not blaming any *individual* for not working on poverty." So, presumably, when we make an observation such as 1, we are not casting moral aspersions on any individual in university U, though we are clearly casting aspersion on the collectivity of individuals in university U. Hence, by analyzing our "language of morals," we find that we do indeed use nonindividualistic judgments since we do often make observations like 1.

A similar dilemma but with a possible solution has been suggested by Dworkin. He argues (1986) that in situations of shared or group responsibility it may be reasonable to *personify* the group or the community. Thus, when a corporation produces a dangerously defective good but it is not possible to pin down the responsibility on any particular individual in the corporation, we may need to treat the corporation as a moral agent and apply "facsimiles of our principles about individual fault and responsibility to it" (Dworkin, 1986: 170). And then, by virtue of the *corporation's* responsibility, we may proceed to hold the *agents* and *members* of the corporation responsible. This is methodologically interesting. Individuals are still essential units in his analysis but, unlike in standard methodological individualism, judgment on the group *precedes* the individual.

Dworkin demonstrates with a very elegant example how we, unwittingly, often use this method. This happens, for instance, when we talk of the state's or the community's responsibility for certain kinds of individual rights. Thus we talk of the state's obligation to ensure that no one is assaulted by others. Moreover, we do this even before agreeing on how this responsibility is to be apportioned across various units of the state, for instance, the police, the bureaucracy and the military. Dworkin (1986: 173) points out how we may reasonably discuss the community's responsibility and "leave for *separate* consideration the different issue of which arrangement of official duties would best acquit the communal responsibility" (my italics).

There is reason for exercising caution in using this approach. To talk of a group's responsibility, without knowing how it is to be apportioned among the individuals in the group, seems to me to be useful only to the extent that such an apportionment is eventually possible. If it were not possible, then we should turn back and question whether it was reasonable in the first place to think of the group as having that responsibility. In other words, the bifurcation of discourse is merely a matter of convenience and there may well be situations where the outcome in the second part requires us to reconsider our conclusions of the first part. This, in turn, means that the personification of the corporation or the community can only be an interim construct, which may need to be dismantled if we are eventually unable to spread the responsibility in some reasonable way across the members of the corporation or the community.

Returning to my example, this means that we cannot first decide that the personification of university U is responsible for a certain neglect and then, by virtue of that, hold professors in university U culpable. So the dilemma mentioned above continues to persist: We have to either admit that methodological individualism does not extend to normative judgments (which in Dworkin's example would mean that we may personify the group but have to stop there and not carry the judgment over to the individuals) or take the position that, though we do in practice pass judgments on *groups*, these are, in fact, meaningless and best resisted.

A6. Determinism and Choice

One philosophical problem that the economist needs to contend with is the alleged conflict between freedom and choice, on the one hand, and causality and determinism on the other. According to the adherents of determinism, whatever happens does so for causes prior to it in time. So nothing can be other than what it is. Counterfactuals are *logically* impossible. If two human beings behave differently, that must be for some causes prior to the moment of the behavior. And those causes must have causes. If we go on tracing the causes further and further back, we will eventually reach causes over which the individuals in question have no control. Thus, according to one strand of determinism – one with which I have considerable sympathy – all human action can be explained, in principle, by heredity and environment, essentially the factors that are beyond the control of the person in question. This seems to suggest that individuals do not have free will. Indeed, a large part of the philosophical debate on the subject has treated free will and determinism as antagonistic to each other.

Even if we push aside the philosophically troublesome question as to whether there is anything called "causality" that links events, research in economics proceeds *as if* there is causality underlying observable phenomena. So the economist, while doing research, acts as if he or she were a determinist. Since economics is also intimately related to choice, the alleged conflict between free will and determinism is something that we need to face up to.

This seeming conflict has troubled social scientists and philosophers (*see, for instance*, Hicks, 1979, and Levi, 1997).[8] Hicks (1979) wanted to hold onto the assumption of free choice and also to causality and determinism, and he was troubled by this conflict. He addressed the problem but the answer he gave was unsatisfactory. He argued that we need to maintain a "double vision." He explained this with the example of the earth and the sun, arguing that whether the sun moves around the earth or the earth around the sun is simply a matter of point of view.[9] The child and the sixteenth-century priest, who believe that it is the Sun that moves, cannot be castigated for stupidity. Hicks argues that a good astronomer needs this double-vision. He then uses this to deliver us from the incompatibility between choice and determinism by saying that we must maintain a double vision by treating the past as determinate but not the future. But this is unsatisfactory. It simply amounts to urging us to look the other way from the problem.

---

[8] Thus Nozick (1981: 293) writes: "Over the years I have spent more time thinking about the problem of free will than about any other philosophical topic except perhaps the foundations of ethics."

[9] And here is George in Tom Stoppard's *Jumpers* (London: Faber, 1972: 66) on this subject: "Meeting a friend in a corridor, Wittgenstein said: 'Tell me, why do people always say it is *natural* for men to assume that the sun went round the earth rather than that the earth was rotating?' His friend said, 'Well, obviously, because it just *looks* as if the sun is going round the earth.' To which the philosopher replied, 'Well, what would it have looked like if it had looked as if the earth was rotating?' "

Fortunately, there are better ways of getting around the problem. I argue below that once we delineate the determinist position more carefully, so as not to unwittingly carry with it corollaries that do not follow from it, we will find that free choice is compatible with determinism. But before going on to it, I want to briefly digress to an implication of determinism that I would like to maintain. People usually show a lot of sympathy for *visible* disadvantages that other people have. Thus, if someone cannot work because of a visible handicap – for instance, not having an arm – we are willing to extend help in the form of social security. But if someone cannot work because he is lazy, we are typically unforgiving. Now, over time, as science progresses, the set of people with whom we are unforgiving has been shrinking. Thus, for instance, as medical research revealed that some of the people whom we took to be just lazy actually suffer from chronic fatigue syndrome (CFS), we came to realize that they need support just like the person with a visible handicap. But this should warn us that the one who has no visible handicap and does not suffer from CFS, but nevertheless is too lazy to work, must also have an undiscovered cause that can be traced to factors beyond his control. Just because someone's cause of laziness is invisible and does not yet have a name does not make that person undeserving of support.[10] Determinism also suggests that the only reason to punish people is to create factors in other people's environment that deter them from crime and other antisocial activities. Punishment ought not to take the form of vengeance.

Let me now return to the alleged conflict between rational choice and determinism, discussed above. According to a closely-related, popular view: "If determinism is true, then one's future is predetermined and hence one need not make any effort." Similar arguments have led to allegations of inconsistency in Marxist thinking. Since, for a Marxist, socialism is inevitable, why does he advocate that people strive towards it? Is it not like an astronomer advocating the eclipse he predicts? I shall argue that this paradox and the one that Hicks (1979) refers to – the conflict between rationality and determinism – arise from the same root cause.

---

[10] There are situations where for *strategic* reasons we have to restrict social support to only the *visibly* disadvantaged. Thus car parks that are reserved for the handicapped cannot be extended to the invisibly disadvantaged (for instance, the lazy) simply because there is no way of distinguishing between the invisibly disadvantaged and the nondisadvantaged. (If there were a way to ensure that the nonlazy persons would not misuse this facility, I would be in favor of car parks being reserved for the lazy.) There are, however, other kinds of social support where people self-select themselves. Welfare for the unemployed is one such example. Those capable and willing to do regular work and earn more would, on their own, reject such support. This realization makes it easier to maintain that society has a collective responsibility for its disadvantaged, and government ought to execute this responsibility.

It has been argued by Lyons (1975) that paradoxes of this kind stem from "a belief that all causality must be at the billiard ball level." His argument, while correct, lacks catholicity. What is it that makes a billiard ball different from a human being, in the context of determinism? This question will be answered in the process of examining the problem raised by Hicks.

In taking on Hicks' problem, it is useful to begin by defining determinism a little more sharply than was done above. It can be said, risking oversimplicity, that an agent is determined if the agent's actions are totally dependent on causes outside the agent's control. In the case of human beings, as mentioned above, determinism adopts the view that an individual's thoughts and actions are totally determined by his heredity and environment, which will be referred to, for brevity, as "external factors."

The alleged incompatibility between choice and determinism stems from an *implicit* belief that determinism precludes the possibility that any incident in a human being's life could depend on factors which are *not* external. That is, there is a tendency to believe that since (assuming determinism) whether Suzanne reads *Macbeth* or not depends on external factors, it cannot depend on Suzanne's penchant for Shakespeare. But, clearly, this need not be. Certainly, x is a function of y does not imply that x is *not* a function of z. A composite function is also a function. Hence, x could be a function of z, which in turn could be a function of y. This fallacy will be referred to, in brief, as FIB: the Fallacy of the Ignored Bridging function.

Now, consider the problem of determinism and effort. The belief that if determinism is true then one need not make any effort in life could be illustrated with an example. Suzanne is about to take an examination and she wants to pass it. The question is whether she should study or not. It may seem that if determinism were true, then she need not. This conclusion is a consequence of the following belief:

> (A) If determinism is true, then Suzanne cannot alter the outcome of the examination by studying or not studying.

But (A) is false and stems from FIB. (A) implies a denial of the existence of a function or mapping between the set consisting of studying and not studying to the set consisting of passing and failing. Clearly, determinism does not necessitate this. Determinism merely says that whether Suzanne will pass or fail is predestined. In fact, it is quite possible that there exists an immutable natural law that an examinee will pass if, and only if, he or she studies. In deciding whether to study or not, *all Suzanne needs to know is this natural law*, which implies:

> (B) If Suzanne wants to pass her exam, then she should study.

If determinism were true, then whether she will pass or not is predetermined, but that is only because whether she will study or not is predetermined. Hence, determinism is compatible with (B), and (A) is therefore false. So when Suzanne asks whether she should study for her examination, a determinist need not be in a quandary. The fact that the outcome of the examination is predetermined in no way affects the answer, "You should study if you want to pass." This answer is unchanged whether or not one is a determinist. Similarly, there is no contradiction in saying that socialism is inevitable, and that people must strive for socialism. It does, of course, imply a belief that it is inevitable that the people will strive towards socialism. And when an astronomer advocates the eclipse he predicts, it is thought to be foolish, not because it is foolish to advocate predestined events, as seems to be implied by Magee (1973), but simply because eclipses, unlike socialism, cannot be brought about by human striving.

Now consider the problem of rationality and determinism. It is worth noting at the outset that if rationality is taken to mean – as is frequently done in the social sciences – some sort of consistency in a person's behavior, then, clearly, rationality need not contradict determinism. A magnetic needle, which always points to North, behaves consistently, though its behavior is undoubtedly determined. The conflict is supposed to be between determinism and rationality, when rationality is defined in terms of some sort of a motivation, like the motivation to maximize happiness or utility.

The alleged incompatibility can be expressed as follows. Consider the statements:

(a) An agent's actions are determined by external factors.

(b) Faced with a set of alternatives, an agent selects so as to maximize his happiness or preference.

Statement (b) should not be viewed as a tautology. What it says is that an agent has a preference relation over the domain of alternatives, and he chooses so as to maximize his preference (i.e. he chooses from his choice set).

The problem arises from the belief that if (a) is true, then (b) is false. Lucas (1970: 27) writes, "If determinism is true, then my actions are no longer really my actions, and they no longer can be regarded as having been done for reasons rather than causes." This is not true. Reasons and causes are not mutually exclusive. Determinism does not imply that an agent's actions are *not* determined by external factors. It is clearly possible that an agent's action is a function of his preference, which in turn is a function of external factors. This implies that both (a) and (b) above may be true. These statements had seemed incompatible because of FIB. Now it is clear why a billiard ball and a human being are different in spite of the fact that the actions of both are determined. In both cases (a) is true, but (b) is true only for human beings. For both, external factors totally determine behavior, but only for human beings does the causal chain run through reason and preference on its journey from external factors to behavior. Similarly, determinism does not imply that there is no difference between a fettered man and a man who is sitting still, because the latter, unlike the former, can walk off *if he wants to*.

References

Acemoglu, D. and Robinson, J. A. (1998), "Why Did the West Extend the Franchise? Democracy, Inequality and Growth in Historical Perspective," mimeo: MIT.

Ainslie, G. and Herrnstein, R. J. (1981), "Preference Reversal and Delayed Reinforcement," *Animal Learning and Behavior*, 9: 476–82.

Akerlof, G. A. (1976), "The Economics of Caste and of the Rat Race and Other Woeful Tales," *Quarterly Journal of Economics*, 90: 599–617.

Akerlof, G. A. (1991), "Procrastination and Obedience," *American Economic Review*, 81: 1–19.

Akerlof, G. A. and Kranton, R. E. (1999), "Economics and Identity," *Quarterly Journal of Economics*, forthcoming.

Anderson, T. J. and Hill, P. J. (1975), "The Evolution of Property Rights: A Study of the American West," *Journal of Law and Economics*, 18: 163–79.

Aoki, M. (1999), "Toward a Comparative Institutional Analysis," manuscript: Stanford University.

Arce M, D. G. (1997), "Correlated Strategies as Institutions," *Theory and Decision*, 42: 271–85.

Arrow, K. J. (1959), "Rational Choice Functions and Orderings," *Economica*, 26: 121–7.

Arrow, K. J. (1972), "Gifts and Exchanges," *Philosophy and Public Affairs*, 1: 343–62.

Arrow, K. J. (1977), "Extended Sympathy and the Possibility of Social Choice," *American Economic Review*, 67: 219–25.

Arrow, K. J. (1982), "A Cautious Case for Socialism," in Howe, I. (ed.), *Beyond the Welfare State*, New York: Schocken Books.

Arrow, K. J. (1994), "Methodological Individualism and Social Knowledge," *American Economic Review*, 84: 1–9.

Arrow, K. J. (1995), "A Note on Freedom and Flexibility," in Basu, K., Pattanaik, P. and Suzumura, K. (eds.), *Choice, Welfare and Development*, Oxford: Clarendon Press.

Asheim, G. B. (1999), "On the Epistemic Foundation of Backward Induction," mimeo: University of Oslo.

Aumann, R. J. (1976), "Agreeing to Disagree," *Annals of Statistics*, 4: 1236–9.

Aumann, R. J. (1995), "Backward Induction and Common Knowledge of Rationality," *Games and Economic Behavior*, 8: 6–19.

Austen-Smith, D. (1990), "Information Transmission in Debate," *American Journal of Political Science*, 34: 124–52.

Austen-Smith, D. and Banks, J. (1996), "Information Aggregation, Rationality and the Condorcet Jury Theorem," *American Political Science Review*, 90: 34–45.

Austin, J. L. (1962), *How to Do Things with Words*, New York: Oxford University Press.

Axelrod, R. (1984), *The Evolution of Cooperation*, New York: Basic Books.

Baird, D. G., Gertner, R. H. and Picker, R. C. (1995), *Game Theory and the Law*, Cambridge MA: Harvard University Press.

Banerjee, A. V. (1992), "A Simple Model of Herd Behavior," *Quarterly Journal of Economics*, 107: 797–817.

Banerjee, A. V. and Weibull, J. (1995), "Evolutionary Selection and Rational Behavior," in Kirman, A. and Salmon, M. (eds.), *Learning and Rationality in Economics*, Oxford: Blackwell Publishers.

Bardhan, P. K. (1989), "Alternative Approaches to the Theory of Institutions in Economic Development," in Bardhan, P. K. (ed.), *The Economic Theory of Agrarian Institutions*, Oxford: Clarendon Press.

Bardhan, P. K. (1992), "Some Reflections on the Use of the Concept of Power in Economics," in Basu, K. and Nayak, P. B. (eds.), *Development Policy and Economic Theory*, Delhi: Oxford University Press.

Bardhan, P. K. and Mookherjee, D. (1998), "Expenditure Decentralization and the Delivery of Public Services in Developing Countries," mimeo: University of California, Berkeley.

Barrett, C. B. (1999), "On Pluralistic Ethics and the Economics of Compassion," *Bulletin of the Association of Christian Economists*, Spring, 20–35.

Barro, R. J. (1984), "Discussion," *American Economic Review*, 74: 179–87.

Basu, K. (1977), "Information and Strategy in the Iterated Prisoner's Dilemma," *Theory and Decision*, 8: 293–8.

Basu, K. (1980), *Revealed Preference of Government*, Cambridge, England: Cambridge University Press.

Basu, K. (1983a), "Cardinal Utility, Utilitarianism and a Class of Invariance Axioms in Welfare Analysis," *Journal of Mathematical Economics*, 12: 193–206.

Basu, K. (1983b), "On Why We Do Not Try to Walk Off Without Paying After a Taxi Ride," *Economic and Political Weekly*, 18: November, 2011–2.

Basu, K. (1986), "One Kind of Power," *Oxford Economic Papers*, 38: 259–82.

Basu, K. (1987), "Monopoly, Quality Uncertainty and 'Status Goods'," *International Journal of Industrial Organization*, 5: 435–46.

Basu, K. (1989), "A Theory of Association: Social Status, Prices and Markets," *Oxford Economic Papers*, 41: 653–71.

Basu, K. (1990), "On the Non–existence of a Rationality Definition for Extensive Games," *International Journal of Game Theory*, 9: 33–44.

Basu, K. (1991), "The International Debt Problem, Credit Rationing and Loan Pushing," *Princeton Studies in International Finance*, No. 79.

Basu, K. (1993), "Comment," *Proceedings of the 1992 World Bank Annual Conference on Development Economics*, Washington, DC: World Bank.

Basu, K. (1994a), "The Traveler's Dilemma: Paradoxes of Rationality in Game Theory," *American Economic Review*, 84: 391–5.

Basu, K. (1994b), "Group Rationality, Utilitarianism and Escher's Waterfall," *Games and Economic Behavior*, 7: 1–9.

Basu, K. (1994c), "On Interpersonal Comparison and the Concept of Equality," in Eichhorn, W. (ed.), *Models and Measurement of Welfare and Inequality*, Berlin: Springer-Verlag.

Basu, K. (1995a), "Civil Institutions and Evolution: Concepts, Critiques and Models," *Journal of Development Economics*, 46: 19–33.

Basu, K. (1995b), "A Paradox of Knowledge and Some Related Observations," mimeo: Cornell University.

Basu, K. (1996), "Notes on Evolution, Rationality and Norms," *Journal of Institutional and Theoretical Economics*, 152: 739–49.

Basu, K. (1997), "On Misunderstanding Government: An Analysis of the Art of Policy Advice," *Economics and Politics*, 9: 231–50.

Basu, K. (1998a), "The Role of Norms and Law in Economics: An Essay on Political Economy," Paper presented at the conference, "25 Years: Social Science and Social Change," Institute for Advanced Study, Princeton, May 9–11, 1997.

Basu, K. (1998b), "Social Norms and the Law," in Newman, P. (ed.), *The New Palgrave Dictionary of Economics and the Law*, London: Macmillan.

Basu, K. (1999), "Child Labor: Cause, Consequence and Cure with Remarks on International Labor Standards," *Journal of Economic Literature*, 37: 1083–119.

Basu, K., Bhattacharya, S. and Mishra, A. (1992), "Notes on Bribery and the Control of Corruption", *Journal of Public Economics*, 48: 349–59.

Basu, K., Jones, E. L. and Schlicht, E. (1987), "The Growth and Decay of Custom: The Role of the New Institutional Economics in Economic History," *Explorations in Economic History*, 24: 1–21.

Basu, K. and Van, P. H. (1998), "The Economics of Child Labor," *American Economic Review*, 88: 412–27.

Basu, K. and Weibull, J. (1991), "Strategy Subsets Closed under Rational Behavior," *Economics Letters*, 36: 141–6.

Bates, R. H. and Weingast, B. R. (1996), "Rationality and Interpretation: The Politics of Transition," mimeo: Harvard University.

Beck, A., Bleicher, M. N. and Crowe, D. W. (1969), *Excursions into Mathematics*, New York: Worth Publishers.

Becker, E. F. (1975), "Justice, Utility and Interpersonal Comparison," *Theory and Decision*, 6: 471–84.

Becker, G. S. (1991), "A Note on Restaurant Pricing and Other Examples of Social Influences on Price," *Journal of Political Economy*, 99: 1109–16.

Becker, G. S. and Murphy, K. M. (1988), "A Theory of Rational Addiction," *Journal of Political Economy*, 96: 675–700.

Benabou, R. and Tirole, J. (1999), "Self-Confidence: Intrapersonal Strategies," mimeo: IDEI, Toulouse.

Benoit, J.-P. and Kornhauser, L. A. (1996), "Game Theoretic Analysis of Legal Rules and Institutions," C.V. Starr Center Working Paper No. RR96-30, New York University.

Bentham, J. (1789), *An Introduction to the Principles of Morals and Legislation*. All references are to the 1996 edition, Oxford: Clarendon Press.

Bernard, J. (1954), "The Theory of Games of Strategy as a Modern Sociology of Conflict," *American Journal of Sociology*, 59: 411–24.

Bernheim, B. D. (1984), "Rationalizable Strategic Behavior," *Econometrica*, 52: 1007–29.

Bernheim, B. D. (1994), "A Theory of Conformity," *Journal of Political Economy*, 102: 841–77.

Bernstein, L. (1992), "Opting Out of the Legal System: Extralegal Contractual Relations in the Diamond Industry," *Journal of Legal Studies*, 21: 115–57.

Besley, T. and Coate, S. (1992), "Understanding Welfare Stigma: Tax Payer Resentment and Statistical Discrimination," *Journal of Public Economics*, 48: 165–183.

Bhagwati, J. N. (1990), "The Theory of Political Economy, Economic Policy, and Foreign Investment," in Scott, M. and Lal, D. (eds.), *Public Policy and Economic Development*, Oxford: Clarendon.

Bhagwati, J. N., Brecher, R. and Srinivasan, T. N. (1984), "DUP Activities and Economic Theory" in Collander, D. (ed.), *Neoclassical Political Economy*, Cambridge, MA: Ballinger.

Bhargava, R. (1993), *Individualism in Social Science: Forms and Limits of Methodology*, Oxford: Oxford University Press.

Bicchieri, C. (1989), "Self-Refuting Theories of Strategic Interaction: A Paradox of Common Knowledge," in Balzer, W. and Hamminga, B. (eds.), *Philosophy of Economics*, London: Kluwer.

Bikhchandani, S., Hirshleifer, D. and Welch, I. (1992), "A Theory of Fads, Fashion, Custom and Cultural Change as Information Cascades," *Journal of Political Economy*, 100: 992–1026.

Binmore, K. G. (1987), "Modeling Rational Players," *Economics and Philosophy*, 3: 179–214.

Binmore, K. G. and Brandenburger, A. (1990), "Common Knowledge and Game Theory," in Binmore, K. G. (ed.), *Essays on the Foundations of Game Theory*, Oxford: Blackwell Publishers.

Black, D. (1983), "Crime as Social Control," *American Sociological Review*, 48: 34–45.

Blackorby, C., Donaldson, D. and Weymark, J. (1984), "Social Choice with Interpersonal Comparisons: A Diagrammatic Introduction," *International Economic Review*, 25: 327–56.

Blau, P. M. (1964), *Exchange and Power in Social Life*, New York: Wiley.

Blume, L. E. and Easley, D. (1995), "What has the Rational Learning Literature Taught Us?" in Kirman, A. and Salmon, M. (eds.), *Learning and Rationality in Economics*, Oxford: Blackwell Publishers.

Borel, E. (1921), "La Théorie du Jeu et les Equations Intégrales à Noyau Symmetrique," *Comptes Rendu Hebdomadaires des Séances de l'Académie des Sciences*, 173: 1304–8. Translated as "The Theory of Play and Integral Equations with Skew Symmetric Kernels," *Econometrica*, 21: 97–100.

Bowles, S. and Gintis, H. (1992), "Power and Wealth in a Competitive Capitalist Economy," *Philosophy and Public Affairs*, 41: 324–53.

Bowles, S. and Gintis, H. (1993), 'The Revenge of the Homo Economicus: Contested Exchange and the Revival of Political Economy," *Journal of Economic Perspectives*, 7: 83–102.

Boyd, R. and Richerson, P. J. (1994), "The Evolution of Norms: An Anthropological View," *Journal of Institutional and Theoretical Economics*, 151: 269–85.

Brandt, R. B. (1959), *Ethical Theory*, Englewood Cliffs, NJ: Prentice Hall.

Breiger, R. L. (1990), "Social Control and Social Networks: A Model from Georg Simmel," in Calhoun, C., Meyer, M. W. and Scott, W. R. (eds.), *Structure of Power and Constraint*, Cambridge: Cambridge University Press.

Bresnahan, T. F. (1981), "Duopoly Models with Consistent Conjectures," *American Economic Review*, 71: 934–45.

British Parliamentary Papers (1968), *Report from the Select Committee [1831–32] on the "Bill to Regulate the Labour of Children in the Mills and Factories of the United Kingdom" with Minutes of Evidence* (*Industrial Revolution: Children's Employment*, 2), Shannon, Ireland: Irish University Press.

Brock, W. A. and Magee, S. P. (1978), "The Economics of Special Interest Politics: The Case of the Tariff," *American Economic Review*, 68: 246–50.

Buchanan, J. M. (1968), "An Economist's Approach to 'Scientific Politics'," in M. Parsons (ed.), *Perspectives in the Study of Politics*, Chicago: Rand McNally.

Buchanan, J. M. (1973), "The Coase Theorem and the Theory of the State," *Natural Resources Journal*, 13: 579–94.

Burt, R. S. (1992), *Structural Holes: The Social Structure of Competition*, Cambridge, MA: Harvard University Press.

Calvert, R. L. (1995), "Rational Actors, Equilibrium and Social Institutions," in Knight, J. and Sened, I. (eds.), *Explaining Social Institutions*, Ann Arbor: University of Michigan Press.

Cao, L. (1999), "Looking at Communities and Markets," *Notre Dame Law Review*, 74: 841–924.

Caplow, T. (1968), *Two Against One: Coalitions in Triads*, Englewood Cliffs, NJ: Prentice-Hall.

Capra, C. M., Goeree, J. K., Gomez, R. and Holt, C. A. (1999), "Anomalous Behavior in a Traveler's Dilemma?" *American Economic Review*, 89: 678–90.

Carneiro, R. L. (1970), "A Theory of the Origin of the State," *Studies in Social Theory*, 3: 3–21.

Chambers, R. G. and Quiggin, J. (1998), "Exploitation and Agency in Agrarian Contracts," mimeo: University of Maryland.

Chandra, N. K. (1977), "Monopoly Legislation and Policy in India," *Economic and Political Weekly*, 12, Special Issue.

Coleman, James S. (1990), *Foundations of Social Theory*, Cambridge MA: Harvard University Press.

Coleman, Jules L. (1982), "The Economic Analysis of Law," in Pennock, J. R. and Chapman, J. W. (eds.), *Ethics, Economics and the Law*, New York: New York University Press.

Colombo, F. (1999), "Paradoxes of Rationality in Simultaneous Move Games: The Game Take-or-Play," mimeo: Universita Cattolica del Sacro Cuore, Milan.

Cooper, B. and Garcia-Penalosa, C. (1999), "Status Effects and Negative Utility Growth," mimeo: Oxford University.

Cooter, R. D. (1998), "Expressive Law and Economics," *Journal of Legal Studies*, 27: 585–608.

Cooter, R. D. (2000), "Law from Order," in Olson, M. and Kahkonen, S. (eds.), *A Not-so-dismal Science: A Broader, Brighter Approach to Economies and Societies*, New York: Oxford University Press.

Copp, D. (1999), "The Idea of a Legitimate State," *Philosophy and Public Affairs*, 28: 3–45.

Cozzi, G. (1998), "Culture as a Bubble," *Journal of Political Economy*, 106: 376–94.

Crawford, V. and Sobel, J. (1982), "Strategic Information Transmission," *Econometrica*, 50: 1431–51.

Crozier, B. (1969), *The Masters of Power*, London: Eyre and Spottiswoode.

Dahl, R. (1957), "The Concept of Power," *Behavioral Science*, 2: 201–15.

Dasgupta, P. (1988), "Trust as a Commodity," in Gambetta, D. (ed.), *Trust: Making and Breaking Cooperative Relations*, Oxford: Blackwell Publishers.

Dasgupta, P. (1997), "Economic Development and the Idea of Social Capital," mimeo: University of Cambridge.

D'Aspremont, C. and Gevers, L. (1977), "Equity and the Informational Basis of Collective Choice," *Review of Economic Studies*, 44: 199–210.

David, P. (1985), "Clio and the Economics of QWERTY," *American Economic Review*, 75: 332–7.

Dawkins, R. (1976), *The Selfish Gene*, London: Paladin.

Deb, R. (1994), "Waiver, Effectivity and Rights as Game Forms," *Economica*, 61: 167–78.

Debreu, G. (1959), *Theory of Value*, New York: Wiley.

de Jasay, A. (1985), *The State*, Oxford: Blackwell Publishers.

de Meza, D. and Gould, J. R. (1992), "The Social Efficiency of Private Decisions to Enforce Property Rights," *Journal of Political Economy*, 100: 561–80.

Denzau, A. T. and North, D. C. (1994), "Shared Mental Models: Ideologies and Institutions," *Kyklos*, 47: 3–31.

Desai, M. (1984), "Power and Agrarian Relations: Some Concepts and Measurement," in Desai, M., Rudolph, S. H. and Rudra, A. (eds.), *Agrarian Power and Agricultural Productivity in South Asia*, Oxford: Oxford University Press.

Deshpande, A. (1999), "Loan Pushing and Triadic Relations," *Southern Economic Journal*, 65: 914–26.

Diamond, J. (1997), *Guns, Germs and Steel: The Fates of Human Societies*, New York: W.W. Norton and Co.

DiMaggio, P. J. and Powell, W. W. (1983), "The Iron Cage Revisited: Institutional Isomorphism and Collective Rationality in Organizational Fields," *American Sociological Review*, 48: 147–60.

Dixit, A. (1996), *The Making of Economic Policy*, Cambridge, MA: MIT Press.

Dixit, A. (1997), "Economists as Advisers to Politicians and Society," *Economics and Politics*, 9: 225–30.

Dixit, A. and Nalebuff, B. J. (1991), *Thinking Strategically: The Competitive Edge in Business, Politics and Everyday Life*, New York: W. W. Norton and Co.

Dixit, A. and Norman, V. (1978), "Advertising and Welfare," *Bell Journal of Economics*, 9: 1–17.

Durlauf, S. N. (1996), "Statistical Mechanics Approaches to Socioeconomic Behavior," mimeo: University of Wisconsin.

Dworkin, R. (1986), *Law's Empire*, Cambridge, MA: Harvard University Press.

Eaton, J. and Engers, M. (1992), "Sanctions," *Journal of Political Economy*, 100: 899–928.

Eggertson, T. (1990), *Economic Behavior and Institutions*, Cambridge: Cambridge University Press.

Eisenberg, M. A. (1999), *Reasons and Persons*, Oxford: Clarendon Press.

Ellerman, D. (1992), *Property and Contract in Economics*, Cambridge, MA: Blackwell.

Ellickson, R. C. (1991), *Order Without Law: How Neighbors Settle Disputes*, Cambridge, MA: Harvard University Press.

Elster, J. (1989), "Social Norms and Economic Theory," *Journal of Economic Perspectives*, 3: 99–117.

Emigh, R. J. (1999), "Means and Measures: Property Rights, Political Economy, and Productivity in Fifteenth-Century Tuscany," *Social Forces*, 78: 461–91.

Engerman, S. L. (1992), "Coerced and Free Labor: Property Rights and the Development of the Labor Force," *Explorations in Economic History*, 29: 1–29.

Ensminger, J. (1998), "Anthropology and the New Institutionalism," *Journal of Institutional and Theoretical Economics*, 154: 774–89.

Fafchamps, M. (1992), "Solidarity Networks in Pre-industrial Society," *Economic Development and Cultural Change*, 41: 147–74.

Fagin, R., Halpern, J. Y., Moses, Y. and Vardi, M. Y. (1995), *Reasoning about Knowledge*, Cambridge, MA: MIT Press.

Farrell, J. and Rabin, M. (1996), "Cheap Talk," *Journal of Economic Perspectives*, 10: 103–18.

Fehr, E. and Gachter, S. (1997), "Reciprocity and Economics: The Economic Implications of *Homo Reciprocans*," *European Economic Review*, 42: 845–59.

Ferejohn, J. (1995), "Law, Legislation and Positive Political Theory," in Banks, J. S. and Hanushek, E. A. (eds.), *Modern Political Economy*, Cambridge, England: Cambridge University Press.

Fershtman, C. and Weiss, Y. (1998), "Social Rewards, Externalities and Stable Preferences," *Journal of Public Economics*, 70: 53–73.

Field, A. J. (1984), "Microeconomics, Norms and Rationality," *Economic Development and Cultural Change*, 32: 683–711.

Findlay, R. and Wellisz, S. (1982), "Endogenous Tariffs," in Bhagwati, J. N. (ed.), *Import Competition and Response*, Chicago: Chicago University Press.

Fish, S. (1994), *There Is No Such Thing as Free Speech: and It's a Good Thing, Too.* New York: Oxford University Press.

Fiss, O. (1996), *The Irony of Free Speech*, Cambridge, MA: Harvard University Press.

Fleurbaey, M. and Gaertner, W. (1996), "Admissibility and Feasibility in Game Forms," *Analyze and Kritik*, 18: 54–66.

Frank, R. H. (1985), *Choosing the Right Pond: Human Behavior and the Quest for Status*, Oxford: Oxford University Press.

Frank, R. H., Gilovich, T. and Regan, D. T. (1993), "Does Studying Economics Inhibit Cooperation?" *Journal of Economic Perspectives*, 7: 159–71.

Friedman, D. (1994), "A Positive Account of Property Rights," in Paul, E. F., Miller, F. D. and Paul, J. (eds.), *Property Rights*, Cambridge: Cambridge University Press.

Friedman, M. (1953), *Essays in Positive Economics*, Chicago: Chicago University Press.

Friedman, M. (1962), *Capitalism and Freedom*, Chicago: Chicago University Press.

Friedman, M. (1986), "Economists and Economic Policy," *Economic Inquiry*, 24: 1–10.

Friedman, M. and Friedman, R. (1980), *Free to Choose*, London: Secker and Warburg.

Fukuyama, F. (1996), *Trust: The Social Virtues and the Creation of Prosperity*, New York: Free Press.

Fuller, L. L. (1969), "Human Interaction and the Law," *American Journal of Jurisprudence*, 20: 1–36.

Gaertner, W., Pattanaik, P. K. and Suzumura, K. (1992), "Individual Rights Revisited," *Economica*, 59: 161–77.

Galbraith, J. K. (1983), *The Anatomy of Power*, Boston: Houghton Mifflin.

Gallie, W. B. (1955), "Essentially Contested Concepts," *Proceedings of the Aristotelian Society*, 56: 167–98.

Gambetta, D. (1993), *The Sicilian Mafia: The Business of Private Protection*, Cambridge, MA: Harvard University Press.

Gardenfors, P. (1981), "Rights, Games and Social Choice," *Nous*, 15: 341–56.

Genicot, G. (1998), "Bonded Labor and Serfdom: A Paradox of Voluntary Choice," mimeo: Cornell University.

Ghatak, M. and Guinnane, T. (1998), "The Economics of Lending with Joint Liability," Economic Growth Center Discussion Paper No. 791, Yale University.

Gibbard, A. (1965), "Rule Utilitarianism: A Merely Illusory Alternative?" *Australasian Journal of Philosophy*, 93: 211–20.

Gibbons, R. (1997), "An Introduction to Applicable Game Theory," *Journal of Economic Perspectives*, 11: 127–50.

Gilligan, T. W. and Krehbiel, K. (1987), "Collective Decisionmaking and Standing Committees: An Informational Rationale for Restrictive Procedures," *Journal of Law, Economics and Organization*, 3: 287–335.

Gluckman, M. (1955), *The Judicial Process Among the Barotse of Northern Rhodesia*, Oxford: Blackwell Publishers.

Goffman, E. (1959), *The Presentation of Self in Everyday Life*, New York: Doubleday.

Goldsmith, J. L. and Posner, E. A. (1999), "A Theory of Customary International Law," John, M. Olin Law & Economics Working Paper No. 63, University of Chicago.

Goldstein, J. and Keohane, R. O. (1993), "Ideas and Foreign Policy: An Analytical Framework," in Goldstein, J. and Keohane, R. O. (eds.), *Ideas and Foreign Policy*, Ithaca, NY: Cornell University Press.

Goyal, S. (1996), "Interaction Structure and Social Change," *Journal of Institutional and Theoretical Economics*, 152: 472–94.

Granovetter, M. (1985), "Economic Action and Social Structure: The Problem of Embeddedness," *American Journal of Sociology*, 91: 481–510.

Granovetter, M. and Soong, R. (1983), "Threshold Models of Diffusion and Collective Behavior," *Journal of Mathematical Sociology*, 9: 165–79.

Green, D. P. and Shapiro, I. (1994), *Pathologies of Rational Choice: A Critique of Applications in Political Science*, New Haven: Yale University Press.

Green, E. J. (1993), "On the Emergence of Parliamentary Government: The Role of Private Information," *Federal Reserve Bank of Minneapolis Quarterly Review*, 17: 2–16.

Greif, A. (1993), "Contract Enforceability and Economic Institutions in Early Trade: The Maghribi Traders' Coalition," *American Economic Review*, 83: 525–48.

Greif, A., Milgrom, P. and Weingast, B. R. (1994), "Coordination, Commitment, and Enforcement: The Case of the Merchant Guild," *Journal of Political Economy*, 102: 745–76.

Grindle, M. S. (1991), "The New Political Economy: Positive Economics and Negative Politics," in Meier, G. M. (ed.), *Politics and Policy Making in Developing Countries*, San Francisco: ICS Press.

Grossman, H. (1991), "A General Equilibrium Model of Insurrections," *American Economic Review*, 81: 912–21.

Gul, F. and Pesendorfer, W. (1999), "Temptation and Self-Control," mimeo: Princeton University.

Habermas, J. (1989), *On Society and Politics: A Reader*, Boston: Beacon Press.

Hadfield, G. (1995), "Rational Women: A Test for Sex-based Harassment," *California Law Review*, 83: 1159–89.

Hahn, F. (1984), *Equilibrium and Macroeconomics*, Cambridge, MA: MIT Press.

Halmos, P. (1974), *Naive Set Theory*, New York: Springer-Verlag.

Hammond, P. J. (1976), "Equity, Arrow's Conditions, and Rawls' Difference Principle," *Econometrica*, 44: 793–804.

Hardin, R. (1997), "Economic Theories of the State," in Mueller, D. C. (ed.), *Perspectives on Public Choice*, Cambridge: Cambridge University Press.

Hare, R. M. (1952), *The Language of Morals*, Oxford: Oxford University Press.

Harrington, J. E. (1999), "Rigidity of Social Systems," *Journal of Political Economy*, 107: 40–64.

Harrod, R. F. (1936), "Utilitarianism Revisited," *Mind*, 45: 137–56.

Harsanyi, J. C. (1955), "Cardinal Welfare, Individualistic Ethics, and Interpersonal Comparisons of Utility," *Journal of Political Economy*, 63: 309–21.

Hart, H. L. A. (1979), "Are There Any Natural Rights?" in Lyons, D. (ed.), *Rights*, Belmont, CA: Wadsworth Publishing Co.

Hatlebakk, M. (2000), "A New Robust Subgame Perfect Equilibrium in Basu's Model of Triadic Power Relations," mimeo: University of Bergen.

Havel, V. (1986), "The Power of the Powerless," in Vladislav, J. (ed.), *Living in Truth*, London: Faber and Faber.

Hayami, Y. (1998), "Norms and Rationality in the Evolution of Economic Systems: A View from Asian Villages," *Japanese Economic Review*, 49: 36–53.

Hayek, F. A. (1960), *The Constitution of Liberty*, Chicago: University of Chicago Press.

Hicks, J. R. (1956), *A Revision of Demand Theory*, Oxford: Clarendon Press.

Hicks, J. R. (1979), *Causality in Economics*, Oxford: Blackwell Publishers.

Hirsch, F. (1977), *Social Limits to Growth*, London: Routledge.

Hirschman, A. O. (1985), "Against Parsimony: Three Easy Ways of Complicating Some Categories of Economic Discourse," *Economics and Politics*, 1: 7–21.

Hobbes, T. (1651), *Leviathan*. All references are to the 1994 edition, Indianapolis: Hackett Publishing Co.

Hodgson, D. H. (1967), *Consequences of Utilitarianism*, New York: Oxford University Press.

Hoff, K. and Sen, Arijit. (1999), "Home-ownership, Local Interactions, and Inequality," mimeo: World Bank.

Hoff, K. and Stiglitz, J. (2000), "Modern Economic Theory and Development," in Meier, G. and Stiglitz, J. (eds.), *Frontiers of Development Economics*, New York: Oxford University Press, forthcoming.

Hofstede, G. (1991), *Cultures and Organizations*, New York: McGraw-Hill.

Holmes, R. (1995), "Voltaire's Grin," *New York Review of Books*, 42 (19): 49–55.

Hume, D. (1739), *A Treatise of Human Nature*. All references are to the 1969 edition, London: Penguin.

Hume, D. (1758), "Of the First Principles of Government," in *Essays: Moral, Political and Literary*. All references are to the 1987 edition, Indianapolis: Liberty Fund.

Janakarajan, S. and Subramanian, S. (1992), "A Model of 'Triadic' Power Relations in the Interlinkage of Agrarian Markets," Appendix to the paper by S. Janakarajan in S. Subramanian (ed.), *Themes in Development Economics*, New Delhi: Oxford University Press.

Jervis, R. (1976), *Perception and Misperception in International Politics*, Princeton: Princeton University Press.

Kagel, J. H., Battalio, R. C., Rachlin, H., Basmann, R. L., Green, L. and Klemm, W. R. (1975), "Experimental Studies of Consumer Demand Behavior Using Laboratory Animals," *Economic Inquiry*, 8: 22–38.

Kahneman, D. (1994), "New Challenges to the Rationality Assumption," *Journal of Institutional and Theoretical Economics*, 150: 18–36.

Kandori, M., Mailath, G. J. and Rob, R. (1993), "Learning, Mutation, and Long Run Equilibria in Games," *Econometrica*, 61: 29–56.

Kaneko, M. (1984), "On Interpersonal Utility Comparison," *Social Choice and Welfare*, 1: 165–75.

Katzenstein, P. (1993), "Coping with Terrorism: Norms and Internal Security in Germany and Japan" in Goldstein, J. and Keohane, R. O. (eds.), *Ideas and Foreign Policy*, Ithaca, NY: Cornell University Press.

Kautilya (c. 300 BC), The Arthashastra. All references are to the 1992 edition, New Delhi: Penguin.

Knight, J. (1998), "The Bases of Cooperation: Social Norms and the Rule of Law," *Journal of Institutional and Theoretical Economics*, 154: 754–63.

Kranton, R. E. and Swamy, A. V. (1999), "The Hazards of Piecemeal Reform: British Civil Courts and the Credit Market in Colonial India," *Journal of Development Economics*, 58: 1–24.

Kreps, D. M. (1990), *Game Theory and Economic Modelling*, Oxford: Oxford University Press.

Kreps, D. M., Milgrom, P., Roberts, J. and Wilson, R. (1982), "Rational Cooperation in the Finitely-Repeated Prisoner's Dilemma," *Journal of Economic Theory*, 27: 245–52.

Kuran, T. (1988), "Ethnic Norms and Their Transformation Through Reputational Cascades," Journal of Legal Studies, 27: 623–59.

Kuran, T. (1995), *Private Truths, Public Lies: The Social Consequences of Preference Falsification*, Cambridge, MA: Harvard University Press.

Larson, M. S. (1977), *The Rise of Professionalism: A Sociological Analysis*, Berkeley: University of California Press.

Lazear, E. P. and Rosen, S. (1981), "Rank-order Tournaments as Optimum Labor Contracts," *Journal of Political Economy*, 89: 841–64.

Lerner, A. P. (1944), *The Economics of Control*, London: Macmillan.

Levi, I. (1997), "Advising Rational Agents," *Economics and Politics*, 9: 221–4.

Lewis, D. (1969), *Convention: A Philosophical Study*, Cambridge, MA: Harvard University Press.

Leibenstein, H. (1950), "Bandwagon, Snob and Veblen Effects in the Theory of Consumers," *Quarterly Journal of Economics*, 64: 183–207.

Lindbeck, A. Nyberg, S. and Weibull, J. (1999), "Social Norms and Economic Incentives in the Welfare State," *Quarterly Journal of Economics*, 114: 1–35.

Lively, J. (1976), "The Limits of Exchange Theory," in Barry, B. (ed.), *Power and Political Theory*, New York: Wiley.

Lopez-Calva, L.-F. (1999), "A Social Stigma Model of Child Labor," CAE Working Paper #99-13, Cornell University.

Lorenz, K. (1977), *Behind the Mirror: A Search for a Natural History of Human Knowledge* (translated by Taylor, R.) New York: Harcourt Brace Jovanovich.

Loury, G. (1994), "Self-Censorship in Public Discourse: A Theory of 'Political Correctness' and Related Phenomena," *Rationality and Society*, 6: 428–61.

Lucas, J. R. (1970), *The Freedom of the Will*, Oxford: Oxford University Press.

Lukes, S. (1974), *Power: A Radical View*, London: MacMillan.

Lyons, D. (1975), "Determinism and Knowledge," *Analysis*, 35: 200–4.

Lyons, D. (1979), "Introduction," in Lyons, D. (ed.), *Rights*, Belmont, CA: Wadsworth Publishing Co.

Lyons, D. (1982), "Utility and Rights," in Pennock, R. J. and Chapman, J. W. (eds.), *Ethics, Economics and the Law*, New York: New York University Press.

Macey, J. R. (1997), "Public and Private Ordering and the Production of Legitimate and Illegitimate Rules," *Cornell Law Review*, 82: 1123–49.

Magee, B. (1973), *Popper*, New York: Viking Press.

Magee, S. P. and Brock, W. A. (1983), "A Model of Politics, Tariffs and Rent-Seeking in General Equilibrium," in Weisbrod, B. and Hughes, H. (eds.), *Human Resources, Employment and Development*, London: Macmillan.

Maggi, G. (1999), "The Role of Multilateral Institutions in International Trade Cooperation," *American Economic Review*, 89: 190–214.

Malinowski, B. (1921), "The Primitive Economics of the Trobriand Islanders," *Economic Journal*, 31: 1–16.

Malinowski, B. (1957), "The Principle of Give and Take," in Coser, L. A. and Rosenberg, B. (eds.), *Sociological Theory*, London: Macmillan.

Mansbridge, J. J. (1990), "Expanding the Range of Formal Modeling," in Mansbridge, J. J. (ed.), *Beyond Self-Interest*, Chicago: Chicago University Press.

Maskin, E. (1978), "A Theorem on Utilitarianism," *Review of Economic Studies*, 45: 93–6.

May, E. R. and Zelikow, P. D. (1997), *The Kennedy Tapes*, Cambridge, MA: Harvard University Press.

Maynard Smith, J. (1964), "Group Selection and Kin Selection," *Nature*, 201: 1145–7.

Maynard Smith, J. (1982), *Evolution and the Theory of Games*, Cambridge: Cambridge University Press.

Maynard Smith, J. and Price, G. R. (1973), "The Logic of Animal Conflict," *Nature*, 246: 15–8.

McGuire, M. (1972), "Private Good Clubs and Public Good Clubs: Economic Models of Group Formation," *Swedish Journal of Economics*, 74: 84–99.

McMillan, J. and Woodruff, C. (1999), "Dispute Prevention Without Courts in Vietnam," *Journal of Law, Economics and Organization*, 15: 637–58.

Meier, G. M. ed., (1991), *Politics and Policy Making in Developing Countries: Perspectives on the New Political Economy*, San Francisco: ICS Press.

Menger, C. (1883), *Untersuchungen uber die methode der Sozialwissenschaften und der Politischen Oekonomie insbesondere*. English translation by Nock, F.J., *Investigations into the Method of the Social Sciences with Special Reference to Economics*, New York: New York University Press.

Mill, J. S. (1848), *Principles of Political Economy*. All references are to the 1970 edition, Harmondsworth: Penguin.

Moore, G. E. (1902), *Principia Ethica*. All references are to the 1988 edition, Amherst, NY: Prometheus Books.

Morris, S. and Shin, H. S. (1995), "p-Dominance and Belief Potential," *Econometrica*, 63: 145–57.

Mosca, G. (1939), *The Ruling Class*, New York: McGraw-Hill.

Munzer, S. R. (1994), "An Uneasy Case Against Property Rights in Body Parts," in Paul, E. F., Miller, F. D. and Paul, J. (eds.), *Property Rights*, Cambridge: Cambridge University Press.

Nalebuff, B. J. and Stiglitz, J. E. (1983), "Information, Competition and Markets," *American Economic Review*, 73: 278–83.

Naqvi, N. and Wemhoner, F. (1995), "Power, Coercion and the Games Landlords Play," *Journal of Development Economics*, 47: 191–205.

Nee, V. and Strang, D. (1998), "The Emergence and Diffusion of Institutional Norms," *Journal of Institutional and Theoretical Economics*, 154: 706–15.

Ng, Y. K. (1973), "The Economic Theory of Clubs: Pareto Optimality Conditions," *Economica*, 40: 291–98.

North, D. C. (1989), "Comments," in Stiglitz, J., *The Economic Role of the State*, Oxford: Blackwell.

North, D. C. (1990), *Institutions, Institutional Change and Economic Performance*, Cambridge: Cambridge University Press.

Nozick, R. (1972), "Coercion," in Laslett, P., Runciman, W. G. and Skinner, Q. (eds.), *Philosophy, Politics and Society*, Fourth Series, Oxford: Blackwell Publishers.

Nozick, R. (1974), *Anarchy, State and Utopia*, Oxford: Blackwell Publishers.

Nozick, R. (1981), *Philosophical Explanations*, Cambridge, MA: Harvard University Press.

Nussbaum, M. (1997), "Flawed Foundations: The Philosophical Critique of (a Particular Type of) Economics," *University of Chicago Law Review*, 64: 1197–214.

O'Donoghue, T. and Rabin, M. (1999), "Doing It Now or Later," *American Economic Review*, 89: 103–124.

O'Donoghue, T. and Rabin, M. (2000), "The Economics of Immediate Gratification," *Journal of Behavioral Decisionmaking*, forthcoming.

O'Flaherty, B. and Bhagwati, J. (1997), "Will Free Trade with Political Science Put Normative Economists Out of Work?" *Economics and Politics*, 9: 207–19.

Olson, M. (1993), "Dictatorship, Democracy, and Development," *American Political Science Review*, 87: 567–76.

Osborne, M. J. and Rubinstein, A. (1994), *A Course in Game Theory*, Cambridge, MA: The MIT Press.

Ostrom, E. (1990), *Governing the Commons: The Evolution of Institutions for Collective Action*, Cambridge: Cambridge University Press.

Parfit, D. (1984), *Reasons and Persons*, Oxford: Clarendon Press.

Parsons, T. (1963), "On the Concept of Influence," *Public Opinion Quarterly*, 27: 37–62.

Pattanaik, P. K. (1968), "Risk, Impersonality and the Social Welfare Functions," *Journal of Political Economy*, 76: 1152–69.

Pearce, D. (1984), "Rationalizable Strategic Behavior and the Problem of Perfection," *Econometrica*, 52: 1029–50.

Phelps, E. S. and Pollak, R. A. (1968), "On Second-Best National Saving and Game-Equilibrium Growth," *Review of Economic Studies*, 35: 185–99.

Platteau, J. P. (1994), "Behind the Market Stage where Real Societies Exist: The Role of Public and Private Order Institutions," *Journal of Development Studies*, 30: 533–77.

Platteau, J. P. and Abraham, A. (1987), "An Enquiry into Quasi-Credit Systems in Traditional Fisherman Communities," *Journal of Development Studies*, 23: 461–90.

Polanyi, K. (1944), *The Great Transformation*, Boston: Beacon Press.

Posner, E. A. (1998), "Symbols, Signals and Social Norms in Politics and the Law," *Journal of Legal Studies*, 27: 765–98.

Posner, R. A. (1981), *The Economics of Justice*, Cambridge, MA: Harvard University Press.

Posner, R. A. (1997), "Social Norms and the Law: An Economic Approach," *American Economic Review*, 87: 365–9.

Putnam, R. D. (1993), *Making Democracy Work*, Princeton: Princeton University Press.

Rainwater, L. (1974), *What Money Buys: Inequality and the Social Meanings of Income*, New York: Basic Books.

Ray, D. (1998), *Development Economics*, Princeton: Princeton University Press.

Reny, P. J. (1986), Rationality, Common Knowledge and the Theory of Games, PhD dissertation, Princeton University.

Robbins, L. (1938), "Interpersonal Comparison of Utility: A Comment," *Economic Journal*, 48: 635–41.

Roberts, K. W. S. (1980), "Interpersonal Comparability and Social Choice Theory," *Review of Economic Studies*, 47: 421–39.

Robinson, Joan (1962), *Economic Philosophy*, Chicago: Aldine.

Robinson, J. A. (1996), "Theories of 'Bad Policy'," mimeo: University of Southern California.

Rosenthal, R. W. (1981), "Games of Perfect Information, Predatory Pricing and the Chain Store Paradox," *Journal of Economic Theory*, 25: 92–100.

Rubinstein, A. (1989), "The Electronic Mail Game: Strategic Behavior Under Complete Uncertainty," *American Economic Review*, 79: 385–91.

Russell, B. (1938), *Power: A New Social Analysis*, London: Allen and Unwin.

Russell, B. (1967), *The Problems of Philosophy*, London: Oxford University Press.

Rutherford, M. (1994), *Institutions in Economics: The Old and the New Institutionalism*, Cambridge: Cambridge University Press.

Rutten, A. (1997), "Anarchy, Order, and the Law: A Post–Hobbesian View," *Cornell Law Review*, 82: 1150–64.

Samuelson, P. A. (1938), "A Note on the Pure Theory of Consumers' Behavior," *Economica*, 5: 61–71.

Samuelson, P. A. (1963), "Comments," *American Economic Review*, 53: 231–6.

Sandler, T. and Tschirhart, J. T. (1980), "The Economic Theory of Clubs," *Journal of Economic Literature*, 18: 1481–521.

Satz, D. and Ferejohn, J. (1994), "Rational Choice and Social Theory," *Journal of Philosophy*, 91: 71–87.

Schelling, T. C. (1960), *The Strategy of Conflict*, Cambridge, MA: Harvard University Press.

Schelling, T. C. (1984), "Self-Command in Practice in Policy and in a Theory of Rational Choice," *American Economic Review*, 74: 1–11.

Schelling, T. C. (1985), "Enforcing Rules on Oneself," *Journal of Law, Economics and Organization*, 1: 357–74.

Schick, F. (1977), "Some Notes of Thinking Ahead," *Social Research*, 44: 786–800.

Schlicht, E. (1998), *On Custom in the Economy*, Oxford: Clarendon Press.

Schotter, A. (1981), *The Economic Theory of Social Institutions*, Cambridge, England: Cambridge University Press.

Schrecker, E. (1994), *The Age of McCarthyism: A Brief History with Documents*, Boston: Bedford Books.

Seabright, P. (1996), "Accountability and Decentralization in Government: An Incomplete Contracts Model," *European Economic Review*, 40: 61–89.

Selten, R. (1975), "Reexamination of the Perfectness Concept for Equilibrium Points in Extensive Games," *International Journal of Game Theory*, 4: 25–55.

Sen, A. (1966), "Hume's Law and Hare's Rule," *Philosophy*, 41: 75–80.

Sen, A. (1970), *Collective Choice and Social Welfare*, Edinburgh: Oliver and Boyd.

Sen, A. (1973), "Behavior and the Concept of Preference," *Economica*, 40: 241–59.

Sen, A. (1987), *On Ethics and Economics*, Oxford: Blackwell Publishers.

Sen, A. (1992), "Minimal Liberty," *Economica*, 59: 139–59.

Sen, A. (1993), "Internal Consistency of Choice," *Econometrica*, 61: 495–521.

Sethi, R. and Somanathan, E. (1996), "The Evolution of Social Norms in Common Property Resource Use," *American Economic Review*, 86: 766–88.

Shedler, J. and Block, J. (1990), "Adolescent Drug Use and Psychological Health," *American Psychologist*, 45: 612–30.

Shepsle, K. A. and Bonchuk, M. S. (1997), *Analyzing Politics: Rationality, Behavior and Institutions*, New York: W. W. Norton and Co.

Shin, H. S. (1993), "Logical Structure of Common Knowledge," *Journal of Economic Theory*, 52: 190–207.

Simmel, G. (1950), *The Sociology of Georg Simmel*, edited by Wolff, K. H., New York: Free Press.

Simmel, G. (1971), *On Individuality and Social Forms* (edited by Levine, D. N.), Chicago: University of Chicago Press.

Simon, J. L. (1974), "Interpersonal Welfare Comparisons can be Made and Used for Redistribution Distributions," *Kyklos*, 27: 63–98.

Singh, N. (1997), "Governance and Reform in India," *Journal of International Trade and Economic Development*, 6: 179–208.

Skaperdas, S. (1992), "Cooperation, Conflict, and Power in the Absence of Property Rights," *American Economic Review*, 82: 720–39.

Smart, J. J. C. and Williams, B. A. O. (1973), *Utilitarianism: For and Against*, Cambridge, England: Cambridge University Press.

Solow, R. M. (1995), "Mass Unemployment as a Social Problem," in Basu, K., Pattanaik, P. K. and Suzumura, K. (eds.), *Choice, Welfare and Development*, Oxford: Clarendon Press.

Sorensen, R. A. (1988), *Blindspots*, Oxford: Clarendon Press.

Srinivas, M. N. (1955), "The Social System of a Mysore Village," in Marriott, M. (ed.), *Village India*, Chicago: University of Chicago Press.

Stein, J. C. (1989), "Cheap Talk and the Fed: A Theory of Imprecise Policy Announcements," *American Economic Review*, 79: 32–42.

Steiner, H. (1994), *An Essay on Rights*, Oxford: Blackwell Publishers.

Stigler, G. J. (1966), *Theory of Price*, London: Macmillan.

Stiglitz, J. E. (1989), *The Economic Role of the State* (edited by Heertje, A.) Oxford: Blackwell.

Stiglitz, J. E. (1999), "Whither Reform? Ten Years of the Transition." Paper presented to the Annual Bank Conference on Development Economics, April 28–29, 1999, The World Bank.

Strasnick, S. (1976), "Social Choice Theory and the Derivation of Rawls' Difference Principle," *Journal of Philosophy*, 73: 85–99.

Strayer, J. R. (1970), *The Medieval Origins of the Modern State*, Princeton: Princeton University Press.

Subramanian, S. (1994), "A Paretian Liberal Dilemma without Collective Rationality," *Theory and Decision*, 37: 323–32.

Sugden, R. (1989), "Spontaneous Order," *Journal of Economic Perspectives*, 3: 85–97.

Sunstein, C. R. (1996), "On the Expressive Function of Law," *University of Pennsylvania Law Review*, 144: 2021–53.

Sunstein, C. R. (1999), "The Law of Group Polarization," mimeo: Law School, University of Chicago.

Sussman, H. (1993), *The Trial: Kafka's Unholy Trinity*, New York: Twayne Press.

Suzumura, K. (1983), *Rational Choice, Collective Decisions, and Social Welfare*, Cambridge, England: Cambridge University Press.

Taylor, M. (1976), *Anarchy and Cooperation*, London: John Wiley.

Taylor, M. (1982), *Community, Anarchy and Liberty*, Cambridge, England: Cambridge University Press.

Thompson, E. P. (1993), *Customs in Common*, New York: W. W. Norton and Co.

Tirole, J. (1994), "The Internal Organization of Government," *Oxford Economic Papers*, 46: 1–29.

Trebilcock, M. J. (1993), *The Limits of Freedom of Contract*, Cambridge, MA: Harvard University Press.

Trubek, D. M. (1972), "Toward a Social Theory of Law: An Essay on the Study of Law and Development," *The Yale Law Journal*, 82: 1–50.

Ulmann-Margalit, E. (1977), *The Emergence of Norms*, Oxford: Clarendon Press.

Veblen, T. (1899), *The Theory of the Leisure Class*, London: Macmillan.

Villanger, E. (1999), "A Theory of Bonded Labor in South Asia," mimeo: University of Bergen.

von Neumann, J. and Morgernstern, O. (1944), *Theory of Games and Economic Behavior*, Princeton: Princeton University Press.

Wade, R. (1988), *Village Republics: Economic Conditions for Collective Action in South India*, Cambridge, England: Cambridge University Press.

Warneryd, K. (1990), Economic Conventions: Essays in Institutional Economics, PhD dissertation: Stockholm School of Economics.

Warneryd, K. (1995), "Language, Evolution and the Theory of Games," in Casti, J. L. and Karlqvist, A. (eds.), *Cooperation and Conflict in General Evolutionary Processes*, New York: John Wiley.

Weber, M. (1922), *Wirtschaft und Gesellschaft*. All references are to the English translation by Fischoff, E. *et al.*, *Economy and Society*, I, New York: Bedminster Press, 1968.

Weibull, (1995), *Evolutionary Game Theory*, Cambridge, MA: MIT Press.

Wicksteed, P. H. (1910), *The Common Sense of Political Economy*, II, London: Macmillan.

Williamson, O. E. (1985), *The Economic Institutions of Capitalism*, London: Macmillan.

Williamson, T. (1994), *Vagueness*, London: Routledge.

Wittgenstein, L. (1922), *Tractatus Logico-Philosophicus*. All references are to the 1961 edition, London: Routledge.

Wynne-Edwards, V. C. (1962), *Animal Dispersion in Relation to Social Behavior*, Edinburgh: Oliver & Boyd.

Young, H. P. (1998), *Individual Strategy and Social Structure*, Princeton: Princeton University Press.

Zambrano, E. (1998), "The Algebra of Inexact Knowledge with an Application to the Game of Hermes," mimeo: Notre Dame University.

Zambrano, E. (1999), "Formal Models of Authority: Introduction and Political Economy Applications," *Rationality and Society*, 11: 115–38.

Zermelo, E. (1913), "Uber eine Anwendung der Mengenlehre auf die theorie des schachspiels, *Proceedings of the Fifth International Congress of Mathematicians*, 2: 501–5.

Name Index

Subject Index